MICRODRAMAS

T0386105

THEATER: THEORY/TEXT/PERFORMANCE
Series Editors: David Krasner, Rebecca Schneider, and Harvey Young
Founding Editor: Enoch Brater

Recent Titles:

Microdramas: Crucibles for Theater and Time
  by John H. Muse

Immersions in Cultural Difference: Tourism, War, Performance
  by Natalie Alvarez

Performing the Intercultural City by Ric Knowles

Haunted City: Three Centuries of Racial Impersonation in Philadelphia
  by Christian DuComb

Long Suffering: American Endurance Art as Prophetic Witness
  by Karen Gonzalez Rice

Alienation Effects: Performance and Self-Management in Yugoslavia, 1945–91
  by Branislav Jakovljević

After Live: Possibility, Potentiality, and the Future of Performance
  by Daniel Sack

Coloring Whiteness: Acts of Critique in Black Performance
  by Faedra Chatard Carpenter

The Captive Stage: Performance and the Proslavery Imagination of the Antebellum North
  by Douglas A. Jones, Jr.

Acts: Theater, Philosophy, and the Performing Self
  by Tzachi Zamir

Simming: Participatory Performance and the Making of Meaning
  by Scott Magelssen

Dark Matter: Invisibility in Drama, Theater, and Performance
  by Andrew Sofer

Passionate Amateurs: Theatre, Communism, and Love
  by Nicholas Ridout

Paul Robeson and the Cold War Performance Complex: Race, Madness, Activism
  by Tony Perucci

The Sarah Siddons Audio Files: Romanticism and the Lost Voice
  by Judith Pascoe

*The Problem of the Color[blind]: Racial Transgression and the Politics of
  Black Performance* by Brandi Wilkins Catanese

Artaud and His Doubles by Kimberly Jannarone

No Safe Spaces: Re-casting Race, Ethnicity, and Nationality in American Theater
  by Angela C. Pao

Microdramas

CRUCIBLES FOR THEATER AND TIME

John H. Muse

UNIVERSITY OF MICHIGAN PRESS

Ann Arbor

Published in the United States of America by the
University of Michigan Press
Manufactured in the United States of America
⊚ Printed on acid-free paper
2020   2019   2018   2017   4   3   2   1

A CIP catalog record for this book is available from the British Library.

Library of Congress Cataloging-in-Publication Data

Names: Muse, John H., author.
Title: Microdramas : crucibles for theater and time / John H. Muse.
Description: Ann Arbor : University of Michigan Press, 2017. | Series: Theater: theory/text/performance | Includes bibliographical references and index.
Identifiers: LCCN 2017023312 | ISBN 9780472073634 (hardback) | ISBN 9780472053636 (paperback) | ISBN 9780472123148 (e-book) Subjects: LCSH: One-act plays—History and criticism. | One-act plays—Technique. | Theater—Production and direction. | BISAC: PERFORMING ARTS / Theater / General. | LITERARY CRITICISM / Drama. Classification: LCC PN1661 .M87 2017 | DDC 808.2/41—dc23 LC record available at https://lccn.loc.gov/2017023312

For Sadie & Jack

Acknowledgments

I am so grateful to those who have given their time and attention to this project. I owe a debt to Elinor Fuchs for setting the fuse—unwittingly—with her offhand remark that modernist theater teems with fascinating short plays. Joseph Roach and Marc Robinson were there at the very beginning and have been brilliant and patient guides: enthusiastic in their support, unfailingly generous with their time, and incisive in their comments.

Early work on the project was supported by fellowships in the names of Andrew W. Mellon and Mrs. Giles F. Whiting; I am grateful to both benefactors. I thank the Beinecke Library for a research fellowship that introduced me to a trove of useful material on Symbolism and Italian Futurism. A number of colleagues at Yale offered advice about the project in its early stages, including James Leverett, Caleb Smith, Elliott Visconsi, Paul Fry, Ruth Yeazell, and especially Sam See, whom we all miss. Wes Davis and Elizabeth Alexander each volunteered to read chapters, and I am grateful for their time and insight. Pericles Lewis, who has been a mentor since my undergraduate years, taught me much of what I know about literary modernism. I owe a profound debt to my amazing compatriots working on theater and performance studies at Yale, including Nick Salvato, Julia Fawcett, Christopher Grobe, Ariel Watson, Rachel Rusch, Jason Fitzgerald, Joseph Cermatori, Nathalie Wolfram, Christine Mok, Uri McMillan, Liz Son, Jacob Gallagher-Ross, and Miriam Felton-Dansky. Amerigo Fabbri taught me much about Italian Futurism and helped with a few crucial translations. Small sections were presented as talks or papers at Yale's Twentieth Century Colloquium, at the American Society for Theatre Research Conferences in Boston, San Juan, Seattle, Nashville, and Baltimore; at the Modernist Studies Association conference in Montreal; the Radical Intersections Conference at Northwestern University Performance Studies; the Theatrephobia symposium and the Theater and Performance Studies Graduate Workshop at University of Chicago; and the Structures of Digital Feeling conference at SUNY Buffalo. I thank all of my interlocutors at those meetings for refining my thinking. I am grateful for the invaluable feedback I received on the Beckett chapter from the faculty working group of the first Mellon School for Theater and Performance Studies at Harvard: Martin Puchner, Corey Frost, Mirabelle Ordinaire, Heidi Bean, T. Nikki Cesare Shotzko, Julia A. Cassidy, Sasha Colby, Bertie Ferdman, Jeffrey Leichman, Holly Maples, and Magda Romanska. Colleagues in the field have sustained me throughout the process and offered helpful advice both online and at conferences. Thanks in particular to Kate Bredeson, Aaron Thomas, Brian Herrera, Darren Gobert, Ellen Mackay, Daniel Sack, and Robin Bernstein.

This would not be the book it is without the University of Chicago and its intellectual community. I thank especially my wonderful senior colleagues and mentors in the English department, who have been so generous with their time and expertise, especially Debbie Nelson, Bill Brown, Loren Kruger, Lauren Berlant, Lisa Ruddick (whose encouragement always buoys me), Bradin Cormack (whose intuitive sense of the book's project still impresses me), Maud Ellmann, Josh Scodel, Ken Warren, Elaine Hadley, Patrick Jagoda, Jennifer Scappettone, and Chicu Reddy. I have learned so much from David Bevington both about theater and about how to be in the world; you will never find a more gracious and helpful scholar. I could never have expected how much my time and work at Chicago would be shaped by the camaraderie of junior faculty from University of Chicago and across the city. Thanks to everyone who read my work through the Chicago Junior Faculty Working Group, especially my colleagues Richard So, Benjamin Morgan, Hilary Chute, Raúl Coronado, Adrienne Brown, Sonali Thakkar, Zach Samalin, Timothy Harrison, Julie Orlemanski, Rachel Galvin, Edgar Garcia, Heather Keenleyside, Timothy Campbell, and Nicole Wright, but also, of course, Neil Verma, Andrew Leong, Harris Feinsod, Nassar Mufti, Megan Heffernan, Jon Cutler, Rebecca Johnson, and Jim Hodge, among others. All of these colleagues give me hope for the future of the humanities.

A yearlong fellowship from the University of Chicago's Franke Institute for the Humanities came at just the right time, affording space, time, and companionship as I revised the book and reconceived its conclusions. For this, I offer thanks not only to Barbara and Richard Franke, but to Director Jim Chandler and the Franke's inimitable staff, Margot Browning, Mai Vukcevich, Bertie Kibreah, and especially Harriet Moody, who always had a key when I forgot mine and always asked after my daughter. My fellow fellows from across the Division were exceptionally thoughtful and generous readers. Thank you Emily Osborn, Steven Rings, Na'ama Rokem, Malte Willer, Peter Ericsson, Joela Jacobs, Ilanit Shacham, Benjamin Morgan, Benjamin Laurence, and Justin Sternberg.

The burgeoning Theater and Performance Studies (TAPS) community at University of Chicago has been a key intellectual home for me over the past few years. Thanks especially to my fellow faculty members from the Committee on TAPS, David Levin, Christopher Wild, Larry Norman, Heidi Coleman, Seth Brodsky, Agnes Lugo-Ortiz, Sarah Nooter, Reggie Jackson, Rocco Rubini, and Judith Zeitlin. Members of the TAPS Graduate Workshop read the Beckett chapter and a draft toward the introduction. Thanks in particular to student coordinators Amy Stebbins, Matthew Stone, Artemis Willis, Anne Rebull, and Brian Berry.

I have learned so much from my exceptional students at Chicago, especially Nahuel Telleria, David Lurie, Evan Garrett, Hannah Brooks-Motl, Sharvari Sastry, and Marissa Fenley, as well as everyone else from my seminars on Staging Modernism, Impossible Theaters, Beckett, Short Attention Span Fictions, and Virtual Theaters. Three PhD candidates in particular, Amanda Shubert, Rachel Kyne, and Nell Pach, have been invaluable research assistants for the book. I am forever grateful for their diligent and inspired work. Chiara Montanari provided crucial assistance with Italian sources and translated a number of previously unpublished Futurist plays.

An earlier version of chapter 2 was published in *Modern Drama* and is reprinted here with permission. Material from chapter 5 appeared in *The Journal of American Drama and Theatre* and *The Journal of Dramatic Theory and Criticism*, and appears with permission. I want to thank the editors of those pieces—Alan Ackerman, David Savran, and coeditors Erin Hurley and Sara Warner—for their close attention and helpful suggestions. Anne Bramley provided sage counsel and sane advice during the final stretches of revision, and helped remind me why I do this work. It has been a privilege to work with LeAnn Fields, Christopher Dreyer, and Jenny Geyer at the University of Michigan Press, as well as Rebecca Schneider and David Krasner, editors of the Theory/Text/Performance series.

Margaret and Ken Muse, to whom I owe so much more than this project, have been unwavering in their love and support. Ken's comments reminded me what an exceptionally thoughtful teacher he is and inspired me to strive to be as helpful to my students. I am grateful to Jayne and Peter Hunt for pitching in to afford me precious time to write, and for much else. Finally, I owe the most to Kathy Hunt Muse—who has made these years a joy—for her keen editorial acumen, her unwavering support, her inexhaustible patience, and for making the time fly.

Contents

Abbreviations

DW   Samuel Beckett. *Dramatic Works*. Vol. 3 of *Samuel Beckett: The Grove Centenary Edition*. Edited by Paul Auster. New York: Grove, 2006.

FP   *Futurist Performance*. Edited by Michael Kirby. Italian texts translated by Victoria Nes Kirby. New York: PAJ Publications, 1986.

FST   "The Futurist Synthetic Theater," in Lawrence Rainey, *Futurism: An Anthology*. Edited by Rainey, Christine Poggi, and Laura Wittman. Translated by Rainey (New Haven: Yale University Press, 2009), 204–9.

M   Samuel Beckett. *Molloy*. In *Novels*, vol. 2 of *Samuel Beckett: The Grove Centenary Edition*. Edited by Paul Auster, 1–170. New York: Grove, 2006.

TB   Filippo Marinetti, et al. "A Futurist Theater of Essential Brevity." In *Critical Writings*. Edited by Günter Berghaus. Translated by Douglas Thompson, new edition, 200–7. New York: Farrar, Straus, and Giroux, 2006. Originally published as *Teatro futurista sintetico*. Leaflet. Direzione del Movimento Futurista. January 11, 1915.

ONE | Introduction

Time Pieces

CHARACTER: A BULLET.
Road at night, cold, deserted.
A minute of silence. — A gunshot.
CURTAIN.

This is, in its entirety, Francesco Cangiullo's 1915 Futurist play, *Detonation: Synthesis of All Modern Theater*. *Detonation* looks like a joke, and many have mistaken it for little more than one. This book attempts to take Cangiullo's subtitle seriously by exploring the potential of theatrical brevity to distill lessons about modern theater and, more widely, to teach us about the experience of time in theater and in general. A sort of opening salvo for the theatrical avant-garde, *Detonation* explodes previous conventions while distilling several hallmarks of modern theater: atmosphere trumps character, expectations are under attack, and an empty stage resonates beyond itself. The play's structure, minimal as it is, condenses the most reliable and timeworn formula for nineteenth-century theater: create a period of rising suspense followed by a gunshot. At the same time, *Detonation* abandons traditional character in favor of atmosphere, effect, and action divorced from human agency. It presents a barren, generic space whose desertion reifies a world without the consolations of religion or traditional morality. It leverages assumptions about theatrical action to create frustration and then surprise. The gunshot—simultaneously the play's inciting incident and climactic moment—followed by an abrupt curtain forces the audience to invent situation and resolution, perpetrator and victim. Perhaps they realize the play's attack is aimed at them, that they are one of its intended victims.

Detonation is one of the more extreme examples of the selective diminution of modern theater.[1] Although brief performances have existed since theater's beginnings, the late nineteenth century saw a growing number of playwrights reshaping the minimum boundaries of dramatic form and insisting that a short play might be equal or even superior to a long one. This book charts the outsized influence this line of minimalist thinking had on modern theater, but does so without taking for granted its underlying assumption that less is always more. I ask instead what very short plays, which I call microdramas, reveal about theater and about time. The reward for paying attention to pieces that might seem like historical footnotes or distractions is a fuller sense of the complexities of temporal experience, both in theater and in general. The book's central argument is that certain microdramas provide laboratories in which the idiosyncratic operations of lived time and of theater are isolated and revealed in their oddity and complexity. Placing unique demands on an audience's attention, memory, and even patience, they make visible the shape of temporal conventions that inform any theatrical performance.

For my purposes, a microdrama is a play crafted to be considerably shorter than its audience's likely horizon of temporal expectation. Most of the audiences I discuss consider plays that last less than twenty minutes to be short. But it is not my intention to define a subgenre. On the contrary, an exploration of brief theater over more than 125 years underscores the subjectiveness and historical contingency of brevity as a concept. Shortness becomes legible on a case-by-case basis from a confluence of emotional reactions and learned expectations that depend on personal, contextual, and historical factors.[2] The audiences for quarter-hour plays in France in the 1880s were so accustomed to clocks that chimed every fifteen minutes that they used the phrase "quarter hour" as a synonym for a moment.[3] Now that our sense of time is tied to the second hand, the fifteen-minute plays that struck August Strindberg as momentary might seem ponderous to the audiences of the two-minute Neo-Futurist plays performed in Chicago since 1985.

The book focuses on a period in Western theatrical and cultural history — the years from roughly 1880 to the early twenty-first century — in which both the experience of time and theatrical conventions were especially visible and contested. In this period, the various temporal revolutions of industrial modernity (technological acceleration, standardized time, Taylorism and factory time, train schedules, telegraphic speed, and, later, the rhythms of television and the Internet), together with innovations in theater technology such as controlled lighting, as well as a growing sense of exhaustion with stale theatrical forms like the well-made play, prompted many artists to reconsider the operations and effects of theatrical time. Self-consciously brief theater provided a particularly intense site for such investigations, and as a result, brevity and compression became vital tools in the renovation of theatrical form on both sides of the Atlantic. Playwrights embraced brevity for a variety of reasons: in response to a sense that dramaturgical conventions were becoming outworn, as a revaluation of ostensibly low cultural forms like vaudeville and cabaret sketches, as a reaction to a cultural milieu they perceived to be accelerating, and in order to estrange an audience's subjective sense of time.

The list of notably short plays by modern and contemporary writers is long.[4] Among the many authors of microdramas, this book focuses on six influential artists for whom brevity became both a structural principle and a tool to investigate theater itself: August Strindberg, Maurice Maeterlinck, Futurist founder F. T. Marinetti, Samuel Beckett, Suzan-Lori Parks, and Caryl Churchill. This focus makes the book not only a study of brevity on modern stages, but a study of what brevity promised theater artists, and an account of the different conceptions of theater that come into focus through their varied attempts to reduce it to essential properties. The book's four central chapters explore four episodes in the history of very short theater, each in a different country and period, but all characterized by the self-conscious embrace of brevity. The story moves from the birth of the modernist microdrama in French little theaters in the 1880s (chapter 2), to the explicit worship of speed in the Italian Futurist synthetic theater some twenty-five years later (chapter 3), to Samuel Beckett's well-known but often-misunderstood short plays written between the 1950s and 80s (chapter 4), and finally to a range of contemporary American and British playwrights whose long compilations of shorts offer a newly mammoth take on momentary theater (chapter 5). The historical breadth of these chapters provides a selective cultural history of the way notions of brevity have changed over time, and have shaped aesthetic reception in historically specific but often undiscussed ways. Taken together in chronological order, these cases suggest that modern and contemporary theater were shaped to a significant extent by a varied and escalating series of assaults on generic and cognitive conventions, assaults that in each case exfoliated the predictable perversity of both theater and time.

Given the variety and abundance of short theater in the long twentieth century, the relative critical silence on this phenomenon is nearly as surprising as the long, empty minute before Cangiullo's gunshot. In published theater criticism, one finds isolated discussions of brevity within studies of particular modernist "–isms," in film studies, and in studies of particular authors, especially Samuel Beckett.[5] But no one has adequately described or theorized the temporal dimension of the various modernist revolutions in dramatic form.[6] Scholars routinely discuss short stories, films, and poems, but short plays have gained little critical attention. Like many audiences and critics, prevailing narratives of modern drama and performance tend to underestimate shorts. The tendency among producers, publishers, and sometimes artists themselves to dismiss short works as trifles, exercises, or as concept pieces has helped efface short performance from the historical record. Outside of educational contexts short plays are performed and anthologized less often than their normative cousins, and those that are recorded often hide in manuscripts, pamphlets, or obscure journals. In the case of Futurist and Dada shorts, the anti-textual prejudices of the artists themselves prevented some of the work from being preserved. Short works deserve more extended consideration than they have been given, even when, or especially when, they seem thin or disappointing, because such shortcomings often expose unspoken assumptions about what makes drama and theater satisfying.

While theater historians largely ignore the late nineteenth-century revolution in time, those who diagnose that revolution tend to ignore questions of time and speed in theater, or to assume straightforward answers to them. Stephen Kern's *The Culture of Time and Space*, for example, undertakes a broad and pioneering survey of the European obsession with space and time in the four decades from 1880 to 1918, but its breadth obviates close attention to the particulars of each genre. When Kern discusses theater, he applies now familiar explanations for the spatial and temporal manipulations of modernist theater: that new forms were needed for new ideas, and that in liberating themselves from the constraints of form (standard plotlines, the division between audience and spectator, etc.), artists freed themselves from time and space.[7] Paul Virilio's *Speed and Politics: An Essay on Dromology* (1977) diagnoses and explores the implications of a technologically inflected modern experience of acceleration, but he does not discuss live performance.[8] Ronald Schleifer's *Modernism and Time* comes to similar conclusions as this study, namely that the crisis of modernity was temporal and gave rise to new manipulations of time.[9] But Schleifer's omission of theater, an art shackled more than most to time, is notable. Paul Ricoeur's *Time and Narrative* shares my sense that storytelling asserts human agency against the vagaries of time. But Ricoeur does not elucidate the ways theater engages in a direct, multifaceted, and medium-specific struggle with and against time.[10] This will be a central focus of the present work. The paucity of scholarship on theatrical engagements with modern time is especially significant because theater's live action and ostensibly shared time offer artists an ideal venue in which to re-create or resist emergent conceptions of temporal experience.[11]

CRUCIBLES FOR THEATER AND TIME

Precisely because microdramas so often define themselves against normative expectations about length and time, they both invite and enact investigations into the perceived fundamental properties of theater. Brief plays often struggle to build complex characters, to incorporate more than one or two plotlines, to involve large casts, and to generate the sort of absorption that animates longer forms. But by testing the minimum requirements for dramatic presence, for emotional identification, for tragic action, and for persuasive argument, microdramas simultaneously dismantle and reinforce basic properties of theatrical and dramatic form. In doing so, these plays represent especially clear examples of an idea that has gained widespread currency among playwrights since the late nineteenth century, the notion that the stage is an experimental space. The authors I feature are especially committed to the notion that the modern stage is, even more than previous stages, a laboratory, a controlled space where time and action could be isolated and subjected to manipulation. In 1880, Émile Zola called for a theater that would "put a man of flesh and bones on the stage, taken from reality, scientifically analyzed"; Marinetti insisted in 1913 that variety theater provided a "melting pot of the many elements of a new sensibility in the making"; Samuel Beckett wanted his short mime *Act Without Words I* to provide a "last extremity of human meat . . . thinking and stumbling and sweating, under our noses"; and Suzan-Lori Parks went so far as to render playful equations that represent the investigations her early plays undertook.[12]

For these authors and others, brevity becomes a means to isolate constituent elements like framing, light, and time, as well as dramatic conventions like reversal and resolution, and to put them forward as potentially fundamental. As spectators grow uneasy during the long, empty minute of Cangiullo's *Detonation*, for example, the play highlights the strength of an unspoken contract governing most commercial theater: in return for the price of admission, theatergoers expect activity that will fill time and, with luck, distract them from its passage. When the silence persists after the opening curtain, it generates conflict not on stage but in the audience, in the friction between the expected scenario and this departure from it. The lack of a story becomes the story. In the process, the play demonstrates an even more fundamental feature of the modern theatrical event: the way framed time cannot help but generate a narrative, even if, or especially if, the frame appears to be empty.

My focus on brevity's metatheatrical potential directs attention to a subtle form of reflexiveness that I call implicit metatheater. By and large, these plays do not represent or discuss theatrical production, but they make theater's materials and habits unusually visible by paring them down. Jonathan Kalb's 2011 study of marathon theater argues that performances lasting more than four hours deserve critical attention because they place theater under unique stress. Marathon productions

> are unforgiving crucibles from which artistic ideas and approaches emerge either hopelessly broken and disproved or unforgettably bright and persuasive. The theater is more itself in them, one might say, because it has a chance to realize essential powers and potentialities that shrink from view when the art must serve the strictures of compulsory brevity.[13]

Kalb's point about extraordinary length is well taken, but his dismissal of compulsory brevity—a category that for his purposes includes two-hour performances—overlooks the way brevity's strictures, when pushed to an extreme, put similar strain on theater's powers and potentialities. Expansion and compression are rival aspects of a common experimental impulse to reinvigorate theater by reinventing its time signatures. Some projects, like Suzan-Lori Parks's massive collection of 365 tiny plays discussed in chapter 5, explore both impulses at once. When duration becomes remarkable, theater becomes "more itself" precisely when it occupies more or less time than we expect.

This line of argument resembles in some ways Clement Greenberg's depiction of modernist formal intervention as a self-critical reduction to essential properties, but the story of microdramas departs from Greenberg's in several crucial respects, not least that the authors of minimal plays rarely agree about what might be unique or irreducible about theater. I do find, much as Greenberg concludes about the reflexive reductions of modernist painting, sculpture, and poetry, that abbreviated theater rejects norms so strenuously that it reinforces their visibility and importance, so that "the further back these limits are pushed the more explicitly they have to be observed and indicated."[14] But the process of reduction to essentials is especially complicated in theater, a hybrid practice combining elements of visual art, music, literature, dance, sculpture, and everyday life. Theater events are shaped by a range of literary conventions—stage directions, character prefixes, act and scene structures—as well as a host of institutional and social conventions that provide a default scenario for a given era. Despite obvious exceptions, the rough outlines of this scenario have been fairly durable since the late nineteenth century: one travels to a purpose-built building and pays to enter a darkened auditorium with seats facing a curtain; that curtain opens onto a raised, lighted stage where professional actors impersonate others for several hours while ignoring the spectators. An artist looking to reduce theater to an essence, then, has numerous possibilities to choose from. As we might expect, microdramas present multiple answers, and sometimes competing answers, about what if anything might be essential to theater. In so doing, they reveal the ramifications of the common but seldom nuanced idea that theater is made of time, space, and attention.

Cultural and theater history provide necessary context for a discussion of modernist shorts, but I focus primarily on the plays themselves, both on the page and in performance, because their moments—alternately fast and slow, thin and dense, radical and conventional—provide evidence in time and space of the elusive and multifaceted nature of temporal experience, and especially the lived experience of live performance. For these authors, formal brevity registers their engagement with temporality as such. The authors of modernist shorts rarely draw direct inspiration from contemporaneous philosophers, psychologists, sociologists, and scientists who were developing more empirical and philosophical approaches to the nature of time itself (William James, Heidegger, Henri Bergson, Einstein, and Husserl). The authors in this book share with these thinkers an interest in exploring temporal experience and a resistance to conventional ways of accounting for it, but their preferred forum for investigation is the stage. While photographic and filmic technology played only a distant role in the development of shorts, the rise of new theatrical technologies, including electric lighting and naturalist sets, catalyzed the urge to compress. Controlled lighting and realistic environments compressed more information into a given scene by creating spaces that spoke for themselves.

In the pages that follow, I entertain skeptical notions about time and reveal many of its wrinkles, but my methodology aims to keep within view a relatively conventional understanding of theatrical experience, the sort of understanding a given script seems to expect from its original readers and audiences, because my ultimate interest is in the sorts of temporal experiences theater provides. To that end, I read play scripts with an eye to the performance conditions they imply. We tend to think of performance choices as an independent realm subject to the whims of directors, actors, or designers, but I emphasize instead the relatively formalized and historically specific experiences generated from the interplay among a dramatic text and the theatrical conventions of its day. W. B. Worthen calls this interplay "the rhetoric of theater," the historically specific "relationship between the drama, stage production, and audience interpretation" within which audience reaction unfolds and in relation to which elements of a play become significant or fade from view.[15] *Microdramas* explores what plays written since the late nineteenth century can tell us about the temporal rhetoric of theater.

As living laboratories for theater and time, microdramas teach a variety of lessons. These insights cluster around four related concepts, which the four sections below discuss in turn: theater's spatialization of time, the heterogeneity of brief time, the riddle of eventfulness, and the pace of absorption. Each of these ideas is loosely associated with a particular chapter, but they also extend across the chapters and grow more nuanced as they appear in different cases. As a result, the four sections below offer both a tour of the book's central ideas and a summary of how its chapters advance those ideas. Together, these observations aim to contribute to a more robust vocabulary for describing the experience of theatrical moments and the affective implications of duration. In reassessing theatrical time, *Microdramas* complements previous work on the phenomenology of theater, including in particular Bert States's insightful *Great Reckonings in Little Rooms*, Jonathan Kalb's *Beckett in Performance* and *Great Lengths: Seven Works of Marathon Theater*, Rebecca Schneider's *Performing Remains*, David Wiles's *Theatre & Time*, and Matthew Wagner's *Shakespeare, Theatre, and Time*. Reading fast plays slowly so as to reveal the complexity of even the briefest and most minimal theatrical moments, the present study aims to suggest just how much work remains to be done in order to describe the temporal dimensions of aesthetic experience, or to say what theater is.

DIMENSIONS OF THE MOMENT: SPACES THICK WITH TIME

The central argument of chapter 2 is that the beginnings of modern drama involved a shrinking of focus that revealed the interdependence of the time-bound and the timeless on stage. The chapter recasts the two rival factions who founded modern drama in Europe's little theaters—the naturalists and the symbolists—as partners in a mutual retreat from the perceived gigantism of the nineteenth century and its totalizing historical narratives, Wagnerian spectacles, and hypertrophied melodramatic plotlines. Although frequently portrayed as rivals, naturalists and symbolists shared an interest in short stretches of time and in using brief performances to ask how much activity constituted a noteworthy event. The chapter focuses on quarter-hour *faits-divers* plays, a theatrical subgenre popular in late nineteenth-century France and named after minuscule newspaper items relating news of accidents, misfortune, or death. Like the newspaper items from which they took their name, theatrical *faits-divers* may seem like the epitome of hard-boiled naturalism, but in fact they present parables of modern urban vulnerability whose reticence reveals symbolic overtones. The less background we are given about a character, the more her plight becomes emblematic of a type of person, or of people generally. The thinner the realistic slice of life, the more easily we see through it and catch glimmers of abstract or existential concerns. Conversely, although symbolist shorts aim to retreat into abstraction, they cannot suppress the time and material space of the stage.

Symbolic overtones become the subject of Maurice Maeterlinck's *Interior*, a short one-act I discuss at some length in chapter 2. *Interior* estranges the naturalist living room by enclosing a typical bourgeois nuclear family within the walls of their house, and following instead two men in the backyard who peer through the rear windows and hesitate to disrupt the tranquil scene by breaking the news to the family that their eldest daughter has drowned. After protracted handwringing, one of them enters the house to deliver the bad news, and the play ends. *Interior* isolates theater's tendency to frame everyday experience so as to convert an undramatic moment into a riveting one, either by singling it out for attention or by offering a privileged perspective on its import. Almost nothing happens inside the oblivious family's living room, but the fact that nothing is happening, that they assume their walls keep them safe, constitutes their crisis.

By dividing the stage space into interior and exterior, the play highlights theater's capacity to spatialize time. The tragedy in this play is not the daughter's death, but the unevenness of time's unfolding, the impossibility of instant knowledge. *Interior* amplifies the temporal dramatic irony that undergirds all suspense: the audience's present time includes this family's future, and we watch with excruciating anticipation as an unfortunate event that has already happened once happens to the family. The spatialization of time has been a staple of dramatic form since Oedipus, whose groping toward knowledge introduces him to a past event and a future fate already known to the audience. *Interior* and other *faits-divers* plays suggest that the dramatic interest at the heart of theater—a form many associate with shared or real time—is the pleasurable tension between overlapping or competing temporalities. Matthew Wagner's account of theatrical time argues that theater magnifies two related impressions of time familiar from everyday life, temporal dissonance ("the juxtaposition of differing temporal schemes") and temporal thickness (the "weighting of the present with the past and the future.").[16] For Wagner, the audience's impression of a given moment in time thickens to the extent the moment is burdened with memory and expectation. One surprise of *faits-divers* plays is that time can thicken as plays grow thinner. A second insight these plays adumbrate is that the thickness of a particular theatrical moment may be relative: it might be thicker for one character or audience member than another, or thicker for everyone in the audience than it is for the characters. Compression leads both naturalists and symbolists to expose a fundamental complexity of theatrical moments: their balance of material reality and symbolic significance, and the related tension between present moments and the various times that intrude on them.

Brief theater reveals time's lumpiness, but does so in more than one way. Mario Dessy's Futurist microdrama *Waiting*, discussed in chapter 3, for instance, suggests that genre also affects time's thickness. *Waiting* uses simultaneous action to juxtapose the very different temporal experiences of two unrelated men waiting for their lovers. For the nervous young man stage right who imagines himself caught in a romantic tragedy, the few minutes before the lover arrives feel endless: "The time is passing? But how? How is time measured? (*Falls on his chair thoughtful*) Is time long?"[17] It feels long to him. But for the elegant dandy stage left who thinks of the delay as a comedy of errors, the time flies. Through the dual lens of this play, a single space has multiple times, and the thickness of the same few minutes varies according to an individual's affective engagements and generic expectations. Samuel Beckett's short play *Footfalls*, discussed in chapter 4, also spatializes time, but does so by making pacing literal. Its central figure, a disheveled and distracted woman called May, shuffles with "clearly audible rhythmic tread" to and fro on a thin strip of light in the middle of a darkened stage and carries on weary conversations with herself and with an offstage voice we presume to be her mother's. May's shuffling footsteps on a strip of light become an irregular metronome that carefully directs attention to the beats of time but measures them idiosyncratically. As the disjointed clock of May's movements unwinds, it suggests more radically than Dessy's *Waiting* the subjectiveness and artificiality of temporal experience.

THE HETEROGENEITY OF BRIEF TIME

By the late nineteenth century, the arrangement and timing of events in well-made-play dramaturgy seemed so mechanical and predictable that one could claim about the playwright Victorien Sardou that "play-making is not merely as much a trade as clock-making; it is the same trade."[18] To some extent, all playwrights are clockmakers whose creations shape and mark time. But to linger in the moments marked off by modern microdramas, plays which often work more like unpredictable egg timers than trusty grandfather clocks, is to uncover the oddity and variability of the temporalities that theatrical timepieces set into motion.[19] We tend to forget that a viewer's experience of any play involves a proliferation of timers that run concurrently and sometimes interfere with each other: the pace of immediate action, that action's place in a chronology, its place in the piece's structure, when the play was written, when it is set historically, how its events resonate with the present and other periods, the time and timing of its style or styles, its rhythmic relation to other plays or media, its relation to conventional rhythms of social life or language, its degree of metatemporal awareness, and so on. In most performances—as in most everyday situations—these overlapping clocks operate mainly beneath conscious awareness. A viewer's temporal experience of a theatrical event depends on the interplay among these clocks and others as they intrude on the attention or fade from view.

Both detractors of short plays and their champions frequently think in narrow ways about the experiences short plays are likely to generate. Critics tend to assume that brief presentations will be trivial and commercially unviable. In his 1938 introduction to a collection of essays on the one-act play, the playwright William Kozlenko ventriloquizes the frequent assumption that brevity denotes immaturity and appeals only to elite idealists. Broadway professionals, he writes, see the short play as "an amateur drill exercise, a sort of romping, precocious adolescent whose outpourings were intended for the delectation of a small, high-brow audience."[20] Here biological metaphors mingle with gastronomic: shorts are adolescent, but also frivolous delectations—appetizers, amuse-bouches, or petits fours rather than substantial fare. By contrast, proponents of theatrical brevity, including many of the authors in this book, attempt to turn these assumptions on their heads by arguing that brevity intensifies, increases shock, or even that it completely renovates theatrical experience. Behind such rhetoric lies a minimalist fantasy of aesthetic experience as pure intensity and immediacy, rapture without rupture. Charting a balanced course between these two extremes, my readings suggest instead that short theater—like all brief experience—produces a variegated range of temporal experiences that mirror and clarify the diversity of theatrical time in general.[21] In microdramas, time can be accelerated or decelerated, intensified or evacuated, unified or granular, parodic or deliberative, and linear or cyclical. Microdramas might seem to abandon conventions of theatrical time, but more often magnify them in all of their diversity.

Chapter 3 takes up an especially clear case of this disparity between brevity in theory and in practice: the synthetic theater of the Italian Futurists. More than any theater artists before or since, Futurists embraced speed and compression as virtues in themselves and as tools to reinvent theater. In a 1915 manifesto on Futurist Synthetic Theater, Filippo Marinetti and his collaborators declared that "mechanically, by force of brevity, we can achieve an entirely new theater perfectly in tune with our swift and laconic Futurist sensibility. Our acts [atti] can also be moments [attimi], only a few seconds long."[22] In a burst of composition from roughly 1915 to 1922, Futurists wrote hundreds of microdramas called sintesi, or syntheses, dozens of which were performed by professional acting troupes in a series of tours around Italy. Some syntheses lasted only a few seconds; none were longer than six hundred words. In the Futurist imagination, brevity would be the primary tool in a wholesale attack on theater, an attack that, if successful, would make possible Marinetti's dream of a theatricality liberated from theater.

But close readings of manifestos and plays reveal Futurist microdramas to be both richer and more slippery than their authors assumed. The abridgment that they insisted would intensify the present tended instead to work in proliferating and contradictory ways: to parody the past, to deflate moments rather than amplifying them, to slow perception, or to reject theatrical tradition so strenuously that they highlighted its basic elements. Consider the blank opening minute of Cangiullo's Detonation. For an audience expecting a show, the short wait becomes interminable because it is evacuated. Its emptiness makes time crawl and magnifies the conventional shape of melodramatic suspense.

Some of the microdramas I discuss feel quick and comic, but just as often we find shorts that are taxing rather than distracting, that evoke existential mysteries, that seem to last forever, or that sear images into the memory. Microdramas often run surprisingly slowly. Beckett's short plays frequently enforce a sluggish pace and decelerate toward stasis. In his *Rockaby*, the slow mechanical rocking of the chair that holds the play's lone figure creaks like a weary clock, and three times comes to a stop after the line "time she stopped," as if time were stopping along with the chair.[23] Brevity's capacity to decelerate time is one reason microdramas in fact rarely cater to short attention spans. More often than not, they demand greater attention from audiences than plays that unfold more predictably. Whether microdramas cram proportionally more information into less time, or leave so much unsaid that they force spectators to supplement the play with their imaginations, they often demand concentrated and consistent attention.

ESTRANGING THE EVENT

Moving from late nineteenth-century drama through the historical avant-garde into the world of postwar and contemporary theater, this book focuses attention on three terms — short, theater, and event — that its narrative increasingly subjects to scrutiny. The implicit struggle to define these terms, and the resistance to defining them, animates many microdramas. To call a play short is to invoke by contrast an unspoken norm of length, generally two or three hours, which has remained remarkably consistent for most of the last five hundred years in Western history. Many assumptions about length stretch back much farther than that, to Aristotle in the fourth century BCE. Aristotle's account of the appropriate length of drama in the *Poetics*, not unlike his discussion of time in the *Physics*, imagines duration in visible terms. A beautiful plot, like a beautiful animal, should be visible as a whole, neither so small as to be imperceptible, nor so large that it "cannot be perceived at once" in the memory. But within these limits, is Aristotle's ideal length long or short? Two contradictory goals drive his analysis: magnitude and unity of time. On the one hand, beauty correlates with magnitude. Length must be sufficient to represent a probable sequence of events depicting a change from bad fortune to good or from good fortune to bad. Once that minimum requirement has been satisfied, "the greater the length, the more beautiful will the piece be by reason of its size, provided that the whole be perspicuous."[24] On the other hand, compared to epic, drama is preferable because its relatively "concentrated effect is more pleasurable than one which is spread over a long time and so diluted."[25] For Aristotle, dramatic composition is a balancing act between extension and compression that should use an audience's memory as its guide. But since his system takes the viewer's subjective perspective as its yardstick, it leaves open the possibility that conceptions of appropriate scale could change over time.

Considered in its broadest form to include everyday performances, storytelling, political speeches, protests, courtship performances, and sexual performance, short performance genres are likely the oldest and most ubiquitous forms of performance, and certainly predate theater. But the rise of purpose-built commercial theaters in the early modern period helped cement the idea that a satisfying theatrical entertainment must be long enough to justify an audience's expenditure of time and energy. For most of theater history, the names of short forms registered their subordinate positions: interludes and entr'actes came between longer sections, inductions introduced a multi-act play, divertissements distracted from it, curtain-raisers stage-managed the audience still being seated, and afterpieces followed feature presentations. Late nineteenth-century playwrights set out to overturn the assumptions that lay behind these terms by writing brief pieces intended to stand on their own.[26] What was new in this period was not the short play *per se*, but rather the notion that brevity mattered, that it could be significant, that it was of the moment, and that it would be essential to renovating theater. As the second and third chapter will show, the flourishing of short drama in the modernist period resulted in part from an embrace by those with artistic cachet of the commercial success of ostensibly low pop cultural forms, including the variety show, vaudeville sketches and blackouts, and cabaret scenes.[27] In this sense, we owe the existence of those few shorts that were published in the late nineteenth century to a self-conscious revolt against the assumption that short work was unstageable, unimportant, or unpublishable. The embrace of brevity coincided with a renewed appreciation for the aesthetic potential of the mundane, an appreciation that blurred divisions between purportedly high and low subject matter in art forms both long and short. But the same logic underlying the conception that any life, however ordinary, may contain hidden depth also supports the idea that no moment is beneath notice. Modernist shorts written under this assumption stage the democratization of time.[28] As a result, preconceptions about what constitutes full length, and what constitutes a play, remain in the front of these authors' minds. In a fascinating paradox, many of their plays simultaneously demand we notice their shortness and insist we disregard it. They gain attention by highlighting their insufficiency relative to conventional length, and use that attention to argue that wholeness or completion is *not* tied to a particular number of acts, scenes, or minutes. In other words, they often ask us to register them as short in order to debunk the designation "short." The pressure these plays put on conventional temporal structures, such as the act and the scene, helps explain why this book is not a study of one-act plays. Several chapters consider works that fit that designation, and the label "one-act" was coined in the modernist period to describe self-consciously brief plays (one act rather than three or five), but the one-act is simultaneously too narrow and too broad for my purposes. Short plays are not always limited to a single act, and one-acts are not always short. On the contrary, the ideal length suggested by Strindberg for a one-act play, ninety minutes, has become the default length for feature films.

For Maeterlinck, what characterized "The Modern Drama" in his 1890 essay by that title was the modesty of its events: "It is in a small room, round a table, close to the fire, that the joys and sorrows of mankind are decided. We suffer, or make others suffer, we love, we die, there in our corner."[29] The old man in a chair from Maeterlinck's later essay "The Tragedy of Everyday Life" (1896) distills Maeterlinck's ideal of a static theater that would accommodate the uneventful:

> I have come to believe that an old man sitting in his armchair, simply waiting beneath his lamp, listening, without realizing it, to all the eternal laws which rule over his home . . . I have come to believe that this motionless man in reality lives a life that is more profound, more human, and more universal than the lover who strangles his mistress, than the captain who comes home victorious or "the husband who avenges his honor."[30]

One of the surprises of the present study is that the motionless figure seated in an armchair would become a recurring character in modernist microdramas, many of which employ stasis to test the minimum limit for eventfulness. The father in *Interior* sits quietly in an armchair, unaware that his daughter has drowned. A similarly static figure returns as a parody of symbolist contemplation in Pratella's *Nocturnal* (1915), a Futurist synthesis in which a husband stares into darkness contemplating the stars and remains impassive even as thieves accost his wife. Later in the century, Beckett's shorter plays offer a succession of immobile contemplative figures—from Krapp giving ear to earlier accounts of himself in *Krapp's Last Tape* (1958); to the seated motionless Joe in *Eh Joe* (1965); to the aged figures subjected to memory in *That Time* (1974), *A Piece of Monologue* (1979), and *Rockaby* (1980)—in a series that increasingly resembles Maeterlinck's ideal. In 2006, Suzan-Lori Parks wrote a two-line play that includes less action than any of these, and yet extends into infinity:

> Someone standing still. They could be dressed in mourning.
> The sound of wind or whales forever.[31]

One author after another tests Maeterlinck's contention that modern theater begins with the recognition that minimal action or even inaction might be considered action, and that an event might not look eventful. When Parks decided to write a new play every day for a year as part of a project she would call *365 Days/365 Plays*, the massive collection of short scenes became an ideal vehicle for an ethos she called "radical inclusion." Converting life into theater every day required a capacious view of what might qualify as theater. Other writers of shorts demonstrate different versions of radical inclusion: naturalists include unremarkable people, symbolist plays telescope eschatological time into brief presentations, and the Futurists assert that "everything of any value is theatrical."[32] These writers understand that putting a theatrical frame around a series of actions implies that they deserve attention, and therefore, that putting less material in the frame implicitly redefines eventfulness. Under such pressure, it becomes increasingly difficult to distinguish between the noteworthy and the trivial.

George Bernard Shaw went so far as to claim that a shift in focus from shocking events to slices of quotidian life invalidates the logic of conventional endings:

> The moment the dramatist gives up accidents and catastrophes, and takes "slices of life" as his material, he finds himself committed to plays that have no endings. The curtain no longer comes down on a hero slain or married: it comes down when the audience has seen enough of the life presented to it to draw the moral, and must either leave the theatre or miss its last train.[33]

Many of the playwrights I discuss resist the satisfactions typically provided by climactic endings. Nevertheless, contra Shaw, the readings that follow show that, more often than not, even momentary or fragmentary scenes call persistent attention to endings and rely on conventional strategies for closure. The habit of coming to an end, of making an ending, is strong enough to impose itself on remarkably slight or inconclusive material. This is no wonder: ending from the moment they begin, shorts are haunted by the imminence of their own demise.

Brief theater's capacity to put pressure on the concept of ending reaches its apotheosis in chapter 4's discussion of work by Samuel Beckett, the best-known author of short plays in the twentieth century. Over his career, Beckett turned from wandering and exhausting novels to the relative compression of dramatic form, and then set about shrinking drama to its vanishing point, crafting increasingly evacuated plays, some of which he called *dramaticules*. Theater promised Beckett a tangible and temporal medium in which the experience of time could be used to defamiliarize itself. His short plays dramatize struggles to wrestle mere duration into more tolerable shapes, and suggest in the process that conventional understandings of time are themselves comforting constructions. In particular, Beckett's late plays radically undermine the constituent elements of dramatic storytelling—beginnings, development, and endings—by fracturing time into tiny repeated bits or grains that recur cyclically.

Beckett's frustration with assumptions about dramatic time began early in his career. In February of 1931, while he was teaching at Trinity College in Dublin, he made his first recorded appearance as an actor in an amateur send-up of Pierre Corneille and Henri Bergson. Together with French exchange student George Pelorson, Beckett condensed Corneille's four-act tragedy *Le Cid* (1636) into a parody they called *Le Kid*, winking at Charlie Chaplin's 1921 film *The Kid*. Corneille had written *Le Cid* in part to demonstrate neoclassical theatrical ideals, including the unity of time, but the play ended up embroiling him in a remarkably heated controversy when Cardinal Richelieu and other members of the French Academy complained that its efforts to maintain the unity of time crowded too much action into too short a time to be believable. Beckett and Pelorson's *Le Kid* restaged parts of Corneille's tragedy as a hopeless race against an onstage clock in order to suggest that theatrical time displays neither Corneille's unity nor Bergson's flux. An enormous clock was painted on the upstage backdrop. Pelorson sat on a ladder and manually adjusted the clock's hands as time passed in the play. When Beckett's character, an aged Don Diègue dressed as Father Time, gave a long soliloquy while holding an alarm clock, Pelorson began moving the upstage clock gradually faster and faster. As the clock accelerated, Beckett glanced nervously over his shoulder at it, and struggled to speak the lines fast enough to keep stage time in step with clock time. Suddenly the alarm in his hands began ringing. He turned it off and picked up the pace, but it rang again, and Beckett's speech accelerated into uproarious incoherence, not unlike Lucky's famous accelerating speech in *Waiting for Godot.*[34] Beckett's first experiment with theater-making, then, began from the premise that strict adherence to clock time on stage can be more estranging and absurd than the conventions of selective abridgment and dilation that theatrical tradition had naturalized.

Beckett's later temporal manipulations in theater follow *Le Kid* in making clock time an imagined enemy and using the oddity of theatrical time to dramatize the difficulty of accounting for time's passage. By atomizing action into snatches of repetitive dialogue or gesture, and by reducing the length of plays to arbitrarily short stretches, Beckett questions the logic by which a succession of instants coheres into an event. On Beckett's stages, the business of life is the doomed struggle to give a tolerable shape to mere duration, to make a series of endings out of time's elapsing. Beckett's formal repetitions often seem to offer the pleasures that Bergson located in repetition—"the pleasure of mastering the flow of time and of holding the future in the present"[35]—or the related pleasure of holding the past in the present, but they ultimately suggest that any structure we impose on time, including Bergson's vision of time as a steady flow, misrepresents it.

THE PACE OF ABSORPTION

The book's fifth chapter considers a recently popular theatrical phenomenon—the very long compilation of short plays—that tests the limits of the theatrical event at both its minimum and maximum. These productions, which I call microthons, register a contemporary urge to break experience into its constituent parts and also to contain everything at once. Chapter 5 explores a number of extreme compilations but focus sustained attention on two cases, Suzan-Lori Parks's *365 Days/365 Plays* (2006) and Caryl Churchill's *Love and Information* (2011).

365 Days/365 Plays began as Parks's quest to write a play a day for a year and later became a yearlong international performance event. Some of *365*'s plays are among the shortest ever written, but as a whole it is among the longest scripts ever published. As both a marathon race to the finish and a recurring daily practice, *365* offers a contrasting take on the questions of repetition and cyclical time raised by Beckett's theater. While Beckett's microdramas are strictly orchestrated to hold recognizable time at a distance, Parks's tests of theatrical possibility are wedded to the calendar and aim to be radically inclusive and flexible. Churchill's *Love and Information*, which includes more than fifty discrete scenes played in an uninterrupted two hours, offers a series of meditations on knowing and feeling in a digital culture, presented in a format designed to test one's ability to deal with information overload.

A central thread of the fifth chapter is a discussion of the pressures microthons place on audience's affective capacities by beginning again and again. Both *365* and *Love and Information* ask audiences to invest attention in a series of mostly unrelated plays ranging in length from a few sentences to a few pages. Although both projects illustrate theater's capacious flexibility, their tiny plays demonstrate the difficulty of relying on emotional identification to drive home a message quickly. More than other work by Parks and Churchill, the individual plays in *365 and Love and Information* tend to appeal to the head more than the heart. They may ask audiences to recognize or appreciate a problem, but they only rarely depend on emotional identification with the characters and their struggles. Those plays in the collection that do seem to beg for feeling become useful test cases exposing the emotional challenges of short form.

Momentary plays have no trouble generating surprising insights, humorous reversals, or powerful images. Futurist syntheses accomplish all of these goals, sometimes in a matter of seconds. And microdramas that last more than a few minutes often leave considerable room for absorption; the suspense that builds over the fifteen minutes of Maeterlinck's *Interior* depends on the deep identification by the presumed bourgeois audience with the middle class nuclear family on stage. Similarly, audiences of Beckett's play *Not I*, subjected to ten minutes of compulsive monologue from a lighted mouth isolated in the dark void of the stage, may register the event as powerful and moving in part because the piece prompts them to identify even with the barest fragment of a human subject. Nevertheless, in extreme cases, brevity tends to interfere with the partial loss of self we call absorption. Strindberg, the Futurists, and others take for granted that a play's energies are contained in a few intense moments and that everything else is unnecessary filler. But the affective challenges of short form suggest that filler helps prepare spectators to appreciate pivotal moments. Brevity interferes with absorption not only because it disrupts expectations, but also because it reduces the time available for the enchantment of vicarious storytelling to take hold. To be sure, some performances encourage identification more quickly than reading does because live human bodies can produce affective responses almost instantly. But my readings suggest that abridgment tends to reduce the depth of identification with a play's figures. Even as microdramas tend to frustrate some modes of identification — such as the gradual absorption into another person's story — they often provide other axes of engagement, whether intellectual, lyrical, comic, structural, or metatheatrical. By drawing attention to the rhythm of accumulation, for instance, microthons challenge memory and attention in ways that feel familiar to audiences accustomed to information overload. In this way, they suggest that one can identify with a process or a pace as much as a character. I call this phenomenon rhythmic identification.

A 2005 microthon by the Chicago-based Neo-Futurists conducts something like a controlled experiment in abbreviation and absorption. *The Last Two Minutes of the Complete Works of Henrik Ibsen* stages the conclusions of all twenty-six Ibsen plays in chronological order from *The Burial Mound* (1849) to *When We Dead Awaken* (1899). Each of the excerpts radically exaggerates theater's conventional late point of attack, throwing the audience immediately into moments of high tension but denying them the gradual emotional and intellectual engagement that undergirds those moments in Ibsen's plays. Piling one climax atop another, this compilation of endings exaggerates the abruptness and absurdity of Ibsen's endings—from *Brand*'s obliterating avalanche, to Nora's slammed door, to Hedvig's suicide in *The Wild Duck*. Offering the high emotion, the ring of finality, and the decisive action without the gradual development that renders them significant, the piece's brevity converts pathos into bathos, and helps to underline what it is that fills full length.

I use these cases to suggest that it is more than an accident of convention that there are countless short comic sketches and so few five-minute tragedies. Rather, I argue, the horizon of emotional possibility is tied to duration, if only loosely. When Aristotle defined tragedy as an imitation that achieves catharsis through pity and fear, he built the capacity to induce a satisfying emotional experience into his understanding of an admirable play, and many have followed his lead. By this logic, the term *short* connotes not only a temporal lack but also some emotional shortcoming, suggesting that short performances sometimes feel insufficient precisely because they give us insufficient time to feel. In a recent interview, Parks was asked how she knows when a play she is writing is finished. Alluding to the character from Tennessee Williams's *Cat on a Hot Tin Roof*, she replied that she writes like Brick drinks: until she hears the click in her head.[36] This book sheds overdue light on the complexities and limitations of very short plays, pieces that sometimes resist conclusion and sometimes reveal the tenacity of the impulse to conclude, and in the process illuminate the mysterious logic by which playwrights and audiences either do or do not feel the click of a definitive ending.

TWO | The Dimensions of the Moment

Short Spaces and the Birth of the
Modernist Microdrama

The parish priest of La Compôte, Savoie, was walking through the
hills alone. He lay down, naked, under a beech tree, and died of an
aneurysm.
–Félix Fénéon, *Novels in Three Lines*

The above account appeared in a Parisian daily newspaper, *Le Matin*, in
1906 among a list of *faits-divers*, sundry incidents too minor to warrant full
stories. Offering only a bare description of the scene and without preface or
commentary, the miniature narrative says little about the victim yet speaks
volumes. Nestled among other reports of accident or misfortune from
across France, the anonymous story reminds the newspaper reader of
shared vulnerability: even a priest is not safe from the capriciousness of
fate. The tale's swiftness reinforces the abrupt arrival of death. An event
almost too insignificant to mention suggests universal mysteries. Fact-
based, unsparing, and ironic, this *fait-divers* resembles journalistic naturalism. At the same time, it exemplifies what Belgian symbolist playwright
Maurice Maeterlinck called the tragedy of everyday life; with minor altera-
tion, it could preface his static one-act, *The Blind*, which opens on a dead
priest leaning against a hollow oak in an ancient forest.

This chapter suggests that any similarity of *faits-divers* to Maeterlinck's
short drama is neither uncanny nor contradictory. While traditional criticism categorizes naturalism and symbolism as modernist species at opposite ends of a spectrum, I argue that considering aspects of both movements
as part of a shared impulse toward compression reveals unexpected and
significant similarities between the two styles. Dramatists of shorts from
both camps replaced length with intensity, reduced the amount of plot and
character while increasing the role of atmosphere, and eschewed absorption in favor of concentrated suspense and effect. More surprisingly, as
plays shrank they started in certain respects to resemble their "other": naturalist shorts revealed symbolic underpinnings, and symbolist shorts increasingly came to rely on the legibility of the material world of the stage.

After a brief discussion of the shared material and historical conditions out of which modernist shorts emerged, I focus on two cases where naturalism and symbolism in theater converge at their minimal boundaries: the *faits-divers* plays of Oscar Méténier, and Maeterlinck's early one-acts, especially *Interior*. A subset of the naturalist *quart d'heure* genre, theatrical *faits-divers* borrowed their name and spirit from the newspaper items after which they were modeled. Offering only the who, what, and where of an incident, *faits-divers* plays rely on specificity and idiosyncrasy, but these minimal slices of life are cut so very thin that they reveal allegorical foundations. Like symbolist one-acts, their shadowy, effectively anonymous figures personify anxieties about the unknown, about the whims of fate, and about forces beyond control or comprehension. Dramatizing the irony of all that lies beyond understanding, Maeterlinck's *Interior* contributed to his reputation as the foremost symbolist playwright, but the spaces and methods of his microdrama bear uncanny resemblance to those of naturalist shorts. Maeterlinck's play—which suspends a naturalist interior within a symbolist void—can be understood as a parable about contemporary theatrical style that exposes the interdependence of the material and the immaterial on stage.

Considered together, these minimal plays illuminate an understudied turn to brevity during the genesis of modern drama and expose the ontological complexity of dramatic activity in general. In both camps of the early French avant-garde, drama, stripped to its minimum, reveals the persistent, uneasy coexistence of time-bound bodies and timeless ideas.

SHORT SPACES

In the last decades of the nineteenth century, Paris witnessed the birth of two forms of short theater often considered diametric opposites—the naturalist *quart d'heure* ("quarter-hour") and the symbolist one-act. Both were made possible by new spaces—the fast-paced urban metropolis and the semi-private spaces of independent theaters and cabarets—and by new conceptions of theatrical space accompanying the advent of modern scenic design. These plays surprised, confused and impressed audiences with their brevity. Writing about the Théâtre Libre in 1888, August Strindberg recorded the birth of a new genre:

> . . . they made the suffering as brief as possible, let the pain pour forth in one act, sometimes in a single scene. One such small master-

piece was, for example, *Entre frères* by Guiches and Lavedan. The play is so short that it is performed in fifteen minutes, and the genre was immediately called *quart d'heure* . . .

The taste of this period, this headlong, hectic period, seems to be moving toward the brief and expressive . . .[1]

Strindberg had experimented with compression earlier that year in *Miss Julie*, but after encountering the *quarts d'heure*, he confessed that the single, unified scene seemed "set to be the type of play for contemporary theatergoers."[2] Some eighty years before Andy Warhol diagnosed the shrinking attention span of modern mediatized consumers, early avant-garde playwrights earned fifteen minutes of fame in fifteen minutes of theatrical time.

The rise of little theaters, first in Paris and then across Europe, created laboratories for diverse experiments in theatrical form and content.[3] Largely supported by subscriptions and insulated from censors who regulated larger commercial theaters, independent theaters were small spaces that allowed expansive thinking about what a play could be and how long one might last. Most independent theaters were small, usually accommodating a few hundred people instead of one or two thousand, and this relative intimacy allowed closer contact with the audience and lessened the need to exaggerate gesture and speech. Spatial constriction did not necessitate brevity, but various kinds of metaphorical smallness in independent theaters—including exclusivity, idiosyncrasy, intimacy, impoverishment, and an interest in detail and nuance—created conditions appropriate for the development and success of very short plays. The plays produced in little theaters were by no means exclusively short, and some, like Auguste Villiers de l'Isle-Adam's philosophical behemoth *Axël*, were exceedingly long. Nevertheless, in terms of dramatic form, the most important revolution fostered by independent theaters like the Théâtre Libre and the Théâtre d'Art was the proliferation and popularization of the one-act play and its shorter cousins. I focus on Paris as the crucible of the little-theater movement, but what began in Paris soon became an international movement with the founding of Germany's Freie Bühne in 1889, Strindberg's Scandinavian Experimental Theater in Copenhagen in 1889 and his Intimate Theater in Stockholm in 1907, J. T. Grein's Independent Theatre in London in 1891, the Moscow Art Theater in 1898, the Irish National Theatre (later the Abbey) in Dublin in 1902, and a host of little theaters in America, most prominently the Provincetown Playhouse in New York, founded 1918. These theaters and the scores of short plays written for them registered a widespread reaction to new conditions of life, new theatrical possibilities, and new conceptions of time.

Several of the factors contributing to the abundance of short plays in small theaters were practical: shorts were cheap, they provided variety that diluted the risk of failure, and they allowed theaters to take risks on new talent. Combining a number of one-acts into an evening program spread the risk for a production among its constituent parts, reducing the chance of a total flop. Little theaters and cabarets hoped to harness the vivacity of variety shows while redeploying conventions of the popular variety industry, which had itself become something of a behemoth, to more rarefied ends.[4]

The true roots of the shrinking drama, however, lay not in practicality but in the idealistic struggle to craft a theater consonant with a self-consciously modern world. Such a reevaluation would trace the beginning of modernist drama not to one –ism or the other, but to the general break with formal convention signaled by the shrinking drama and the growing importance of theatrical space. The proliferation of shorts in late nineteenth-century Europe testifies to widespread exhaustion with various kinds of gigantism in the nineteenth century, including imperial expansion, totalizing historical narratives, epic pretensions, multivolume novels, and melodramatic hyperbole. Both naturalist and symbolist playwrights rejected the immense spectacle of Wagnerian opera, the comprehensive sweep of the panorama, and the hypertrophied plotlines and histrionic acting styles of melodrama and the well-made play in favor of more compact themes. In an interesting twist, although Wagner's grandiosity seems antithetical to compression, the concept of the *gesamtkunstwerk* or total work of art provided symbolists with a model for a kind of synthesis only available in performance, a synthetic philosophy they would apply to *contract* their forms.[5] Just as short-story writers were reshaping the minimal requirements for a complete narrative work and Impressionist and Pre-Raphaelite painters were turning away from the grand sweep of academic genre and history painting to more intimate and manageable subjects, a growing number of playwrights turned to smaller frames.[6] Edgar Allan Poe's stories, apparently realistic but infused with mystery, inspired not only writers of naturalist shorts—from Méténier, who admired his use of suspense, to Strindberg, who called his play *Simoom* an "Edgar Poer"[7]—but also symbolist poets and dramatists, including Aurélien Lugné-Poë who adopted Poe's name and claimed to be related to the American writer. Unlike curtain raisers or vaudevilles, which on the whole were not meant to be taken seriously, naturalist and symbolist shorts represented conscious attempts by theater artists to achieve dramatic profundity in less theatrical time. As early examples of the modernist revaluation of the quotidian and the fragment, both naturalist *quarts d'heure* and symbolist one-acts sought to reframe the experience of brief stretches of time so as to reveal the drama already inherent in seemingly unextraordinary moments.

In their cultural context, these theatrical experiments in length are symptoms of an obsession with time that pervaded late nineteenth-century consciousness. In the last decades of that century, one sure way to make art that resonated in its day was to make art that resonated in *time*, that is, art that concerned itself with the issues of time and speed that dominated the zeitgeist.[8] The perceived pace of discovery and progress in that self-consciously modern age led to a sense that historical time itself was accelerating. Carlyle spoke for his generation when he observed that "the series of events comes swifter and swifter, at a strange rate; and hastens unexpectedly . . . so the wisest Prophecy finds it was quite wrong as to the date; and, patiently, or even indolently waiting, is astonished to see itself fulfilled, not in centuries as anticipated, but in decades and years."[9] The establishment of railroad schedules and factory time clocks forced ordinary people to pay unprecedented attention to time. Metropolitan living increased not only the need to be aware of time as it passed but also the speed of everyday interactions. As Simmel noted in "The Metropolis and Mental Life" (1903), "the brevity and scarcity" of urban encounters increased the desire "to appear 'to the point,' to appear concentrated and strikingly characteristic."[10] The burden of time is a practical as well as a philosophical concern for theater artists, whose work imposes an experience of time on audiences. For naturalists who sought to reproduce modern life on stage, brevity reinforced the accuracy of the reproduced metropolitan world; short stage scenes reflected short urban scenes. Although symbolist playwrights strove to create spaces out of time, they shared with the naturalists a sense that theater must be overhauled in order to resonate with modern experience. In other words, they insisted on the timeliness of timelessness.

The prevailing origin myths of modern drama tend to portray the independent theater movement as the cradle of two rival tendencies: naturalism, a hard-nosed stepchild of the realist novel born to Émile Zola and André Antoine, and symbolism, a younger, contemplative sibling, raised by Paul Fort and Lugné-Poë, who rebelled by escaping into poetry, idealist philosophy, dreams, and the occult. Both went on, we are told, to produce large rival clans with little miscegenation. A number of scholars have worked either to qualify or dismantle the perceived dichotomy between the real and anti-real camps.[11]

John Henderson is particularly sensitive to the common aims of the wave of avant-garde dramatists writing for little theaters in the 1880s and 1890s. His chapter on naturalism and symbolism in *The First Avant-Garde* concludes by suggesting that realism and idealism were two sides of a common avant-garde gesture characterized by a spirit of youthful revolt, faith in theater's future, a desire to appeal to a sophisticated audience, an obsession with technical experimentation, amateurism stemming from their suspicion of mere skill, a willingness to draw inspiration from outside theater and outside France, and, finally, a polemical stance ensuring that each faction would staunchly deny it owed anything to the other.[12] I contribute to this dismantling not by showing how artists borrowed from both traditions or synthesized them but by imagining both movements from the beginning as part of a common retreat from the grandiosity of nineteenth-century cultural and theatrical forms. Despite their many obvious differences, naturalist and symbolist playwrights shared an interest in compression, in density, and in the importance of theatrical moments, all in the service of roughly the same goal: to produce a theater truer to the realities of life as the playwrights understood them.

A QUARTER-HOUR IN THE LIFE: NATURALIST SLICES OF TIME

In his 1881 essay "Naturalism on the Stage," Émile Zola prophesies that naturalism will one day reign not only in the novel but also on the stage. In response to the claim that naturalistic detail takes more time and space to unfold than the two or three hours allowed by a typical performance, Zola counters that the nature of theater allows far more compression than the novel:

> The marvelous powers of the theatre must not be forgotten nor must its immediate effect upon the audience. . . . If a novel is read by the fireside, in several instances, with a patience tolerating the longest details, the Naturalistic drama should proclaim above all that it has no relation to this isolated reader, but to a crowd who demand clearness and conciseness. . . . The novel analyzes at length with a minuteness of detail which overlooks nothing; the stage can analyze *as briefly as it wishes* by actions and words. In Balzac's work a word or a cry is often sufficient to describe the entire character. This cry belongs essentially to the theatre.[13]

A picture may be worth a thousand words, but a living, breathing, and sometimes crying person is worth far more. Theater needs fewer words to reproduce real people and things because it is an art populated by real people and things. Zola asks, "Is not the stage set a continual description more exact and startling than the descriptions in a novel?"[14] Zola's question highlights the unavoidable phenomenological density of theater's materials. As Bert States observes, "theater—unlike fiction, painting, sculpture and film—is really a language whose words consist to an unusual degree of things that *are* what they seem to be."[15] For Zola and the naturalists, theater was naturally suited for shorthand because it was a language constructed from actual bits of reality. As with life itself, tremendous stores of information inhered in the syllables of a theatrical moment.[16]

Zola claims that his essay "Naturalism on the Stage" will "foretell the future," and to a remarkable degree it does (9). Although Zola's plays met with mixed reviews and although the sort of rigorous naturalism he favored was rarely successful, he does correctly prophesy the eventual commercial dominance of some form of realist drama. In the time since his 1881 essay, the more or less fully rendered living room has proven the template for the preponderance of commercial dramatic output, from the bourgeois parlors of Ibsen, Strindberg, Chekhov, Wilde, and Shaw in Europe, to the stifling interiors of O'Neill, Glaspell, Odets, Williams, and Miller in America; to the interiors of Hollywood sound stages; to the ubiquitous sitcom living rooms piped through televisions into rooms around the world. More specifically, Zola correctly predicts that the theater of the future could work "as briefly as it wishes" by harnessing the silent vocabularies of material reality (10). Zola lived to see his prophecy fulfilled—however partially—by short naturalist one-acts written for independent theaters in Paris, especially Antoine's Théâtre Libre. The Théâtre Libre produced several Zola adaptations and a score of new one-acts by young naturalists, the shorter of which were dubbed *quarts d'heure*. From the seventeenth through the nineteenth centuries, the phrase *quart d'heure* had become shorthand in French for a short period of time.[17] For a culture not yet accustomed to minute hands on clocks but attuned instead to church bells that rang on the quarter hour, the *quart d'heure* registered not as an accumulation of fifteen minutes, but as a single short block of time, one that was subdivided if at all not into minutes, but half quarter hours.[18] By the late nineteenth century, factory and train schedules and the proliferation of handheld watches among the middle classes had introduced minutes into the vocabulary, but the term *quart d'heure* retained its place as a synonym for a moment.

Quarts d'heure took seriously the naturalist project of recording the minutiae of life as it occurs second by second. It is telling that playwright and critic Jean Jullien was describing a short naturalist *play* when he coined the most famous description of naturalism—*tranche de vie* or slice of life: these incisive performances take biopsies from societal tumors and put the offending portion on display, in the flesh.[19] Naturalist playwrights envisioned themselves as experimental scientists, and the *quart d'heure* was the case study, the microscopic slide that served simultaneously as their evidence and findings. By shrinking the size of the sample to a collection of moments, they pushed the limits of the synecdochic logic underlying all naturalism (scientific, literary, or theatrical), and at times fell prey to the same reductionism that plagued early anthropology. In these plays, a few moments in the life of a thug or a thief come to stand for not only his whole life but for a way of life. If longer naturalist one-acts like *Miss Julie* offset their condensation with psychological depth and nuance, the *quart d'heure*—despite attempting to put accurately rendered people before the audience—tends inevitably to flatten and simplify its characters into types. Kirk Williams has argued that although the method of naturalist playwrights rejects metaphor in favor of metonymy, "considered holistically, their works operate according to a loose form of allegory that treats the figures onstage as representative of whole classes."[20] The case of the *quart d'heure* pushes Williams's paradoxical thesis to its limit: the more naturalist plays are boiled down to their essential elements, the less convincing as individuals their characters become, and the more they operate allegorically. The surprising product is naturalism so distilled it reveals a symbolic core.

The master of the *quart d'heure*, Oscar Méténier, created grim, living political cartoons. The ending of Méténier's *quart d'heure Meat-Ticket* (known as *La brême* in French) is illustrative. Father and Mother Pichard sit in the back room of a wine shop. Although lower class, they have absorbed a patina of bourgeois Christian values—enough to know that the goal of life is a steady job, industry, and upward mobility. They also agree an adult woman should choose her own direction in life, so they magnanimously allow their youngest daughter, Nini, just arrived from her first communion, to choose her own career, and they are tickled when she decides to join her older sister's profession as a card-carrying prostitute.[21] *Meat-Ticket* draws to a sardonic close as the parents toast their industrious daughter: "Here's to a successful career, my girl! . . . Here's to a happy future, my child!"[22] Despite the naturalistic milieu, including real bowls of hot wine, the quickly sketched family Pichard could be any lower class family. The scenario and dialogue aim less for verisimilitude than for realistic absurdity, creating an effect that might remind modern audiences of Edward Albee's work.

The association of the slice of life with titillating cruelty and exposé fueled reactions against naturalism and contributed to the closing of the

Théâtre Libre in 1893. But the *quart d'heure* and its increasingly shocking descendants had long lives on the Parisian stage thanks to the longevity of an offshoot from the Libre, the Théâtre du Grand Guignol.[23] Founded by Oscar Méténier in 1897, the Grand Guignol specialized in its early years not in the horror plays for which it later became infamous but in two subgenres of the *quart d'heure*: popular manners[24] and *faits-divers*. While both subgenres registered the demand among Parisian theatergoers for increasingly up-to-date and unsparing portraits of their city, *faits-divers* plays offer one of the clearest cases of theater's remediation in reaction to the time-conscious medium of newspaper. Méténier, having worked for a police commissioner and contributed to sensationalistic crime papers, found in the newspaper a model of bare-bones naturalistic storytelling. Like tiny variety theaters revealing an overdose of reality through an accumulation of small accounts, daily papers quickened the pace of life, captured the present, and whetted the appetite for salacious detail. Newspaper *faits-divers* described muggings, arrests, animal attacks, break-ins, drug overdoses, deaths, and the like without elaboration but often sculpted to create irony and macabre effect. Two examples from a remarkable author of *faits-divers*, critic and anarchist Félix Fénéon, capture the tantalizing drama and mystery possible in this minuscule newspaper genre:

> Responding to a call at night, M. Sirvent, café owner of Caissargues, Gard, opened his window; a rifle shot destroyed his face.

> A corpse floated downstream. A sailor fished it out at Boulogne. No identification; a pearl-gray suit; about 65 years old.[25]

The theatrical *fait-divers* is one of the earliest examples of a whole family of modernist art inspired by the newspaper, including Picasso's collages, the "Aeolus" chapter of James Joyce's *Ulysses*, the headline typeface of Wyndham Lewis's manifestos, the devastating six-word short story attributed to Ernest Hemingway ("For sale: baby shoes, never worn."), and the Federal Theatre Project's Living Newspaper performances.[26] But unlike bona fide newspaper headlines, *faits-divers* could barely be considered newsworthy; instead, they helped redefine the meaning of newsworthy. Visitors to the early seasons of the Grand Guignol, by extension, paid to see the earliest form of what would eventually become the sensationalistic local television news broadcast or true-crime drama.

Even more than Maeterlinck's static one-acts, *faits-divers* revealed the extent and variety of quotidian tragedy. In Méténier's 1897 quarter-hour

Fig. 1. Printed *faits-divers* as daily Parisian spectacle in Max Radiguet's cover illustration from *L'Assiette au beurre* (September 8, 1906). (General Collection. Beinecke Rare Book and Manuscript Library, Yale University.)

Lui! (*Him!*), a prostitute is locked in a bedroom with a man she soon realizes is a psychopathic murderer. The play self-consciously admits its debt to journalistic *faits-divers*: the performance opens with the matron of the brothel, Madame Briquet, and one of her workers, Violette, reading and quoting from *Le Petit Parisien*, a pulp magazine full of *faits-divers*. They gawk at a story and a picture that relate the grisly decapitation of one Madame Dubois earlier that day, and they worry that the culprit is still at large. Madame Briquet sums up both the police chase and, unwittingly, the project of the play when she says, "It's a race against the clock . . ."[27] This line sets a short fuse, and the play accelerates toward its conclusion. The women hear a newsboy in the street calling "Extra! Evening paper!" and rush off to see if the killer has been caught. Then the onstage *fait-divers* delivers the news we're waiting for: a man fitting the murderer's description arrives as the next customer, bearing the loot that's gone missing from Madame Dubois's house.

Through the onstage reenactment, *Lui!* awakens in the audience anxiety produced by the crime. A murderer has been ripped from the headlines and put before the newspaper reader in the flesh.[28] The play relies on the audience's identification with the characters not as prostitutes but as fellow readers of crime magazines who know the paranoia created by daily intrusions of an often terrifying outside world into the privacy of the bedroom or the breakfast table. As Richard J. Hand and Michael Wilson note, the play feeds off the assumed metrophobia of the spectators, who are surrounded by strangers in the city—and in the theater—and wondering if their personal spaces are secure (84). Méténier wants to rattle his spectators like the crime story has rattled Madame Briquet: "Things like that really get to me . . . I haven't been able to eat a thing all day after seeing *that*" (85, emphasis in original). As the heightened anxiety and over-emotive dialogue reveal, the *fait-divers* genre marries the gritty, fully realized physical spaces of naturalism and the suspense of melodrama. Although young Violette is saved at the last minute by the arrival of a police inspector, her final hysterical words are simultaneously a convincing picture of urban paranoia and a melodramatic exclamation point: "I'm scared—so scared!" (92). Defenders of naturalism's unrelenting attention to the unsavory argued that the essential relationships between man and society could be portrayed more clearly through primitive characters and gritty situations than when obscured by bourgeois trappings like money, psychological development, and affectation.[29] This was certainly the appeal of the *quart d'heure* for Strindberg, who found the "joy of life in its cruel and powerful struggles" and argued that a truly objective view involves the cruelty of an indifferent god.[30]

The *quarts d'heure* proved a significant source of inspiration for Strindberg during his naturalist period, and not only because they shared his unsparing view of the human condition. Strindberg kept track of the work at the Théâtre Libre by reading Georg Brandes's reviews in the Danish daily *Politiken* and Emile Blavet's reviews in *Le Figaro*.[31] Convinced that the new Théâtre Libre's *quart d'heure* was "the type of play for contemporary theatergoers" and that it "may well become the *formula* for the drama of the future,"[32] Strindberg decided to create an experimental theater on the same model in Copenhagen, and between 1889 and 1892, he wrote nine one-acts for the new theater, three of which—*The Stronger, Pariah*, and *Simoom*—are *quarts d'heure*, at least in length.[33] Writing in praise of Gustave Guiches and Henri Lavedan's *Entre frères* in his essay "On Modern Drama and Modern Theater," Strindberg ruminates on the vogue of modern theatrical brevity. As the best contemporary diagnosis of the phenomenon, his thoughts are worth quoting at some length:

> This is dramatic action reduced to a single scene, and why not? Anyone who has had the task of reading plays that have been submitted to a theatre director soon observes that every play would seem to have been written for the sake of a single scene, and that all the author's creative joy involved this scene, which sustained him during the terrible pains which the exposition, presentation, complications, unraveling, peripeteia and catastrophe had caused him. . . .
>
> The taste of this period, this headlong, hectic period, seems to be moving toward the brief and expressive, and Tolstoy's painful *The Power of Darkness* at the Théâtre Libre was unable to retain the audience's interest, even with the help of Franco-Russian politics.
>
> A scene, a *quart d'heure*, seems set to be the type of play for contemporary theatergoers . . . With the help of a table and two chairs one could present the most powerful conflicts life has to offer; and in this type of art, all the discoveries of modern psychology could be applied for the first time in a popular form.[34]

Strindberg explains the vogue for brevity as a return to the ancient unity of action that had defined Greek tragedy for Aristotle, bolstered by a self-consciously modern age and a shrinking attention span. Short plays promised convenient and manageable pieces for a poor experimental theater that intended to tour, but arguably, what appealed most to Strindberg about the *quarts d'heure* was the way their paucity of incident shifted focus toward his true interest: mental conflict.

In fact, Strindberg's quarter-hour pieces resemble the French *quarts d'heure* in little aside from their length and their surface naturalism. If the French plays sought to present case studies from the lives of society's lower strata, set in fully-stocked surroundings and turning on some significant action, Strindberg employs bourgeois characters, dispenses with the naturalist set, and pares the action down to dialogue alone in order to sharpen the psychological conflict. He wanted no superb sets to "blind the eyes" and to "hide the poverty of a form," preferring instead "simple *mise-en-scène*."[35] In an 1888 letter to a colleague, he describes the formula: "Two characters, without plot, with sharp tension, in a Battle of the Brains, struggle between souls."[36] The battle of brains—*hjärnornas kamp*—would become a central Strindbergian obsession.[37] The single-scene short pitting two minds against each other provided a dramatic distillation of the conflicts at the core of early plays like *The Father*.

The Stronger (1889) is a battle of brains between two actresses, Mrs. X and Mademoiselle Y, who we gather have both loved the same man (Mrs. X's husband), but it is also a battle between the verbal and the nonverbal. In this conversation, there are two participants but only one speaker. Mademoiselle Y remains silent throughout, while Mrs. X talks to cover up the silence, filling the emptiness with small talk, with apologies for Mlle. Y's broken engagement with a young man, with pointed stories about her husband and insinuations about an affair between him and Mlle. Y, and finally, with a dismissive announcement of moral victory and a word of thanks to Mlle. Y for having taught her husband how to love. A duet of the spoken and the unspoken, *The Stronger* anticipates later twentieth-century one-acts that stage battles between a talker and a listener, including Eugene O'Neill's late play, *Hughie* (1941), and to a lesser extent Albee's *Zoo Story* (1959). Like these plays, Strindberg's duet asks which character is the stronger, and leaves the question intentionally unanswered. Mlle. Y maintains a dignified and superior silence, but the resilient Mrs. X has recovered from losing her husband and may have won him back. The play asks not only which is the stronger soul but which is the stronger style—the active or the inactive, the spoken or the silent—a question that the play's pared-down dramaturgy may help to answer. If Mrs. X seems transplanted from an adulterous, action-packed melodrama, here she finds herself in a play that, much like Mlle. Y, maintains a dignified inactivity. Just as Mlle. Y uses restraint to wind "all of these thoughts out of [Mrs. X]," the play restrains action and speech in order to lay bare its central psychological conflict.[38]

Strindberg's one-acts were early experiments in dramatic compression, a theme he would return to throughout his career. Earlier in 1888, in the Preface to *Miss Julie*, Strindberg had called for a number of naturalist renovations in lighting and theater space, culminating in a testament to small scale: "if we could have complete darkness during performances; and, finally, and most importantly, a *small* stage and a *small* auditorium, then perhaps we might see a new drama arise."[39] These small plays were his first attempt to find a form to fit such a small, modern theater. Later, and more famously, Strindberg would found the 161-seat Intimate Theatre in Stockholm, an institution in which he could explore what he saw as the central requirement of drama, "the strong, highly significant motif, but with limitations."[40] Although he wouldn't return to the quarter-hour form in his post-*Inferno* period, in later plays Strindberg used asterisks to indicate what John Martin calls each turn-of-idea.[41] Many English translations omit the asterisks, so this small-scale structuring within scenes has been lost to many readers, but it suggests that Strindberg continued to see mental activity as more central than physical, and to assume that moments are dramatic elements as fundamental as scenes or acts.

Peter Szondi has noted that the action of all naturalist drama resembles newspaper *faits-divers* in that the identity of the person to whom the action happens, though specified, is generally unimportant.[42] Although it purports to be the first drama to present actual people on stage, its characters are, in Una Chaudhuri's words, "merely the raw material, the data, of the audience's discoveries."[43] This counterintuitive idea—that a mode of theater insisting on the specificity of people and places presents stories that are essentially anonymous—is nowhere truer than in naturalist *faits-divers*—minimal scenes in which the shape of an incident outweighs the shaping of character. The specificity of the action may heighten the perceived danger, but the vicarious fear these microdramas engender relies on the abstract, impersonal threat of an anonymizing urban landscape. The less information *faits-divers* provide about their victims, the more their stories become parables of modern vulnerability, and the more the portentous figures in their dark corners come to resemble the unnamed shades lurking in the shadows of symbolist drama.

Staging compressed and enigmatic *faits-divers* instead of events with longer historical or narrative arcs allowed playwrights to explore the riddle of eventfulness. For Roland Barthes, newspaper *faits-divers* are compelling because of their liminal position between the remarkable and the irrelevant, a territory charged by the mystery of why things happen and why particular occurrences demand notice. *Faits-divers* appear closed, self-sufficient, and immanent, referring to little or nothing outside themselves, a quality that allies them with short stories, anecdotes, and tales, as well as sketches, skits, and scenes. But every *fait-divers* nevertheless contains a minimal structure that makes it worth mentioning, an implied relation between terms that relies on aberrant causality or coincidence. *Faits-divers* come in many varieties, but they nearly always imply a perverse logic behind events, whether by tweaking stereotypes (a chief of police kills his wife), by suggesting that coincidences are motivated (a prostitute eager for news of the killer is rewarded with a terrifying in-person meeting), or by highlighting the disproportion between an insignificant cause and a great effect (a train is derailed in Alaska when a deer trips a switch). News of a *fait-divers* prompts a cosmic detective story that would connect the event with its cause (189). Underscoring the pervasive influence of causality but simultaneously undermining its predictability, *faits-divers* portray a naturalistic world of events charged with hidden echoes, buried relations, and unseen connections. As such, they distill the paradox of naturalism's debts to the unseen. When Barthes writes that "a god prowls behind the *fait-divers*," he captures their uncanny suggestion that nothing is coincidence and also offers a serviceable description of early naturalist drama.[44]

The paradox in which less material generates more symbolic associations applies as much to the stage world of naturalist microdrama as to its narrative. Minimizing the drama magnifies its essential materials—space, light, movement, and objects—and burdens them with metaphorical significance. In such a world, moments are more momentous because they speak for themselves. Jean Jullien, one of the first to suggest that the essence of drama may be visual rather than verbal, called for reforms in staging that would become conventions of the realist theater, including the darkened auditorium, controlled lighting, and an imagined fourth wall. Such innovations promised to increase verisimilitude, but the creation of a lighted onstage world surrounded by a void had the counter-intuitive effect of encouraging spectators to imagine the stage as a space apart charged with symbolic meaning. This tendency becomes more acute as the amount of material decreases. Minimalism's tendency to magnify subverts what Chaudhuri calls naturalism's "contract of total visibility" by exaggerating it. According to Chaudhuri, the "promise of the well-stocked stage of Naturalism is a promise of omniscience, indeed of a transfer of omniscience from dramatist to spectator."[45] But the promise that observation of a world will produce knowledge about it, when applied to a tiny amount of material, creates spaces in which otherwise insignificant figures or objects—a tramp, a prostitute, a razor, or a gun—point beyond themselves to hidden meanings. As they grow thinner, slices of life reveal glimmers of the ineffable mysteries they purport to exclude.

SPACES OF MIND: SYMBOLIST MICRODRAMAS

During the same period when naturalist shorts were gaining popularity, symbolist writers also used the discovered spaces of independent theaters to experiment with short theater. At first blush, they embraced brevity for very different reasons than did the naturalists. If naturalist shorts aimed accurately to reproduce the pace of modern life's pivotal incidents, symbolist shorts offered what Jean Cocteau later called "poetry of the theatre."[46] Symbolist theater was invented not by theater directors but by poets in collaboration with painters, and it found its small stages in spaces like Paul Fort's Théâtre D'art and Lugné-Poë's Théâtre de l'Oeuvre. Inspired by Charles Baudelaire's translations of Edgar Allan Poe, and especially by Poe's "The Philosophy of Composition," which argued that the desired effect of an artwork should determine its shape and that "brevity must be in direct ratio to the intensity of the intended effect," symbolist playwrights created plays that work in some ways like lyric poems.[47] In her book *Lyric Time*, Sharon Cameron writes eloquently on the way lyric poetry tends to occupy and amplify moments:

> If a poem denies the centrality of beginnings and endings, if it fails to concern itself with the accumulated sequence of a history, it must push its way into the dimensions of the moment, pry apart its walls and reveal the discovered space there to be as complex as the long corridors of historical or narrative time.[48]

Translating this lyric project for the stage, symbolist plays pry apart naturalism's walls and push open the dimensions of the moment to create their own microcosms. Whereas naturalists hewed closely to historical and clock time, symbolists preferred spaces that conjured a moment out of time or beyond time, freed from history. Pushing against the dominance of measurable or scientific time, symbolists eschewed the newly established Greenwich mean time in favor of subjective and syncretic tempos of the mind, of myth and the occult, of poetry, and of dreams.[49] Some playwrights attempted to create through webs of allusion and correspondence a space altogether outside of time, what W. B. Yeats would call "a deep of the mind," and which Beckett would later describe, echoing Yeats, as "pro-founds of mind."[50] Others telescoped huge swathes of mythical time into a few minutes, creating neo-mysteries like Pierre Quillard's *The Girl with Cut-off Hands* (1891), which aims to represent an "infinite multiplicity of time and place" in a short episode, or like Strindberg's aberrant *Coram Populo!* (1877–78) which squeezes into a few minutes a six-act tragedy including the creation of the world, the fall of man, the tower of Babel, and the apocalypse.[51] Many symbolist poems and plays expose the complexity of the momentary, but these telescopic temporalities suggest the obverse, that all time might be imagined within the bounds of a moment. *Coram Populo!* imagines that theater can estrange time as radically as a divine perspective might, shrinking all of biblical time into an episode and converting God's decision to create earth into a sadistic folly soon repented. Its audience gains brief access to a simulated divine temporality, but at the cost of learning that from such a perspective all of creation becomes a cruel accident, a *fait-divers*.

The symbolist desire to free the spectator or reader from the constraints of time could be approximated in a painting or a poem, but it ran into a fundamental tension when deployed in theater, a form tied to time's passage in which bodies occupy more or less the same space and time. Symbolist theater seemed to some a contradiction in terms, an attempt to render bodies into ideas, to harness the visible to evoke the invisible, to organize time-bound spaces so as to escape the clutches of time and space. Symbolist playwrights responded to this seemingly insoluble bind with a particular brand of idealistic anti-theatricality.[52] They sought to occlude, replace, or evacuate theater's persistent materiality using various forms of abstraction, from Maeterlinck's early proposal of a theater of androids, to Edward Gordon Craig's über-marionettes, to the vogue for masks, most enthusiastically embraced by Yeats. They hid stages behind gauze, abstracted voices through incantation or sing-song, estranged bodies through slow-motion movement, and resisted the flow of time by slowing action to a crawl and stripping places and characters of identifying detail.

Although Martin Puchner and others have shown that these anti-theatrical impulses often led to productive innovations in theater, Maeterlinck proved that the best solution to the paradox of symbolism in the theater involved an engagement with, rather than a retreat from, theater's fundamental materials: space, light, bodies, and time. Maeterlinck pioneered this approach and, in doing so, secured a place as the best-known and most commercially successful symbolist in the theater.[53] Although his early writings bemoan the materiality of the stage and propose doing away with actors and action, his microdramas always make the spectator aware of their dual status as material spaces and as spaces of the mind. Maeterlinck's one-acts quote and manipulate elements of the naturalist theater not merely to cater to an audience weaned on realist convention but to expose the *correspondence* in theater between the seen and the unseen.

"ONLY THROUGH TIME TIME IS CONQUERED": MAURICE MAETERLINCK

> But only in time can the moment in the rose-garden,
> The moment in the arbour where the rain beat,
> The moment in the draughty church at smokefall
> Be remembered; involved with past and future.
> Only through time time is conquered.
>   –T. S. Eliot, "Burnt Norton"

> Time and space are two masks of the same enigma, which as
> soon as we look at them fixedly assume the same expression.
>   –Maeterlinck, *The Life of Space*[54]

Maeterlinck sought to create a theater consonant with modern life by shrinking its focus. On his account, outworn tragedies that followed the "extraordinary and violent adventures" of grandiose or royal figures steeped in blood no longer resonated with the self-consciously modern audiences of late nineteenth-century Europe.[55] Popular drama of the nineteenth century directed obsessive attention toward climactic events caused by moral lapses—infidelity, bankruptcy, murder—but in their obsession with scandal overlooked the conflicts found in the minutiae of everyday moments characterized by stasis and silence. What was needed was a drama that "actually stands for the reality of our time," which must, first of all, be small: "It is in a small room, round a table, close to the fire, that the joys and sorrows of mankind are decided. We suffer, or make others suffer, we love, we die, there in our corner."[56] Maeterlinck's assumption that modern drama should be modest, domestic, anonymous, and static found its apotheosis in the image of the old man in a chair from "The Tragedy of Everyday Life" (1896). An excerpt from this passage appears in the introduction, but I quote it more fully here since it is a linchpin in both Maeterlinck's dramatic theory and his dramaturgy:

> I have come to believe that an old man sitting in his armchair, simply
> waiting beneath his lamp, listening, without realizing it, to all the eternal

laws which rule over his home, interpreting without comprehending the silence of doors and windows and the small voice of the light, submitting to the presence of his soul and of his destiny, head slightly bowed, without suspecting that all of the powers of this world are active and watchful in this room, like attentive maid-servants, unaware that the little table he leans on is actually held in place over the abyss by the sun itself, and that there is not a single star in the sky nor a single force of the soul that is indifferent to the movement of an eyelid that droops or of a thought that takes flight—I have come to believe that this motionless man in reality lives a life that is more profound, more human, and more universal than the lover who strangles his mistress, than the captain who comes home victorious or 'the husband who avenges his honor.'[57]

Here is a drama so small it is almost imperceptible, hidden inside the mind and subtle enough to escape notice of its protagonist. Yet it draws its force and profundity from the notion that the infinitesimal is the concave side the infinite, that minutiae are tied to unseen powers so that the faintest action—a drooping eyelid—is yoked to destiny just as it is to gravity's invisible influences. Critics hail Maeterlinck's prescience in describing the central role of inaction and silence in twentieth-century drama, and they often note his theater's undeniable resemblance to Samuel Beckett's, where static figures with bowed heads recur frequently and situation takes precedence over action.[58] Like Beckett, Maeterlinck argues "for the elevation of theatre's intermittent parts into coherent, freestanding, dramatic 'wholes.'"[59]

What has gotten less attention in discussions of Maeterlinck's interest in the quotidian is the uncanny similarity of the synecdochic logic of "The Tragedy of Everyday Life" to that of theatrical naturalism. If, as theater historians explain, symbolism revolts against slavish imitation of the material in order to evoke the spectral, the immaterial, and the unseen, why does Maeterlinck appear to desire a theater that "stands for the reality of our time,"[60] and why does his emblem for that theater so closely resemble a naturalist slice of life, including the table, the armchair, the lamp, indeed the very domestic "corner of life" that Zola used to define naturalism in "Naturalism on the Stage"? (6) What does Maeterlinck mean when he calls for "a kind of new beauty, that shall be *less abstract* than was the old"?[61] Why, too, do several of the little plays he created for independent theaters, especially *The Intruder* (1891) and *Interior* (1894), seem bound to conventions that symbolists are purported to revile, from domestic settings realized onstage, to realistic lighting produced by actual lamps on tables, to contemporary human characters who speak prose dialogue in the idiom, if not the manner, of ordinary speech? One tempting but insufficient answer is that Maeterlinck in his early years was not a representative symbolist playwright. But while his one-acts bear more resemblance to naturalism than most symbolist drama, that resemblance makes them, paradoxically, optimal translations of the symbolist doctrine of correspondences into theatrical form. To examine Maeterlinck's 1894 one-act, *Interior*, in light of naturalist shorts reveals how naturalism and symbolism converge at their minimal limits by relying more heavily on the constitutive elements of theater. This conclusion supplements work by Daniel Gerould and Patrick McGuinness, both of whom argue, against the grain of symbolist pronouncements, that the fervent suppression of contemporary time and space in symbolist drama—its rigid policing of characterization, decor, and locale—paradoxically caused the material time and space of the stage to gain more importance.[62]

As the curtain rises on *Interior*, we see an exterior—the back of a house—and, through its windows, the generic bourgeois sitting room familiar to naturalist drama. Inside, a nuclear family of father, mother, two daughters, and a baby "is pretty distinctly visible, gathered for the evening round the lamp."[63] The house's back wall, partially occluding the interior promised by the play's title, seems to breach Chaudhuri's contract of total visibility. Yet the tangible and fully rendered architecture of the house obeys naturalist conventions. Seeing the house from the outside, and from behind, reminds the audience that it exists in three dimensions, standing on imagined walls that, according to the conventions of realistic staging, extend beyond the visible frame of the stage. An old man and a stranger arrive in the garden and pause to observe the family, who appear strange, distant, and silent. Putting its subjects behind glass, the play seems to follow the empirical logic that binds scientific and theatrical naturalism, subjecting oblivious creatures to observation and recording how they react to stimuli.[64] As the spare plot unfolds, we learn that the old man and stranger have been charged with delivering to the parents news that their daughter has drowned (or has drowned herself). We watch the eavesdroppers observe the family and delay giving them the news, and finally we see the old man, under pressure from the approaching crowd of mourners who have arrived at length, enter the house and deliver his heart-rending message to the family.

Interior dramatizes the delayed announcement of precisely the sort of news related by *faits-divers*. The plot follows rules of probability and possibility that became ideals of theatrical verisimilitude in the seventeenth century, but the amount of action has been drastically reduced. One of

Fig. 2. Obscure shadows engulf a small island of interior space in an 1899 advertisting poster by Catalan painter and symbolist playwright Santiago Rusiñol. (Reproduced by permission of the Documentation Centre and Performing Arts Museum of the Institut del Teatre, Barcelona.)

Fénéon's news items from *Le Matin* relays an everyday tragedy with un-canny resonance: "By accident, or, more probably, suicide, Mme Veit and her daughter Antoinette, 9, drowned in the canal at Nancy" (60). But like someone who has not yet read this newspaper update, the family has through most of the play not yet gotten the news. What makes this unre-markable scene dramatic is our knowledge of their ignorance. The play offers an essentially naturalist vision of theater as nothing more than the framing of everyday experience, the conversion of experience into mean-ing through perspective.

At the same time, numerous clues signal the play's departures from the naturalist aesthetic. The family moves with the stylized gravitas that had already by 1894 become characteristic of symbolist drama. With their cryptic, ominous dialogue and generic names, the old man and the stranger resemble members of the liminal society of old men and strang-ers who haunt symbolist and expressionist drama.[65] The music of their formalized dialogue signals the otherworldly status of the world outside the house:

> THE STRANGER: See, they are smiling in the silence of the room . . .
> THE OLD MAN: They are not at all anxious—they did not expect her this evening.
> THE STRANGER: They sit motionless and smiling. But see, the father puts his fingers to his lips . . .
> THE OLD MAN: He points to the child asleep on its mother's breast . . .
> THE STRANGER: She dares not raise her head for fear of disturbing it . . .
> THE OLD MAN: They are not sewing anymore. There is a dead si-lence . . .
> THE STRANGER: They have let fall their skein of white silk . . .
> THE OLD MAN: They are looking at the child . . . (48–49)

If these lines of roughly equal length tied together by anaphora resemble a poem, it is a strangely narrative one. Much of the oddity of the old man's speech derives from its redundancy and persistent diegetic distance, quali-ties that cause him to resemble a Brechtian narrator.[66] Maeterlinck coined the term *second-degree dialogue* to describe language freed from its plot-furthering role, seemingly superfluous language full of "ineffable im-port."[67] The dialogue in *Interior* is something else. Second-degree dialogue is casual, underdetermined, and irrelevant to the plot; here the dialogue is formal, overdetermined, and details each step of the minimal plot, generating the same sort of suspense that drives Poe's short stories.

A final and vital clue that the play reflects symbolism's deep engagement with materiality is gleaned not from the script itself but from the title of the volume in which it was first published: *Three Little Dramas for Marionettes*. If one were to read only Maeterlinck's early dramatic writings, it would be easy to take the collection's title literally. In "Small Talk," he voices the common symbolist complaint that the abundance of sullied material bodies on stage corrupts the purity of its ideas. In response, he advocates replacing actors with non-human figures:

> The stage is where masterpieces die, because the presentation of masterpieces by *accidental* and *human* means is a contradiction. . . . One should perhaps eliminate the living being from the stage. . . . Will the human being be replaced by a shadow? a reflection? . . . a projection of symbolic forms, or a being who would appear to live without being alive? I do not know; but the absence of man seems essential to me. (145)

But as his career developed, Maeterlinck's resistance to live actors softened, and most critics agree that the phrase "for Marionettes" in the title is meant figuratively.[68] The actors should not be marionettes but should resemble them in their remoteness, silence, and helplessness. The more puppet-like the characters, the more their status as individuals diminishes in favor of the "external nullity which the marionette by its very nature emphasizes," and the more they come to operate as symbols of humanity's submission to forces beyond its control.[69] Arguably, the Old Man's description of the family—"they look like lifeless puppets" (48)—only works if he is describing human actors. In a marionette production, the line would become redundant self-referential comedy. Using live actors in a naturalistic interior but emphasizing their lack of volition, Maeterlinck does not demonstrate symbolist disregard for materiality as much as he illustrates the peculiar submission of all theatrical characters, especially those of naturalism, to external forces. Naturalism makes its characters the puppets of historical, genetic, economic and narrative forces, and thus shifts the locus of recognition from character to audience. This tendency is even more pronounced in very short plays. As a result, both naturalist and symbolist shorts tend to create hollow characters overshadowed by their allegorical significance.

In the case of *Interior*, the obvious allegorical theme is one of Maeterlinck's enduring preoccupations: the obliviousness of human beings in the face of death's inevitable approach. In the remainder of the chapter, a close reading of the spaces of *Interior* will reveal that the play also illustrates the futility of resisting the flow of time, and in the process, that it brokers a compromise between realism and idealism.

The play's sealed interior can be seen as the human mind in time, trapped inside a present defined by stubbornly material objects but moving toward—and at times vaguely aware of—a shadowy yet inevitable future it can never fully grasp. A vital clue to this layer of the play's meaning is Maeterlinck's preoccupation with the idea that the present and the future are separated by a permeable membrane. In the 1904 essay "The Foretelling of the Future," he describes the mind as a vessel that, though it is sealed against the future into which it sails, occasionally allows intimations of that future to leak into its awareness (143). Inside the ship, we have no idea where we're going, or what the sea ahead looks like. Our frustration with the solid walls between our minds and the future has for ages fueled prophecy, prognostication, and mysticism: "man has tried to find crannies in that wall, to provoke infiltrations into that vessel, to pierce the partitions that separate his reason, which knows scarcely anything, from his instinct, which knows all, but cannot make use of this knowledge" (143). In rare cases, Maeterlinck marvels, the vessel leaks, making inner truths that are invisible to our conscious awareness, visible to fortune-tellers or others sensitive enough to see them. As he ponders this situation, he begins to envision the private mind as an almost public space. In doing so, he traces the outlines of several key concepts in *Interior*:

> It is really disconcerting that a stranger should see farther than ourselves into our own hearts. . . . It is vain for us to keep watch upon ourselves, to shut ourselves up within ourselves: our consciousness is not watertight, it escapes, it does not belong to us; and though it requires special circumstances for another to install himself there and take possession of it, nevertheless it is certain that, in normal life, our spiritual tribunal, our *for intérieur*—as the French have called it, with that profound intuition which we often discover in the etymology of words—is a kind of *forum*, or spiritual market-place, in which the majority of those who have business there come and go at will, look about them and pick out the truths, in a very different fashion and much more freely than we would have believed. (157)

The term Maeterlinck uses for consciousness in the essay—*for intérieur*—suggests a retrospective frame for the play's symbolism. Derived from the Latin *forum*, *for intérieur* fractures the single consciousness and, at least for Maeterlinck, implies that the mind is a theatrical space susceptible to the scrutiny of others. More specifically, the passage envisions the mind immuring itself within its own walls, but remaining visible to a stranger.

This situation closely parallels the spatial arrangement of *Interior*. The front of the house is shut to the outside, oblivious to the future. But, as the old man says, "there are no shutters on this side of the house" (46). Somewhere in the back of the mind, there are windows that open onto the unknown, windows that from the inside yield only dark shadows but that nevertheless make us visible and vulnerable, "separated from the enemy by only a few poor panes of glass" (51). The internal faculties may shore up mental defenses against the unknown, much as the family has secured the house—"They have strengthened the walls of the old house; they have shot the bolts of the three oaken doors. They have foreseen everything that can be foreseen" (49)—but in fact very little can be foreseen from inside life's little dramas. The back windows, however, remain unshuttered, and intimations of the future glimmer through "the transparent film of the windowpanes" (46), making brief electric connections between the known and the unknown. When the stranger outside describes the drowned girl's hair swaying with the current, inside the room "the two young girls turn their heads towards the window" as if they can sense the impending news (47). Later, the two girls approach the windows, setting up a stage image that reinforces the house-as-head analogy:

> (*At this moment one of the two sisters comes up to the first window, the other to the third; and resting their hands against the panes they stand gazing into the darkness.*)
> THE OLD MAN: No one comes to the middle window.
> MARY: They are looking out; they are listening . . .
> THE OLD MAN: The elder is smiling at what she does not see.
> THE STRANGER: The eyes of the second are full of fear.
> THE OLD MAN: Take care: who knows how far the soul may extend around the body. (*A long silence*) (50)

The eyes of the house, animated by the daughters, are the childish, nearsighted eyes of the mind, which peer curiously into the darkness but see little. The middle window could be a third eye, but it is empty.

In his essay "The Fourth Dimension," Maeterlinck declares that "time is space that flies" (90). *Interior* arrests the flight of time at the border between two spaces. The distance between the family and the onstage spectators, who "seem to see them from the altitude of another world," is a gulf not just in awareness but also in time (21). The divided stage reifies the distance between the present material world and an immaterial but inevitable future that has paused for a moment as it approaches. In the opening moments of the play, the old man calls attention to the time of the interior—"It is nine on the clock in the corner"—as if to imply that the corner has its own time (46). Walter Benjamin reminds us that any working clock "will always be a disturbance on stage" because "even in a Naturalistic play, astronomical time would clash with theatrical time" (247). In this case, the clock does not register the distance between audience time and stage time, but between two different spaces of time on stage: the private refuge of synchronic, interior time in the domestic corner, and the public time of the stage exterior. The house insulates the family in a slow-motion present while outside time approaches inexorably in the form of the community of mourners:

> MARY: They are coming by the little path. They are moving slowly.
> THE OLD MAN: It is time . . .
> MARY: Have you told them, Grandfather?
> THE OLD MAN: You can see that we have told them nothing. There
> they are, still sitting in the lamplight. (49)

The Old Man's idiomatic expression, "It is time . . . ," followed by a pause, serves both in its everyday capacity and to designate that the mourners, like death carrying an hourglass, bear the symbolic weight of both mortality *and* time. The group is "taking a very roundabout way," but it "will arrive at last, nonetheless" (49, 50). The family inside "cannot bid it stay; and those who are bringing it are powerless to stop it. . . . It has mastered them, too, and they needs must serve it. It knows its goal, and it takes its course. It is unwearying, and it has but one idea" (50). The community of mourners, described as "the crowd," represents a vision of public, historical time, diachronic and inescapable. Trapped inside a naïve present, the father "keeps his eyes fixed on the great pendulum of the clock," as if he recognizes the real enemy (51).

Time may seem at first to be Maeterlinck's enemy as well. This play of hesitation struggles to maintain the sanctity of the interior moment against the intrusion of time. The transparent interior becomes a bubble suspended for a moment in the stream of time. As the delay persists, we understand that the family's refuge is also their prison. The catastrophe in their story has already happened when the play begins, but it has not yet happened *here*. As far as the play is concerned, the real tragedy is not their daughter's death, but the tragedy of time's lumpiness, the impossibility of simultaneous knowledge. Through the lens of this play, we understand events not as instantaneous, but as limping, capricious, and viral. The daughter dies many times as the news spreads across space.

By amplifying the temporal dramatic irony that fuels all suspense, *Interior* highlights theater's ability to capitalize on the unevenness of lived time. *Interior* reduces drama to its central temporal irony, and directs attention to the ways theater makes time uniquely visible, and gives viewers perspective on its approach. *Interior*'s magnifying lens suggests that a fundamental interest of theater is not shared time but the pleasurable friction between competing temporalities. For Matthew Wagner, theatrical time is uniquely thick; its present moments are swollen with awareness of the past and the future.[70] The surprising lesson of *Interior* is that an audience's experience of time can thicken as a play grows thinner. By reducing the amount of action and delaying the arrival of news, *Interior* makes the passage of time inescapable, and makes the family's future visible from within the audience's present. Although audience and characters share a unified performance time, the gap between the audience's and characters' knowledge creates an unavoidable rift in the shape of their temporal experience.

Interior generates interest by delaying the arrival of knowledge, but, as Maeterlinck understands, in the face of historical, narrative, and dramatic necessity, the bubble must burst. The old man knocks, the family opens the door, and as he delivers the news, two spaces and two times come together in a silent climax. Maeterlinck called his early plays static dramas, and in a relative sense, they are; but however much his short plays resist movement and narrative momentum, they ultimately incorporate the demand for action, if only minimally. *The Intruder* (1891), an earlier and less sophisticated take on the drama of a bourgeois family waiting for death, ends predictably with the death of the wife. *The Blind* (1890) is more thoroughly plotless—a fact that has reinforced its many comparisons to Beckett's *Waiting for Godot*—but its closing moments offer rising dramatic tension through the approach of mysterious footsteps as well as a climactic final tableaux, and the play ends just as the footsteps have arrived. Although Maeterlinck claims that real tragedy "begins only when what are called the adventures, sufferings, and dangers have disappeared," his short plays take place in the moments *before* a disaster, and, very much like naturalist shorts, use suspense to dilate those moments.[71] *The Blind* may begin after the death of the priest, but the impending disaster in the play is the danger that awaits the group in his absence, the threat made audible by the approaching footsteps at the play's conclusion. In this respect, Maeterlinck's one-acts share the same overall plot arc as naturalist shorts, though in subdued form. Each has a late point of attack, rising action toward a predictable and expected event, and an abrupt ending just after the event. Both *faits-divers* plays and Maeterlinck's one-acts use the skeleton of a conventional plot to redefine the type of human experience that qualifies as an event—and as a play.

Maeterlinck accommodates the basic demands of theater (visibility, action, and revelation) with goals of the symbolist drama (invisibility, inaction, and insight). He understands, more than many symbolist playwrights, the basic need for performance to speak in languages an audience can read. Despite his early resistance to the materiality of the stage, by 1902 when he wrote the preface to his collected plays, he was more open to compromise. The playwright, he says,

> is obliged to bring the idea that he has created of the unknown down into real life, into everyday life. He must show us how, in what form, in what conditions, according to what laws, to what end, those superior powers, those infinite principles, those unknown influences which as a poet he believes pervade the universe, work upon our lives.[72]

In response to compromises like this one, some contemporaries dismissed Maeterlinck as a popularizer who introduced complex philosophy through his readable collections of essays, represented metaphysical concepts through fairy tale plays, and made symbolism palatable to bourgeois tastes. But while this view of Maeterlinck's theater would account for the presence of suspense and climactic action, however spare, it does not explain why *Interior* encloses a realistic living room inside a world of shadows.

By exposing the unknown, invisible world that lies outside the four walls of the bourgeois living room and outside of the positivist logic that undergirds it, Maeterlinck's metatheatrical construct makes a contemporary theatrical argument: this is not just a play within a play, but a fully rendered naturalist interior sealed up within a symbolist void. Surrounding the bourgeois living room with a dark world of mysterious figures bearing special knowledge, *Interior* defamiliarizes the self-enclosed *fait-divers* by revealing the uncanny potential that inheres in naturalism's overdetermined moments. Maeterlinck, like the most effective naturalist playwrights, Ibsen and Chekhov, understands the essential symbolism within, beneath, and around the naturalist stage. Ibsen compared the symbolism buried within his naturalist plays to "a vein of silver ore in a mountain."[73] Chekhov was an enthusiastic admirer of Maeterlinck and Strindberg, and could have been describing the family in *Interior* when he says of the ideal naturalist play: "People are sitting at a table having dinner, that's all, but at the same time their happiness is being created, or their lives are being torn apart."[74] Similarly, Maeterlinck could have been speaking of Ibsen's late drama or all of Chekhov when some years later in *The Buried Temple* he describes the characters in his "little plays" as

> poor little trembling, elementary creatures, who shivered for an instant and wept, on the brink of a gulf; and their words and their tears had importance only from the fact that each word they spoke and each tear they shed fell into this gulf, and were at times so strangely resonant there as to lead one to think that the gulf must be vast if a tear or a word, as it fell, could send forth so confused and muffled a sound.[75]

The minimal elements of Maeterlinck's dramatic vocabulary—a tear or a word—are the same as those Zola suggested would allow *naturalist* drama to work as briefly as it wants—"a word or a cry" (10). It is noteworthy in this context that a later play set at the vanishing point of symbolist compression, Beckett's thirty-second *Breath* (1969), seems to answer Zola's contention that the "cry belongs essentially to the theater" (10). In a piece of theater stripped to its essentials, the only action is a recorded cry, the rise and fall of lights, and the sound of a single breath. Despite the piles of rubbish littering the stage, the piece hardly resembles naturalist drama. But *Breath* could, much to Zola's surprise, be seen as the extreme endpoint of the sort of dramatic compression he imagines on the naturalist stage.[76]

At the same time, *Interior* diagnoses symbolist playwrights' reliance on, and fascination with, the materials of theater. Tendencies that might seem to mark *Interior* as less symbolist than other contemporary plays—its apparent verisimilitude, its subtle rather than overt poetry, its elevation of everyday space—in fact reveal it as a refinement of one strain of symbolist theater. Symbolism is at its most pure when it outlines the correspondences between visible objects and the unknown; *Interior* makes these correspondences its subject.

The concurrent emergence of very short plays in two rival camps of the Parisian theatrical avant-garde in the late 1880s suggests a reevaluation of the distinction between naturalism and symbolism that takes into account their shared interest in the minor and the brief. Both naturalist and symbolist playwrights agreed with Poe's assertion that a work's "brevity must be in direct ratio to the intensity of the intended effect."[77] *Quarts d'heure* employ shortness to increase acerbity, *faits-divers* use it to cause a sensation, and symbolist one-acts rely on it to give the impression of a dream that overwhelms and quickly disappears. Both naturalist and symbolist shorts display their subjects not by cataloging or containing them, but by aiming to extract their essence, although their methods of distillation vary. *Quarts d'heure* and *faits-divers* isolate the climax of a story and the moments just before it, modern mysteries telescope history, and Maeterlinck's shorts zoom in on a period of waiting before an unextraordinary action in order to plumb the depth lurking beneath the mundane. But in each case, these shorts almost always present a small but cohesive block of time, a singular moment, redefined as a dramatic whole, rather than fragmenting, deconstructing, or frustrating basic dramatic structure as later modernist playwrights would do.

If both kinds of early microdrama sacrifice temporal and geographic breadth, both try—sometimes in vain—to replace them with density or depth. As the plot of a naturalist short grows less complex, more weight falls on the density of the stage world and the depth of the psychological portrait. The old man in an armchair from "The Tragedy in Everyday Life," the archetype both of the generic chair-bound protagonist of the naturalist short *and* the unspecified old man of the symbolist short, is trapped in one time and place, and yet according to Maeterlinck, he lives in reality "a life that is more profound, more human, and more universal than" traditional characters (301–2). Maeterlinck's point is not merely that the quotidian evening at home can be as important as the grand event, but that a nuanced appreciation of the texture of temporal experience may be *more* accessible when presented without the distraction of action. Moments of rest, outside the stream of dramatic action, make visible "the march of time and many other more secret footsteps" (301). Elsewhere in the essay, Maeterlinck calls on dramatists to follow modern painters and musicians, who, unlike dramatists, understand that the compelling frontier of modernity is interior. They know "that all that life has lost, as regards mere superficial ornament, has been more than *counterbalanced by the depth*, the intimate meaning and the spiritual gravity it has acquired."[78] If in everyday life depth, intimacy, and gravity might counterbalance the superficial, on stage, strictly speaking, everything is superficial. Due to the temporal and scenic constraints of dramatic form, playwrights, more than novelists, must generally suggest depth rather than plumb it. As a result, both the naturalist and the symbolist schools of playwriting ask the superficial to stand in for the profound.

Whatever the style, drastic pruning reveals the basic fact that theatrical attention makes matter matter. Martin Esslin makes this capacity a central theme of *The Field of Drama*:

> The stage or screen as a place where significant things are being exhibited elevates the most mundane objects and events to exemplary status, makes them significant beyond their mere individual being: they become signs for multitudes of similar objects and events. Any object, any gesture thus is potentially redolent of possible metaphorical or symbolic meaning, far beyond its literal or factual function in the performance. (163)

Esslin's remarks apply Viktor Shklovsky's concept of defamiliarization, or Marcel Duchamp's insistence that art consists only in the framing, to the stage and the screen.[79] But the scale of the frame also makes a difference. Minimal art revises Esslin's account by teaching us that the natural tendency of artistic framing to make objects significant can increase as the size and complexity of the field decreases. A bushel of apples in the back of Mother Courage's wagon likely means somewhat more than one in your house, but an apple alone on a bare stage cannot help but stand in for the idea of an apple, and is more likely to suggest Eve's temptation or Newton's discovery or New York City, or perhaps all three at once.

This tendency was amplified in the 1880s and 1890s as controlled electric lighting and modern scenic design created closed universes with their own physics. With the replacement of gaslight in theaters with electric light, the elimination of footlights in favor of either realistic or impressionistic lighting, and the advent of modern scenic design spearheaded by Adolphe Appia and Gordon Craig, new and more concise theatrical languages became available for the first time. Appia and Craig were among the first to harness the symbolic potential of these new conventions and technologies. Their designs dispense with attention to detail in favor of fidelity to a pure and concise artistic conception or vision, and insist on the instant communicative potential of form, movement, and light.[80] The use of electric light deified theater artists, allowing them to divide the light from the darkness and create spaces whose suns and moons operated according to independent logic. To a new degree, the stage became a space apart, a confined realm that, like Maeterlinck's *Interior*, invites interpretation as something other than itself. Such spaces allowed dramatists to do more in less time by capitalizing on the human tendency to mythologize, to organize changes in light, space, or time into narratives. In both *quarts d'heure* and symbolist one-acts, brevity reinforces the entrapment of the figures and the transience of life. Both Maeterlinck's characters "who shivered for an instant and wept, on the brink of a gulf" and Méténier's who live a heartbeat away from capricious disaster stand in the light only for an instant. They are akin to Beckett's characters about whom it is said, "They give birth astride of a grave, the light gleams an instant, then it's night once more" (*DW*, 82). For all three dramatists, drastically delimited stage worlds reify drastically delimited lives.

Despite their fervent claims of originality, naturalist and symbolist playwrights did not create new theaters *ab ovo*. Instead, working from opposite directions, they exfoliated theatrical performance to reveal the potential energy hidden in its moments, each of which balances mutually exclusive possibilities. Naturalists stripped away falsity and artifice. Symbolists insisted on the potential for abstraction and poetry. Both embraced compression. Playwrights would continue to argue about the proper balance of realism and antirealism on stage, but one tentative winner of the debate was brevity. I say tentative because, as we will see in later chapters, any victory in the name of brevity attributed to the little theater movement must be considered a qualified victory. To survey the history of microdrama is to study not only the gradual acceptance and popularity of shorts but also the tenacious persistence of temporal norms and, as a result, a century of resistance against norms and accommodation to them. Through the lens of microdramas, modern drama must be seen more as a refinement of theater than a reinvention of it.

THREE

The Future in the Instant

Futurist Synthesis in Theory and Practice

> *Thy letters have transported me beyond*
> *This ignorant present, and I feel now*
> *The future in the instant.*
> —Shakespeare, *Macbeth*

As the curtain rises, a man enters the stage preoccupied, upset, and in a hurry. He removes his overcoat and hat, paces furiously, and erupts in disbelief at some unknown outrage: "Incredible!" Suddenly the audience catches his eye. Irritated, he turns to face them, walks to the edge of the stage, and announces categorically: "I . . . I have absolutely nothing to tell you. . . . Bring down the curtain!"[1] And the curtain falls. This is *Negative Act*, a microdrama written by Italian Futurists Bruno Corra and Emilio Settimelli in 1915 and performed along with dozens of other original shorts in a series of tours around Italy over the following eight years. The Futurists dubbed most of their short plays *sintesi*, or syntheses, because they hoped the compressed plays would synthesize the dynamism of modern life into concise and purified forms.[2] The few seconds of *Negative Act* claim to tell us nothing, but nevertheless distill an image of the on-the-go citizen in an accelerating world, impatient with distractions (268). At the same time, *Negative Act* exemplifies the *via negativa* of Futurist condensation. This is theater so deeply impatient with its foundational assumptions—that it should provide a story, that a person in the midst of a crisis should allow strangers to observe him—it becomes self-canceling. As it self-destructs, it not only snubs the audience but also reminds them just how odd and voyeuristic an activity they are engaged in. Although the play insists it has nothing to say, Futurist shorts like this one have much to tell us, not despite their brevity but on account of it.

The Italian Futurists, European modernism's most fervent disciples of speed, were also the period's most explicit advocates for brevity as a theatrical virtue. In early 1915, Futurist founder Filippo Marinetti collaborated with the authors of *Negative Act*, Corra and Settimelli, to write a manifesto entitled "The Futurist Synthetic Theater" (*Il teatro futurista sintetico*). The manifesto champions short theater as the ideal vehicle through which to deconstruct temporal and spatial conventions underpinning bourgeois theatergoing, and to construct if not the future an accelerated and super-charged present. The synthetic theater (*teatro sintetico*) was the most sustained among a staggering array of live performance forms that became central to Futurism and its dissemination between 1905 and the 1930s. Futurism found its first audiences at raucous theatrical evenings (*serate*) featuring lectures, declamations, poetry readings, art exhibited on stage, and variety acts. But it was also enacted at dance presentations, concerts of *Intonarumori* (noisemakers), and street actions, as well as through touring productions of synthetic theater, through Fillia's mechanical art theater, Enrico Prampolini's Magnetic Theater, and Azari's Aerial Theater.[3] I focus here on the synthetic theater and its close cousins, the theater of surprise and the theater of dilated instants, because these forms made brevity their *raison-d'être*, and because they engaged dramatic tradition most directly and therefore shed the most light on the Futurists' ambivalent negotiations with theater and time.

Futurist microdramas are an elusive species, hard to mistake but difficult to pin down. Although many of the plays are now lost, the several hundred that survive are a wildly diverse set of dramaturgical experiments written by more than fifty authors, many of whom had never written a play before. Critic Mario Verdone calls each of the plays "an expedition in search of a different continent."[4] Like microdramas by Suzan-Lori Parks and Chicago's Neo-Futurists discussed in chapter 5, Futurist syntheses range from realistic to wildly abstract, from political to imaginary, from well-populated to characterless, and from dialogic to speechless. Their authors often assigned the pieces subgenres—the brief synthesis (*sintesi breve*), the copenetration (*compenetratizone*), the theatrical surprise (*sorpresa teatrale*), the drama of objects (*drama d'oggetto*), and so on—but these categories were defined loosely and often overlapped. While the Futurists insisted on synthetic theater's radical novelty, the *sintesi* often recycle, refine, or parody facets of modern drama. Some plays echo symbolism by embracing abstraction and dramatizing states of mind; others borrow from vaudeville and the naturalist *faits-divers* tradition and feature familiar types speaking conventional prose dialogue. Still others sketch trends that would be elaborated in surrealism, dada, absurdist theater, and performance art. At their most radical, such plays call for brief impossible action on a grand scale, featuring hurricanes or hot air balloons as protagonists.[5]

Despite their programmatic variety, Futurist shorts share a single defining characteristic: brevity. More than any theater artists before or since, Futurists embraced speed and radical compression as virtues in themselves and as tools to reinvent theater. The synthetic theater manifesto is unequivocal: "We are certain that mechanically, by force of brevity, we can achieve an entirely new theater perfectly in tune with our swift and laconic Futurist sensibility. Our acts [atti] can also be moments [attimi] only a few seconds long."[6] The longest printed sintesi, Francesco Balilla Pratella's The War, fills only ten pages, and most take up less than a single page and can be performed in one or two minutes. The shortest, like Negative Act, end almost at the moment they begin. Within a movement that embraced hyperbolic rule breaking and advocated "the dynamic leap into the void of total creation," why was brevity the cardinal rule, the sine qua non of Futurist dramaturgy? (FST, 207)

Futurists offered a host of polemical answers to this question in their manifestos on theater—"The Variety Theater," (1913) "The Futurist Synthetic Theater," (1915) "Manifesto of Futurist Dance," (1917) and "The Theater of Surprise" (1921)—documents that both illuminate and trouble the question of brevity on stage.[7] Written to be declaimed with stylized flair, to imply headlong momentum, and to feed the public relations machine Marinetti was so adept at building, the manifestos are a short histrionic genre of their own. As such, they reward readers who approach them with the imagination and skepticism of a drama critic.[8] Their hyperbolic blueprints rarely reflect the precise workings of Futurist shorts, but they reveal the outlines of a fantasy about the potential impact of short performances. In this fantasy, short plays would accomplish two seemingly antithetical goals: they would better reflect the pace of everyday modern life, and they would create enriched and expanded moments that trump quotidian experience. Along the way, brevity would save theater from itself by forestalling the many vices Futurists ascribed to traditional, bourgeois drama—analysis, prolixity, explication, psychology, convention, predictability. In the Futurist imagination, brevity would be the primary tool in a wholesale attack on the theater institution, an attack that, if successful, would enable Marinetti's dream of a theatricality liberated from theater.[9] An appreciation for the dynamism of everyday life would in turn jumpstart the Italian public and rally them behind a proto-Fascist political program.

My readings resist two common reactions to the sintesi. The first reaction takes at face value Futurist pronouncements about what shorts would accomplish, and the second assumes the plays are self-explanatory. Everyone writing about Futurist syntheses mentions their surprising brevity—at least one claims it is their only noteworthy feature—but fewer critics interrogate the nature and mechanics of brief time in the *sintesi*.[10] Many seem to agree with Christiana Taylor's dismissive summation, "The most that can be said of [early Futurist plays] is that they occasionally had humor and that they were capable of rendering a very small vignette of some everyday aspect of life."[11] English language criticism to date is distinguished by its dearth of in-depth readings of the *sintesi*.[12] A notable exception is Gordon Ramsay's "Simultaneity and Compenetration in *sintesi* of the Italian Futurists," which includes close readings of a half dozen plays.[13] The reluctance to submit Futurist play texts to careful scrutiny is not surprising; many *sintesi* seem to insist, like the impatient man in *Negative Act*, that they "have absolutely nothing to tell you."

The disinclination to analyze Futurist scripts has been exacerbated by the tendency among recent scholars to cast Italian Futurism as the founding movement in a twentieth-century turn away from text and toward performance.[14] Many of the Futurists' most influential innovations were nontextual or anti-textual and helped to blur distinctions among received artistic forms.[15] But the focus by critics on interactivity, scenography, and multiple media has distracted attention from the plays. While nontextual elements played a vital role in Futurist productions, their practice remained deeply indebted to the written and printed word, to conventions of dramatic composition, and to assumptions about the shape and nature of theatrical activity. Especially during the brief heyday of the Futurist synthetic drama, from 1914 to 1924, the authors of Futurist microdramas clung as fervently as any innovators in modern theater to the astounding conviction that a revolution in dramatic form—in the shape and size of scripts—could fuel not only a renewed theater but also a restored world.

This chapter disobeys the Futurists by analyzing at some length the brief moments their plays define, reading the scripts against the manifestos and against accounts of tour performances in order to trace the distance between Futurist theory and practice. Such an approach is not without its ironies. Those attempting to pry apart Futurist syntheses using the most passé of tools—analysis—find themselves frequently lampooned by their very objects of study, objects named for a process diametrically opposed to analysis. Francesco Cangiullo's play *The Paunch of the Vase*, for instance, depicts a Scientist who stares "with the eyes of an idiot, mummified" through the rotund bulb of a beaker for two static, three-minute acts until, in the third act, the author of the play enters with a cudgel, whacks him over the head, and exits. The Scientist struggles to stand, asks his typist to bandage his head, dictates a letter to Cangiullo thanking him for being so kind as to bash his head rather than his beaker, and returns to examining the beaker. I aim to subject the Futurists' short theatrical concoctions to similar close scrutiny without repeating the Scientist's mistakes of privileging the objects at the expense of their context or being oblivious to their playfulness. R. S. Gordon rightly identifies reversal as the fundamental structure of the *sintesi*; they thrive by setting up expectations and then subverting them.[16] But Futurist syntheses contain even more reversals than their authors intended, revising or overturning Futurist theories for how short theater should work and, along the way, adumbrating tensions inherent in the experience of time in theater and otherwise.

The following three sections explore in turn three Futurist assumptions about brevity: that it reflects modern speed and simultaneity, that it intensifies experience, and that it dismantles convention. The latter portion of each section tests each assumption against microdramas meant to exemplify it. If Futurist manifestos were exhaustive and accurate accounts of the *sintesi*, we would expect the plays to represent an urbanized and frenetic present; to intensify and purify experience to create "a blinding atmosphere of intellectual intoxication"; to exclude predictable characters and situations; and to systematically reject theatrical and dramatic tradition by abandoning all limits on dramatic form and theatrical protocols.[17] While one can locate each of these tendencies in Futurist play texts and in performance accounts and while creative performance teams could infuse any of the scripts with intoxicating dynamism and unpredictability, a balanced account of Futurist synthetic theater finds a set of practices far more entangled with tradition than their authors claimed: plays less interested in the future or the present than in the past, plays that tend to deflate or defuse moments rather than purifying them, and plays that so firmly reject dramatic and theatrical conventions that they expose their persistence.

SPEED AND SIMULTANEITY: BRIEF MIRRORS
FOR A FAST WORLD

What led the Futurists to make brevity the crucial common denominator of their theatrical output? A necessary but insufficient answer is that short theater was a natural extension of their quasi-religious worship of speed as a tool to master time. In the 1915 manifesto "Birth of a Futurist Aesthetic,"

Marinetti writes, alluding to special relativity: "We are creating a new aesthetic of speed. We have virtually destroyed the notion of space and greatly reduced that of time. . . . We shall thus arrive, by the same token, at the abolition of years, days, and hours."[18] The new aesthetic—sometimes called a religion-morality of speed—dictated a rejection of deliberation in favor of speed, abridgment, and synopsis. Its motto was "Quick, tell me the whole story *in two words!*"[19] Futurist manifestos on theater assert that short drama would more accurately reflect the acceleration of modern life. The notion that a faster world required faster art is familiar. But to linger over the assumptions behind the Futurist embrace of speed offers a clearer picture of the friction between their radical dramaturgical theories and their relatively conventional theatrical practice. As we will see, translating the religion of speed into a dramaturgical method revealed blind spots in the Futurists' naïve embrace of brevity.

For Marinetti and his Futurist cohort, the pace of what they called modern life provoked considerable anxiety. By the futurist account, the industrial revolution, the rise of the metropolis, and the invention of technologies that accelerated transportation and communication had all fundamentally altered the pace of life and thought in discombobulating ways. Some historians argue that the acceleration of modern life began well before mechanization and urbanization; Jeffrey Schnapp, for instance, traces the advent of a thrill-seeking "culture of speed" back to eighteenth-century carriages and coaches.[20] But my goal here is to understand the Futurists' own justifications for their love of speed within a cultural mythology that took a willfully myopic view of the past. Marinetti's rhetorical persona was so obsessed with the problem of living in a time-obsessed age that he complained it was impossible to eat a meal at a railway station in peace while being watched over by the relentless hands of a clock face, that "spinning anxiety-memory-airscrew."[21] Through the lens of this preoccupation with time, pace became a central criterion by which to evaluate a performance. Impatient to jump ahead, Marinetti was convinced that shorter, richer moments would alleviate the temporal awkwardness of conventional dramaturgy.

The synthetic theater manifesto (1915) explains that traditional playwrights, including those figures usually considered modernist innovators—Ibsen, Maeterlinck, Claudel, Shaw—remained behind the times, shackled to "prolixity, detailed analysis, and drawn-out preparation." Predictable plays run slower than the imagination, so each act becomes "as painful as having to sit patiently in a waiting room" for someone important to receive you. "Faced with these authors' works, the audience has assumed the indignant attitude of a circle of bystanders who swallow their anguish and pity as they watch the slow agony of a horse who has collapsed on the pavement" (FST, 205). The simile imagines well-made-play dramaturgy as a lame, exhausted beast of burden whose crises may provoke Aristotelian fear or pity, but whose conclusions are so fore-gone as to make the onlooker wish the ordeal were over as soon as possi-ble. The figure aligns traditional theater with an obsolescent technology, but the imagined scene is oddly modern. One might expect the manifesto to praise the spectacle of a fallen horse as a shocking urban incident. In-deed, the crash that left another snorting beast, Marinetti's Fiat convert-ible, rolled over in a ditch and surrounded by its own circle of onlookers on the outskirts of Milan became, in the founding Futurist manifesto, an icon for the movement's headlong violence and the mythological site of its birth. My argument suggests that just as the muddy "maternal ditch" of Marinetti's car crash could serve as the womb of Futurist modernity, the wheezing beast of traditional dramaturgy might, despite appearances, have provided the beating heart of Futurist *sintesi*.[22]

A prominent strain of Futurist dramaturgy defends new formal techniques—acceleration, improvisation, fragmentation, and non-sequi-turs—on essentially mimetic grounds. According to the Futurists' now fa-miliar rendering of the early twentieth-century life, trains, automobiles, motorcycles, and airships not only reduced the separations of physical dis-tance but also shrank metaphorical distances between objects and ideas. Technologies of speed converted the passenger into a spectator more likely to survey than to ponder and cultivated an ability to look at things system-atically, "to do the job of analogy by mechanical means."[23] Technologies of virtual transport—the telephone, the cinema, the wireless telegraph, and the newspaper ("a synthesis of a day in the world's life")[24]—cultivated similar skills even in those who never left home by allowing the impression of near real-time contact with all points of the world. The imagined Futur-ist spectator would glance, rather than staring, and would understand dis-traction as a mode of intellectual engagement that necessitates new modes of comparison. Skimming was raised to a virtue, and absorption—a central goal of contemplative symbolist theater—became hopelessly passé.

The perceived fragmentation of urban life meant that, for the Futurists and their audiences, short, random scenes without the reassurances of ex-position or context might in fact be more realistic.

It's stupid to want to explain with logical minuteness everything taking place on the stage, when even in life one never grasps an event entirely, in all its causes and consequences, because reality throbs around us, assaulting us with *bursts of fragments of intercon-nected events, interlocking together, confused, jumbled up, chaotic.* . . . in daily life we nearly always experience mere *flashes of argument* which have been rendered *ephemeral* by our activities as modern men, pass-ing in a tram, a café, a railroad station, so that experiences remain cinematic in our minds like fragmentary dynamic symphonies of gestures, words, lights, and sounds (FST 206, emphasis in original).

The window of a tram reveals a series of fragmented encounters and scenes, so the theatrical voyage should do the same, recreating in the mind of the passive audience member the familiar impression of disorienting speed. Modern life barrages all of the senses at once, so a theater true to modern experience would present not a static and sequential story but a cinematic combination of partial gestures, language, light, and sound. The authors draw a straight line in this passage from Georg Simmel's observation of "the brevity and scarcity of the inter-human contacts granted to the metro-politan man" to a dramaturgical method that reflects such fleeting and dy-namic encounters.[25] With the possible exception of August Strindberg, who implied a similar equation when he wrote that the "brief and expressive" single scene seemed "set to be the type of play for contemporary theatergo-ers," no theater artist had made such an explicit or impassioned call for an accelerated theater to reflect accelerated life.[26]

But how should we account for the sustained interest in techniques based on the way things appeared "in daily life," alongside the fervent in-sistence, just a few lines earlier in the synthetic theater manifesto, that "It's stupid to worry about verisimilitude" or the declaration that Futurist the-ater "will resemble nothing but itself"? (FST 206, 207) Günter Berghaus makes sense of the apparent tension between these aims by breaking the movement into two overlapping factions: one group including Marinetti whose goals were primarily didactic and thus invested in the relationship of art to daily life and another group more closely associated with the vi-sual arts, who favored abstraction and the autonomy of the artwork.[27] Like Berghaus, many readers assume that Futurist shorts lacking human charac-ters, logical dialogue, or coherent narrative are as far from the real as the-ater can get. But even at this extreme, mimesis remains a central goal for these works. In a 1922 manifesto, Futurist Franco Casavola reframes the synthetic theater as a "Theater of Dilated Moments." According to Casa-vola, an abstract theater of expanded moments is the most true to life precisely because the most innocuous instants often provoke illogical and fantastic daydreams. We have all had the experience, he claims, in which imagination,

> struck by a reflection, a color, an analogy, stimulated by any impression without interference from the will, and even without our awareness, jumping from an indefinable springboard into the infinite kingdoms of the absurd, has created fantastic layerings of reality in which reality is distorted, reversed, or even destroyed in order to create a new reality. If we isolate these instants and hold them still, while they are dilating, we find, between their endpoint and their starting point, a new form of theater, absolutely illogical, crazy, amusing but nevertheless sprung directly from reality, and even solidly anchored in reality.[28]

This approach folds the irrational back into reality and reveals Futurist dramaturgy, no matter how brief, unreal, or fanciful, as a strategy for improved verisimilitude. This characterization falls in line with Roman Jakobson's claim that Italian Futurists offered merely a reform in the field of reportage.[29] Brevity increased theater's shutter speed and distorted the material it represented, but its innovations remained driven by the urge to harness and record new experiences of automatic and subconscious analogy.

From this perspective, abridging dramatic structure emerges as a crude stand-in for a more radical fantasy of compressing the diversity and intensity of life itself into a surveyable unit (*FP*, 42). The ultimate goal of Futurist compression, at least in theory, was not to harness the future but rather to create an enriched, extended, and more fully available present. In order to create a theater consonant with what the Futurists understood as the modern spectatorial condition, theatrical moments needed to be shorter but also wider and deeper. Theater thus needed to capture not just the speed but also the dynamism and simultaneity of modern life. For the Futurists, dynamism meant not merely motion or momentum, but the kind of unpredictability that ideally keeps one attuned to the sensations and revelations of the moment. Scripting dynamism involved engineering and exaggerating the randomness and spontaneity inherent in live performance, a medium that supported their mimetic project by offering moments actually composed of the reality that "throbs around us" (FST, 206).

Carrying a philosophy of compressed action to its limit led directly to the ideal of simultaneous perception. Futurist experimentation across the arts sought to represent multiple times and spaces within the same perceptual moment. Futurist painters created overlapping images that copied the look of time-lapse photography and made visible the "force lines" that connect disparate objects. In 1913, four years after Italian Guglielmo Marconi won the Nobel Prize in physics for his work in wireless telegraphy, Marinetti hailed a new "wireless imagination" able to forge connections that collapse otherwise distant times and places.[30] In poetry, Futurist "words-in-freedom" abbreviated ideas by omitting words and trusting the reader to connect disparate thoughts as the telegraph connected remote places.[31] The Futurist fantasy of collapsing space and time was fueled by their intoxication with contemporary scientific thinking, which suggested that the physical world in extremis might not follow Newtonian laws.[32] Applying ideas from modern physics with some poetic license, Futurists imagined that one might be trained to conceive of everyday moments as charged with the time-warping properties that recent physics had theorized would pertain near the speed of light, where the distance between objects shrinks to zero, objects blur into one another as their mass approaches infinity, and "all things are simultaneously present to and within each other."[33] Such a dream offers one explanation for the odd abundance of sluggish or frozen time in their microdramas: accelerating thought to superhuman speeds slows the world to a crawl.

Simultaneity in Practice

A number of Futurist syntheses aim to literalize simultaneous perception by juxtaposing unrelated characters or situations within the same place and time. In theory, simultaneity promised to offer the spectator the world all at once and to forge novel connections, but the *sintesi* that feature simultaneity reveal that the technique was more often employed to establish relatively traditional comparisons. Marlo Carli's 1916 play, *Violence: A Symphony* (*Violenza, sinfonia*), comes as close as any *sintesi* to realizing on stage the synthetic theater manifesto's hyperbolic description of a reality that assaults us with fragments of "confused, jumbled up, chaotic" events (FST, 206). The play begins on a city street where drums and cymbals can be heard approaching from the distance. The clamor grows louder until it reaches deafening levels. Suddenly the street explodes into all sorts of simultaneous action while the din continues behind the wings and an unseen hand cracks a whip "violently and repeatedly."[34] The street becomes a caricature of frenetic urban clutter. Vendors, pedestrians, salesmen, police, a boy hawking newspapers describing bombings and disasters, a biker riding in circles, and others all gradually intensify their gestures. Windows slam, glass shatters, two men fight, a man chases a woman and murders her, two actors rehearse a scene, and a despairing lover commits suicide. As the crescendo peaks, a fruit stand vomits fruit onto the ground and a cataclysm shakes the earth, evoking an image of modernity as violent rupture, and in particular the war in which Italy had become involved the previous year. Everyone flees, leaving behind the obscene tableaux of two corpses on a silent street. A deep red sunset descends, there is a dark pause, and then a sunrise. A stooped, frail, and nearly blind old couple emerges from a door with a young boy. The old man informs his grandson that violence does not exist, ". . . it is nothing but an illusion we create when we are young. Don't you see? The world is calm, good, and candid: this is how it was and how it will always be. Otherwise, how could we elderly people live in peace?" The boy resists and directs his grandfather's attention to the corpses. "What are you talking about?" the old man replies, "They must be sleeping."[35] And the play ends.

The play's dynamism and simultaneity do not lead to novel analogies; instead, they magnify what any *flâneur* knows about the sensory overload of urban life and underscore the absurd tenacity of denial in the face of accelerating cultural change and martial violence that feels cataclysmic. *Violence* collapses a dozen *faits-divers* into the same space and time, but rather than deifying the spectator, simultaneous action underlines her helplessness and vulnerability, and likely makes her hope the acceleration will end. The play's emotional effect relies on the spectator's *discomfort* with an influx of simultaneous action. I imagine the contemporary viewer must have been relieved when the play returned to the familiar ground of audible dialogue to make its final point. This symphony of violence exaggerates the shape of well-made-play dramaturgy, with rising tension, violent climax, and denouement. The spectator is meant to marvel at the figurative blindness of the old couple's denial, but ultimately the play backfires by allowing the ostensible fool to give an accurate description of its histrionic violence: the play itself is indeed an illusion created by the young in which the dead bodies are living people with their eyes closed.

Carli's *Violence* collapses a host of actions into the same scene, but most *sintesi* that use simultaneity depict two or three scenes side by side on the stage, with or without a separating barrier, and often with a permeable barrier. This strain of simultaneous action reinforces a related Futurist ideal: interpenetration, the notion that events distant in time or space are metaphysically interconnected. Mario Dessy's play *Lives* (*Vite*) depicts on one side of the stage a domestic scene much like Maeterlinck's *Interior* where a lower middle class family sits around a table, mother sewing, father reading the paper, son reading a book, but juxtaposes that scene with the living room of an unrelated young man dressed in a sharp suit. While the family congratulates themselves on drastically restraining their spending to avoid debt, the dapper man soliloquizes about his recent financial ruin. Without money, the young spendthrift is bereft of hope and feels himself surrounded by "a great darkness and a desperate loneliness."[36] But the simultaneity of the action suggests the man might be less alone than he appears. The two scenes unfold independently until the final moments of the three-minute play: When the desperate man shoots himself, the family hears the shot but cannot be sure what they've heard. It sounds to the son like a gunshot, but the father thinks it must be thunder and returns to his newspaper. In this case, simultaneity intensifies the comparative logic of morality plays. Synchronizing the two scenes implies that the play's parallel cases might not be independent. Perhaps *Lives* diagnoses the solipsism of financial considerations in an interdependent economy, suggesting that the family's stinginess somehow contributed to the young man's ruin. More likely, the play works on a more abstract register to suggest that the specter of destitution looms over the ideal of lower middle-class thrift. In any case, although this morality play presents bourgeois salvation and damnation side by side in the same moment, its moral remains conventional, and its form simply amplifies the logic of a dramatic staple, the double plot.

The Futurists' fascination with spatial and temporal interpenetration yokes them to their ostensible enemies, the symbolists, well known for their interest, following Baudelaire, in correspondences between the seen and the unseen. We saw in the last chapter how Maeterlinck suggests that premonitions of the girl's death in *Interior* might reach her family before news of it does. Dessy's *Lives*, too, makes the domestic sitting room vulnerable to infiltration by precisely the sort of misfortune its comfortable walls presume to keep at bay. Umberto Boccioni's account of simultaneity from the catalog of the first Paris exhibition of Futurist painters makes clear the movement's commitment to rupturing the tidy frame of the domestic scene and implicates the naturalist proscenium in that false tidiness: "You must render the invisible which stirs and lives beyond intervening obstacles, what we have on the right, on the left, and behind us, and not merely the small square of life artificially compressed, as it were, by the wings of a stage."[37] For Futurist painters, the canvas may be square, but it cannot merely frame reality as a conventional painting or proscenium might do. In place of "the small square of life"—an allusion not just to the canvas but also to the little "corner of life" that Zola used to define stage naturalism—

Fig. 3. Umberto Boccioni, *The Street Enters the House*, 1911. Oil on canvas, Sprengel Museum, Hanover. (Photo Credit: BPK, Berlin / Sprengel / Art Resource, NY.)

Futurist frames must remain sensitive to the elusive spatial and temporal borders of everyday moments. Maeterlinck's *Interior*, like Boccioni's statement, evokes the theatrical frame only to suggest that the world pictured on stage is permeated by an invisible world. *Interior*'s single closed scene, then, already suggested the sort of simultaneity Futurists would later render literally in plays like *Lives*. In other words, Futurist simultaneity radicalizes the thickness and resonant metaphoricity that characterized theatrical space and time for the symbolists, and that has always been a hallmark of theatrical experience.

More specifically, simultaneous action allowed controlled experiments in the relativity of short stretches of time and in the temporal dynamics of genre. Like *Lives,* Dessy's two-page play *Waiting* (*Attesa*) (1919) juxtaposes two sitting rooms from different houses, one stage left, the other stage right, with no wall separating them. In each room, a young man awaits a lover who never arrives. The two interiors are similar, but they are furnished in different styles and contain very different characters. Stage right, a nervous, desperate Young Man paces and glances at a clock, convinced his lover, due any minute, will never arrive. Stage left, an unconcerned Elegant Youth in a dinner jacket lounges, reads the paper, and smokes although his date is already half an hour late. As the title suggests, *Waiting* focuses attention on anticipation and its power to heighten one's awareness of time. The play begins at the precise moment that the two characters independently notice that it's nine o'clock, and both men repeatedly check the time and talk about its passage. Over the following few minutes, the audience watches two solo scenes unfolding at the same time in a theatrical answer to split-screen techniques popular in early cinema. The men share a stretch of time on stage (and with the audience), but their subjective experiences of the same few minutes work to complicate any simple notion that time can be shared. Kirby notes that the play's two parallel scenes, printed in facing columns of text, exemplify Futurist simultaneity (*FP*, 47). True enough, but what work does simultaneity do in the play? The manifestos suggest that simultaneous action mirrors the multiple inputs of modern life in an increasingly global village. But Dessy's play arguably involves a more sophisticated yet also more traditional use of simultaneity to conduct an experiment in the relativity of lived and theatrical time.

As the two men wait and talk to themselves, their parallel stories reveal that the anxious Young Man is living through a melodramatic tragedy, while the Elegant Youth finds himself in a comedy of errors. The Young Man—anxious, romantic, and contemplative, not unlike the symbolists— awaits his love, "beautiful like the spring," who will be visiting for the last time before destiny demands that she go "far from here." He knows that when she leaves, he will be frozen in grief: "I will remain thus, suffering, remembering her, crying for her, in this love nest" (284). The pain of awaiting this final meeting, and the growing certainty that she won't arrive at all, stretches moments and makes him bear the whips and scorns of time:

> The time is passing. . . . She isn't coming . . . I feel it. (*Takes a rose from the vase of flowers, pulls the petals off and lets them fall.*) They say these petals that are falling from sadness . . . are my tears! The time is passing. But how? How is time measured? (*Falls on his chair thoughtful*). Is time long? (*Stretches his legs*). I want to shorten the waiting. Wait-

ing for whom? for her? No, for death (*His head falls back on the back of the chair*). (285)

The Young Man's question—"How is time measured?"—is the question of the play, and the temporal dissonance between its two spaces offers a preliminary answer. For the melancholic, decadent Young Man trapped in an interminable moment, it is impossible to measure time according to any objective standard. Like the true lover that Shakespeare's Rosalind imagines in the forest of Arden, this lover would use sighs, groans, and rose petals to "detect the lazy foot of time."[38] But the falling petals offer no escape from sluggish time. Under the shadow of anxious romantic anticipation, a few minutes' wait becomes the beginning of the wait for death.

"Is time long?" The Young Man's behavior answers his rhetorical question in the affirmative, but the other sitting room offers a competing answer. While the Young Man despairs in the minutes *before* his scheduled appointment, the Elegant Youth—dapper, vain, and confident—remains relatively calm. His primary concern, it turns out, is which shoes will pinch his feet less on the date. At the moment when the Young Man loses himself in the wish to "remain thus" for several months, the Elegant Youth glances at his watch: "five after nine . . . for two cents I would change my shoes." A minute or so later in the performance, just when the young man asks in despair, "How is time measured?" the elegant youth checks his watch, "ten after nine." Unlike his desperate counterpart, he has little trouble measuring time, and his periodic announcements prove that time flies on his side of the stage. As the play opens, he is surprised to find it's "already nine o'clock!" A mere five sentences later it's "five after nine," and a half dozen lines after that it is "ten after nine." When his date is forty minutes late, instead of reclining in despair, he quips playfully, "I shall go out with these shoes on . . . but, on my word as a gentleman, when I settle the account with her, I want to deduct ten liras for waiting!" and the play ends, just as on the other side of the stage, the young man's head falls back on the chair (285). In his 1900 essay, *Laughter*, Henri Bergson argued that acceleration produces comedy by making people mechanical and puppet-like.[39] This microdrama suggests the more familiar obverse that a comic outlook accelerates time.

The same brief period, without apparent incident, becomes one man's protracted demise and another's trivial punch line. Rather than emphasizing the shared experience of a standardized global time, revealing the interpenetration of the two spaces, or providing a snapshot of the present, Dessy's simultaneity uses a new technique to make a familiar comparison.

Matthew Wagner's chapter in *Shakespeare, Theatre, and Time* on the wrinkles of theatrical time reminds us that a playwright interested in simultaneity need not go to such lengths. Theater is always already characterized by temporal dissonance—whether between story time and performance time, between the character's experience of time and the audience's, or between the historical time represented and the era in which the play is produced.[40] But Dessy's play presents a brand of temporal dissonance that Wagner does not discuss: the dissonance between two fictional worlds on the same stage. *Waiting* does not have a single "story time." Instead, it sets two tempos against each other, creating a synthetic sense of time constructed from the interplay among three times: the two tempos on stage and the somewhat more neutral five minutes in which the audience watches the piece. The result is a self-conscious exploration of the mechanics behind the felt acceleration or deceleration of stage time. In this play, generically informed impressions of time provide the frames of reference against which clock time is relativized.

Seen through this split lens, time is relative according to one's expectations and in relation to the narrative through which we imagine an experience. Time's thickness varies with a person's affective engagements. In particular, the play suggests that genres, and audience preconceptions about them, warp time: tragedy dilates moments, and comedy accelerates them. The few minutes we spend with the melodramatic young man are freighted with months of imagined abject loneliness: "Destiny wishes to separate us . . . if she goes far from here, after several months nothing will remain of me and my love except vague remembrances. I will remain thus, suffering, remembering her, crying for her . . ." (FP, 284). For this young lover worried he might be abandoned, time congeals unbearably: his suspenseful present is haunted by visions of a static future shadowed by memories of the past. By contrast, the elegant youth's urbane nonchalance leaves him more concerned with his present condition, or at least the condition of his shoes. There's a good chance he's been stood up by the woman who was meant to arrive more than half an hour ago, and yet he's convinced that he'll soon "bear the sweet spasms of love near [her]" (285). In his dandified overconfidence and lustful misogyny, he resembles a typical young Futurist and suggests what a Futurist mastery of time might look like in everyday life.

Dessy's reflexive use of theater to estrange its own temporal manipulations is characteristically modernist, even as it illustrates a set of predictable conventions governing the perceived pace of temporal experience. Dessy shows that different dramatic modes provide what Reinhart Koselleck calls different spaces of experience—distinct patterns of recurrence and repetition—and therefore generate unique horizons of expectation about even the same event. From this perspective, the play dramatizes a microhistorical, apolitical, and everyday version of what Koselleck calls "the simultaneity of the non-simultaneous." That is, a history of even the few minutes from nine o'clock to ten after nine contains layers of time with different "relative velocities" dependent both on subjective perceptions and on conventional dramatic modes.[41]

The play's temporal dramatic irony allows the audience—whose psychological and temporal experience of the play is assumed to be more neutral than the characters'—to understand how each man's state of mind inflects his temporal experience. But that's not to say that watching the play would be uncomplicated. A viewer cannot help but shift attention from one scene to the other, attending at any given moment more closely to one or the other monologue. We might ask whether such a process should be considered simultaneous perception. Does this production meet Bergson's definition of simultaneity—"two or more events entering within a single, instantaneous perception"—or does it produce instead high-speed serial comparison?[42] Whatever the answer, the play reminds us that the same moment seen through different eyes or through the lenses of different expectations can be insufferable, entertaining, or even both at once. The play remains a reflection of a recognizable modern world with heightened time-consciousness, but Dessy employs brevity and simultaneity to highlight old truths. A simultaneous scene promising everything at once relies on the successive rhythms of back-and-forth comparison, a play meant to conquer time highlights the weight and monotony of its passage, and a drama assumed to produce a dynamism never seen in previous theater underscores the persistent relevance of dramatic conventions (melodrama, comedy, paired characters as foils).

A GYMNASIUM FOR THE SPIRIT

The Futurists hoped brief performances would reflect the accelerated world outside of the theater, but—equally important—they also enlisted brevity to intensify reality. Radically foreshortening dramatic structure was part of a proactive and political plan to overhaul life, to forge a new sensibility in a crucible of sensation and surprise that would convert life into a *spettacolo*. The "swift pace of contemporary events" would fuel a theatrical machine that would in turn generate independent momentum, exciting audiences with a "labyrinth of sensations imprinted with the most exacerbated originality and combined in unpredictable ways."[43] Brevity would not simply cater to impatient modern audiences; it would create them. Futurist performance ultimately sought to mobilize the Italian public, to jolt them out of an imagined torpor into vigorous support for the Italian Front of the Great War: "Every night the Futurist theater will be a form of gymnastics that will train our race's mind to the swift, dangerous enthusiasms which have been made necessary by this Futurist year" (FST, 208). The quest for a restorative program of personal and national exhilaration, purgation, and celebration—a proto-Fascist calisthenics for the modern soul—led the Futurists to variety theater.

The authors of the 1913 Futurist manifesto "The Variety Theater" hailed popular theater—including music halls, the circus, vaudeville, French *revues*, *variétés*, and *café-concerts*—as the healthiest of all forms of contemporary spectacle because the speed of such forms drags "the most sluggish souls out of their torpor and forces them to run and leap."[44] The variety show's combination of shock, surprise, and ingenuity promised, more than painting or literature, to attract mass audiences and to subject them to a program of aesthetic hygiene. Variety theater would be the temple of Marinetti's "religion-morality of speed," a venue that translated rhetoric about the virtues of speed into swift action.[45]

Written in 1913 during the height of the popularity of Futurist soirées, the Variety Theater manifesto articulates a set of theoretical commitments (speed, variety, interactivity, surprise) that Futurist synthetic theater would several years later attempt to codify with its scripts. In particular, the manifesto posits a necessary connection between the pace of a performance and its intensity: the "piling up of events that are raced through in an instant, and of stage characters bundled off, from right to left, in a couple of minutes," would naturally generate an atmosphere of astonishment.[46] Variety also promised to obviate tiresome, self-important acting styles. Futurist painter and playwright Bruno Corra praises the structure of vaudeville, which "through its inmost constitution, imposes on the actors a rapid, uninvolved, nimble, modern delivery, absolutely excluding: grave tones, the knowing pause, careful engraving and all the other pedantic slowness that instead fit like a hand in glove with the gloomy Norwegian tradition" exemplified by Ibsen.[47] The music hall fascinated Marinetti most for its liminal position between organized theatrical event and flexible spontaneous gathering. The Folies Bergère, he wrote, was "a theatre which is not a theatre, a promenade where you may sit down, a spectacle which you are not obliged to watch."[48] In looking to popular forms to rejuvenate an experimental art form, the Futurists were adopting a strategy that was somewhat new in Italy but had been in vogue in Paris and Berlin for a quarter century and had animated both Cubist painting and Apollinaire's poetry, to name only a few of the best known examples.[49]

The suggestion that a fast-paced show will necessarily make an audience run and jump reveals the naiveté and conservatism of Futurist poetics. Along similar lines, the metaphors in the synthetic theater manifesto reveal its authors' commitment to a model of spectatorship as predictable as the workings of the digestive system. For the Futurists, traditional plays diluted action with multiple acts, countless insignificant characters, and ponderous acting. Audiences forced to swallow such bloated time suffer spectatorial indigestion, a discomfort only relieved when the conclusion allows them to expel pent up sighs and applause like so much flatulence (FST, 205). Marinetti suggests that Futurist playwrights should instead "boil all of Shakespeare down to a single act," refining aesthetic experience into bite-sized moments.[50] Some viewers of Futurist shorts found that the authors had done so much digesting for them that the result was no better than excrement. But the Futurists insisted that tactical reductions would purify and improve experience. This rhetoric is remarkably inflexible in its assumption that slowness produces ponderous torpor, while speed precludes deliberation and intensifies experience.

Taken to its extreme, the logic of abridgment promised to fulfill a fantasy of pure relevancy in which no moment was insignificant or boring. The true model for the Futurist theater was not everyday modern life, but life in its most extraordinary and overwhelming moments. This yearning for more intense moments inheres in the term *sintesi*, not just an abbreviated account of essential elements, but a literal putting together or fusing of places, people, or ideas into concentrated and more complex form. Although fed by swift actuality, such a theater would afford experiences that life outside the theater rarely can, and would train the audience to live all moments at a higher pitch. Theatrical framing became a metaphor for translating temporal experience into rarefied form. Just as painters and composers discover, "scattered through the outside world, a narrower but more intense life made up of colors, forms, sounds, and noises, so the man gifted with theatrical sensibility discovers his own specialized reality" violently attacking his nerves, a reality "that is called the theatrical world" (FST, 207–8). Short Futurist plays, then, would violently assault the nerves in order to foster a sensibility fully alive to the inherent theatricality of moments. Writing plays based on the premise that "everything of any value is theater" (tutti è teatro quando ha valore) would, the Futurists hoped, create spectators who learned to embrace this premise outside of the theater (FST, 206). Combining the two impulses I have discussed—a passion for contemporary life plus a desire for "a specialized reality" that is "narrower yet more intense"—the perfect Futurist theater would convert the diversity of the present into a forum for perpetual instant delight and a spur for more vigorous and engaged living (FST, 208).

Intensity, Reduced

The Futurists imagined abridgment as a recipe for intensity, but in practice their radical cuts have a tendency to undercut, to parody, to ironize, and to make moments feel less intense. Futurist excerpts have not just been trimmed down but emaciated to an impoverished dramatic structure that relies for its completion on the mental architecture of a public weaned on familiar dramatic pieces. When Giuseppe Steiner rewrites Vittorio Alfieri's well-known five-act history play, *Saul* (1782), so that each act becomes a two- or three-line snapshot, the result travesties history and heroism (*FP*, 307). Similarly, Angelo Rognoni's three-line *Hamlet*, appropriately subtitled a "synthetic devaluation," begins when Hamlet, lost in thought, notices his father stage left. The play ends abruptly when Hamlet shrugs with indifference at his father's suggestion that he's a ghost: "Oh, okay."[51] Rognoni's devaluation defuses the inciting incident of Hamlet's drama by refusing to take it seriously. It replaces the cultural obligation to revenge with a nonchalant Futurist disregard for the death of one's elders. This foreshortening does not intensify the play's essential questions; it forestalls them. A genuine attempt to synthesize Hamlet's epistemological quandaries might stage the same meeting, have Hamlet ask "Who's there?" and bring down the curtain.

Rather than offering experiences "narrower yet more intense," Futurist shorts that cut quickly to the chase expose and short circuit arbitrary conventions of gradual exposition, development, preparation, and elaboration. Cangiullo's 1915 play *Decision* artificially raises the stakes by fancifully abridging an imaginary source text of incredible length, a text referred to only in the play's subtitle: *A Tragedy in 58 Acts and Perhaps More*. The stage directions clarify the situation: "Representing 57 of these acts is unnecessary. The last act is by Francesco Cangiullo." The essential act finds a twenty-five year old protagonist, Giulio, alone in a vestibule at night. All of a sudden, he erupts violently and utters the play's only speech:

Oh, good God! By now, the game has gone on for some time. . . . The Press . . . public opinion. . . . But me, I don't give a damn about the public or the Press! (*Taking his coat and hat from the portmanteau and putting on his coat*) This thing *absolutely* must end!

(*Quickly, he shuts off the light and leaves*).
CURTAIN[52]

The lineaments of a traditional ending are here, but when isolated, they become satire. Like Nora's infamous final slam of the door in Ibsen's *A Doll House*, this character's exit marks the end of the action, but evacuated of referents, the closing exclamations ring hollow. *Decision* exacerbates the tendency of plays to become more self-conscious as they draw to a close. When the entire play is an ending, it refers to little other than the convention of ending itself. Like Giulio, the similarly named Cangiullo couldn't care less about public opinion. The game of commercial theatrical form has gone on for too long, and must end along with this play.

Accounts we have of audience reception during tours of the *sintesi* confirm the sense that their brand of radical compression was more likely to deflate than supercharge. Professional theater critics rarely took the Futurists seriously enough to bother attending their events, so responses to the tour performances come primarily from other newspaper staff. Reviews range from dismissively condescending to sympathetically critical. It's clear that audiences understood the Futurists' experiments as provocative hyperbole and were often ready to grant them considerable credit for making an effort to unsettle the status quo. But even sympathetic reviewers often felt the plays' radical brevity overshot the mark, missing the difference between intensifying compression and idiotic reduction:

These nice, talented avant-garde artists need to understand that not everything can be the subject for theatrical synthesis. They should also understand that it would be inadvisable, by synthesizing and interpenetrating all the time, to reach complete stupidity. There is a limit to everything, unfortunately, even simultaneous and synthetic drama. But considering the intelligence of some of the Futurists, we expect that they will produce something better.[53]

Accounts of Futurist performance by theater historians tend to focus on the movement's transformative goals as expressed in the manifestos and its formal innovation, but contemporary audiences were struck more by the irony of Futurist theater's traditionalism. More than one reviewer dismissed the plays as derivative or backward looking:

> Futurist synthetic theater . . . is nothing more than a condensation of scenes typical of the Grand Guignol with a lot of sentences sounding like D'Annunzio. It has such a passéist tone that it is depressing. A complete bore . . .[54]

> [The audience] felt the syntheses were a curious, obsolete, traditional development, composed of lines that merely set up a dramatic turn.[55]

> The usual parade of sketches . . . half comic, half macabre little farces of a kind that has existed for a long time in the realm of passéist plays, [Octave] Mirbeau's theater, or the Grand Guignol. . . . some syntheses as long-winded as watered-down milk.[56]

> Beauty was not reached and the public did not have any feeling of intensity or rapidity.[57]

For these audience members, Futurist brevity served primarily to amplify and radicalize a well-established strain of modern theater described in the last chapter: the vogue for condensed, acerbic scenes marrying the serial format of cabaret and vaudeville with parodic commentary on the theatrical medium.[58] The suggestion that the Futurists borrowed ideas from late nineteenth-century naturalist tendencies is not far-fetched: Felix Fénéon, the Parisian author of newspaper *faits-divers* featured in chapter 2 was an old friend of Marinetti's and organized the first Futurist exhibition in Paris.[59] But the final observation above is the most astounding: audiences complained that performances of *sintesi* were *too slow*. Despite a mountain of Futurist rhetoric about compression creating an atmosphere of astonishment, technical limitation meant that evenings of *sintesi* often dragged. Despite the best efforts of companies, spectators complained that "the plays were very short, the intervals very long."[60] By one account, "The total length of the ten plays in the program: about thirty minutes. The total length of the intermissions: two hours."[61] Since most Futurist playwrights had little experience in theater, they did not anticipate the logistical difficulty posed by ten to fifteen set changes in less than an hour.

Reviewers like those above tend to assume that such exasperation and delay proves the failure of the Futurist dramaturgical project, and to a large extent, it does. But numerous *sintesi* self-consciously parody past forms and so encourage strategic boredom. Corra and Settimelli's *Passatismo* (Pastism), for instance, represents fifty years in the life of a couple by repeating with minor revisions the same dull conversation three times, separated by blackouts that span many years.[62] A man and a woman, already old when the action begins, sit at a table across from each other, with a calendar nearby.

Act 1

OLD MAN: How are you?
OLD WOMAN: I am content. And you, how are you?
OLD MAN: I am content. (*Pause.*) What a beautiful day it will be tomorrow! (*Pause.*) Let's also remove the usual leaf today: January 10, 1860. (*Pause.*) Have you digested well?
OLD WOMAN: I am content.
OLD MAN: Have you conquered your dyspepsia?
OLD WOMAN: I ate well enough and have digested well. So I am content.

Darkness (*FP*, 269)

The second act repeats the scene precisely as before, except the calendar has leapt forward twenty years to January 10, 1880. The man and woman do not appear to have aged. Their bourgeois platitude, "I am content," already repetitive within each act, grows increasingly absurd and evacuated when repeated in each subsequent act, until their refrain of contentment and satisfactory digestion begins to suggest their misery (the Futurists used the adjective "digestive" as an insulting synonym for bourgeois, that is, interested only in passive consumption). The final act begins and proceeds identically to the first two, until the old man announces the date, January 10, 1910, at which point, one after the other, they suffer identical heart attacks:

OLD WOMAN: Oh God! What a stab in my heart! I am dying . . . (*She falls over and remains immobile.*)
OLD MAN: Oh God! What a stab in my heart! I am dying . . . (*He falls over and remains immobile.*)

CURTAIN

Passatismo dramatizes with self-congratulatory glee the violent death, on or about the end of the first decade of the twentieth century, of the past, its Chekhovian listlessness, and its audience. Corresponding roughly to the advent of Futurism, the year 1910 was singled out by some as a watershed. Virginia Woolf, alluding to the Post-Impressionist exhibition at the Grafton Galleries in London late that year, famously proposed that "on or about December 1910 human character changed."[63] Corra and Settimelli's bourgeois drones, instead of mastering time, are felled by the arrival of change. The synthetic theater manifesto suggested that radical abridgment would excise the empty time from previous drama, leaving only engaging and dynamic action in tune with a modern present. But in this case, abridgment evokes not speed but the painful torpor of the past, highlighting the fatal monotony of an outmoded bourgeois lifestyle (and by extension its drama). As in plays by Ionesco, Beckett, and Pinter, repetition without progress becomes a strategy for figuring life, especially middle class life, as a series of tedious acts "incessantly and exasperatingly repeated."[64] Like Hamm and Clov in Beckett's *Endgame*, this couple repeats "All life long the same questions, the same answers."[65] Instead of rendering action more dynamic, here cutting out swathes of time underscores stasis. Radical excision makes life into a trivial joke, complete with the standard tripartite rhythm.

A similar logic drives *Sempronio's Lunch*, Corra and Settimelli's 1915 parody in digest form of a bourgeoisie who do little more than digest. The play arranges five tiny excerpts from a man's life, punctuated by blackouts that stand in for many years, in order to tell the story of his life as a single five-course lunch. Over a span of perhaps five minutes, the audience sees the child Sempronio eat soup at home, the young man have boiled meat in a restaurant, the adventurer order a roast with vegetables in Africa, the married adult enjoy fruit at a Parisian cabaret, and the aged Sempronio take coffee in bed. Sempronio is waited on by five different servants of a variety of ages and backgrounds (an old maid, a servant named Giovanni, a "negro" Karscia, a Cabaret server, and a young maid Antonietta), he eats in a range of locales that would flummox even the most creative quick-change set designer, and he ages from childhood to infirmity, but the one constant for this bourgeois everyman is a full and satisfying lunch, prepared and served by someone else. The final line of the play—"Thank you, Antonietta . . . I have had a quick breakfast . . . but I've eaten well" (*FP*, 272)—simultaneously drives home the minor tragedy of life's brevity and pokes fun again at the lone criterion for bourgeois contentment: good digestion. As far as the Futurists are concerned, it is only logical that a life lived in pursuit of a decent meal should end as soon as the meal does.

One might assume the play borrows its montage effect from film, collapsing narrative time in the same way that Orson Welles' *Citizen Kane*, for instance, would later condense sixteen years of Kane's first marriage into two minutes by stringing together shorts scenes of the couple at their breakfast table. Futurist playwrights certainly admired film's ability to jump quickly from one time to another, but temporal montage is not unique to film. In fact, Welles borrowed the technique from a one-act play: the idea, he admitted, "was stolen from *The Long Christmas Dinner* of Thornton Wilder."[66] Wilder's 1931 play compresses ninety years in the life of a family into a twenty-five minute one-act structured around a single meal at the same table, offering a more compelling and more tragic version of the conceit behind *Sempronio's Lunch*. *The Long Christmas Dinner* suggests that abridgment need not create comedy, but in the hands of Futurist playwrights at least, editorial scissors remained a tool for parody and deflation more than intensification.

THE ATTACK OF BREVITY

In addition to the desire to reveal more life in less time and to enliven that life, a third motivation behind the Futurist embrace of brevity was its potential to sabotage theatrical and dramatic tradition. Futurist playwrights sang the praises of swiftness as a tool to remake theater and society, but the first step of that renovation was demolition. In particular, brevity became a tool to dismantle the creaky and outmoded theater institution.[67] For all of their performative enthusiasm, the Futurists presented their activities as a full-scale assault on theatrical establishment, on dramatic technique, and on the possibility of a successful performance. Indeed, Arnold Aronson calls the Futurists' assault on theater's fundamental assumptions the very "embodiment of a modernist anti-theatricality."[68] The most abhorrent preconceptions for the Futurists were artificial limits on the content and shape of plays themselves, and the rigidly scripted experience of an evening at the theater. Although by 1915 these complaints were by no means new, the Futurists were among the most vociferous opponents of overstuffed plotlines; the artificial imposition of exposition and denouement; and the frequent assumption that only particular stories, people, or actions merited representation onstage. The play that opened this chapter, Corra and Settimelli's *Negative Act*, distills this radical antagonism; a two-line play insists it has nothing to tell us and demands that the curtain come down. Written for and performed in traditional theaters, this play and others invoke theatrical conventions by pretending to ignore them.

Another strain of Futurist antitheater denies the primacy of the stage action but makes theatergoing into an alternative spectacle, an unfortunate tragedy for a few, but an entertaining diversion to most. The same actions that ruin the stage performance complete the offstage performance. Futurist scripts written along these lines are theatrical time bombs, built to self-destruct on stage but to succeed in staging audience action. The Futurists aimed to subvert expected theatrical activity both from within and without, and to replace it with a new kind of activity, also scripted but following a different set of rules.

Given the Futurists' infatuation with theatricality, it may seem odd to call their innovations anti-theatrical. But to my mind, Futurist impulses that others have alternately identified as either pro-theatrical or anti-theatrical are deeply interrelated. To be sure, Marinetti and his cohort often express profound fascination with theatricality and display. Martin Puchner's influential study of anti-theatricality in modernist drama, *Stage Fright*, singles out Marinetti as a representative of avant-garde *pro*-theatricality. Puchner distinguishes between two impulses in the modern theater: high modernist anti-theatricalism and avant-garde (pro-) theatricalism. Representatives of both groups distrusted existing forms of theater and sought to reform them, but they did so for different reasons and in different ways. High modernist writers (Mallarmé, Yeats, Joyce, Stein, Beckett) maintained recognizable dramatic form while resisting the vagaries of theatrical production in order to maintain control over the work of art, while avant-garde theatricalists, Marinetti chief among them, sought to rescue theater from itself by reinventing both art and life under the sign of theatricality. Puchner contends that although radical theatricalism sometimes led to the same conclusions as anti-theatricalism, one should nonetheless distinguish between "attacks on the theater motivated by a celebration of the value of theatricality and those motivated by a resistance to it."[69] High modernist and avant-garde writers attacked theater for different reasons, but the remarkable similarity of some of their methods prompts questions about how sharply one can distinguish between the two groups.

To be sure, unlike the closet dramatists Puchner discusses, the Futurists celebrate display, revelation, public disclosure, and interaction with audiences, and they laud not only performance in general but theater as a space and as a set of cultural practices. The Manifesto of Futurist Playwrights opens with an unambiguous assertion: "Among all literary forms, the one that has the most immediate significance for Futurism is certainly the theater."[70] Five years later, the synthetic theater manifesto reiterates this idea: "the only way that Italy can be influenced today is through the theater"

(FST, 204). The manifesto argues that theater provided a ready-made popular forum for political and aesthetic propaganda because a majority of Italians frequented theater, compared to the minority who read books or journals. And theater is not just for the masses. The authors of the synthetic theater manifesto express a childlike affinity for the privileged space of theater, praising its architectural (and embodied) dimensions:

> The theater itself is for us an inexhaustible source of inspiration: that infectious, magnetic sensation emanating from the gilded, empty theater during a morning's rehearsal, though one's mind is tired; an actor's intonations suggesting the possibility of a paradoxical line of thought to be built upon it; a movement of scenery that sparks off a symphony of light; the voluptuousness of an actress giving rise to an abundance of exciting suggestions.[71]

Nevertheless, many of the Futurists' incursions against dramatic tradition are the same as those used by high modernist anti-theatricalists, including the dehumanization and suppression of the actor, the rejection of character, the writing of scenarios that seem impossible to stage, and the sabotage of dramatic development. The "Manifesto of Futurist Playwrights" announces almost textbook distrust of the performing actor: "We want to subordinate the actors completely to the authority of writers."[72] Continuing this theme, the Variety Theater manifesto suggests strategies for disrupting actors' performances—"Have actors tied in sacks up to their necks recite [Victor] Hugo's *Hernani*. Soap the floorboards of the stage to cause amusing pratfalls at the most tragic moments"[73]—that are nearly identical to the actor-in-barrel tactics that Puchner identifies as characteristic of the high-modernist anti-theatricality of Yeats and Beckett. These shared techniques begin to suggest a porous boundary between modernist pro-theatricality and anti-theatricality.

The Futurists were equally committed to sabotaging the habits of audiences and proposed a range of delightful subversive tactics to "prevent any set of traditions from becoming established":

> . . . spread a strong glue on some of the seats, so that the male or female spectator will remain stuck to the seat and make everyone laugh . . .—Sell the same ticket to ten people, resulting in traffic jams, bickering, and wrangling.—Give free tickets to men and women who are notoriously unbalanced, irritable, or eccentric and likely to provoke an uproar with obscene gestures, pinching women, or other

freakishness. Sprinkle the seats with dusts that provoke itching, sneezing, etc.[74]

The vicarious enjoyment of practical jokes has long been a staple of theater, from the *lazzi* of *commedia dell'arte* to the more elaborate on-stage mousetraps in Shakespeare's plays, including *Hamlet*, *Twelfth Night*, and *Much Ado about Nothing*. The Futurists' anti-theatrical innovation was to make the audience the butt of the joke. Their disruptive techniques prevent, interrupt, distract from, or ruin the expected theatrical event but simultaneously provoke parallel performances.

The best way to make sense of such thoroughgoing sabotage by artists infatuated with theater is to consider their idealism. The Futurists had enough faith in the *potential* of theatricality to risk a complete rejection of activity previously recognized as theater. Even as they rejected previous theater as irreparably flawed, they embraced the notion of theater as a mystical catalyst for heightened perception, a frame for experience that compels attention to the workings of the thing itself in time and space. Such a position sounds viable in theory, but in practice, Futurist anti-theatricality struggled to liberate itself from its target. While the manifestos insist that brevity would create an "entirely new theater" by allowing a "leap into the void of total creation" (FST, 205, 207), the *sintesi* remain deeply entangled with late-nineteenth-century and early-twentieth-century European theater. In the remainder of this chapter, I turn to two plays that simultaneously reject modern theater and distill it.

Explosion as Synthesis

Let us return to the play that opened the book, Cangiullo's *Detonation: Synthesis of All Modern Theater* (1915):

> CHARACTER: A BULLET
> *Road at night, cold, deserted.*
> *A minute of silence. — A gunshot.*
> CURTAIN
> (*FP*, 268)

Look past the wink and you see a play that, true to its subtitle, both lampoons and crystallizes several hallmarks of modern drama. The play's structure condenses the most reliable formula for nineteenth-century drama: create a period of rising suspense followed by a gunshot. The authors of the synthetic theater manifesto complain that in traditional theater, and even in ostensibly modern plays by authors like Ibsen, "each act is as painful as having to sit patiently in a waiting room" for an important guest, creating interminable boredom before the inevitable "*coup de théâtre*: a kiss, a shot, a word that reveals all" (FST, 205). *Detonation* isolates and magnifies this experience but does not fundamentally alter its shape. For an audience expecting a show and primed for shock by the title *Detonation*, the long empty minute may feel even longer and more exasperating than the acts of a traditional play, and the eventual *coup de théâtre* quite literally reveals all there is. Cangiullo's gunshot estranges the concept of the sudden turn of events by isolating it. Taken on its own, the *coup de théâtre* becomes at once a *coup* revolting against theater and an essentially theatrical punch in the gut.

The choice of a gunshot as the single action synthesizing modern theater is exemplary. Andrew Sofer's transhistorical study of objects on stage, *The Stage Life of Props*, identifies the gun as *the* representative prop in modern theater.[75] Sofer argues that pistols on the modern stage both evoke and subvert the rigid conventions of dramatic closure inherited from nineteenth-century melodrama. As a result, guns in modern drama—from Hedda Gabler's pistols to Winnie's out-of-reach gun in Beckett's *Happy Days*—"threaten, distort, and even rupture stage time."[76] *Detonation* suggests that one need not even bring the gun onstage: the gunshot alone, the audible yet invisible trace of the gun, dislocates and ironizes stage time. When the gunshot is all there is, it becomes both inciting incident and climactic action, a dramatic arc closed into a self-referential loop. This beginning that is also an ending converts one of the most traditional strategies for dramaturgical culmination—the suicidal pistol shot—into a suicidal attack by the drama on itself. Yet the means of attack is familiar in theater history: Cangiullo's play condenses and parodies the use of the gunshot on stage as a convenient device to end both the protagonist and the play.[77]

In this case, however, the gun is not only a prop or a plot device but also an offstage supporting actor. *Detonation* abandons human character in favor of dehumanized action. The very short list of dramatis personae—"Character: A Bullet"—pokes fun at a reader's conditioned need to follow the fate of a character. But at the same time, Bullet is only slightly more ridiculous than characters in other Futurist plays (Biplane, Dirigible, Tall Armchair), and Bullet has the advantage, along with Biplane, of being one of the agents that the proto-Fascist Futurist movement hoped would execute extraordinary actions, offstage as much as on. Performed in Italy in 1915 and the few years following it, *Detonation* could not help but evoke the violence of the Great War. In that context, the bullet may be the archetypal Futurist character: a relentless, mechanized agent harnessing technology to move at great speed and make a violent impact. This *sintesi* interprets literally Marinetti's claim three years earlier that the "heat of a piece of iron or wood is now more thrilling for us than the smile or the tears of a woman."[78] Here again, the Futurists amplify a current found elsewhere in early twentieth-century theater. Elinor Fuchs argues in *The Death of Character* that theater since the late nineteenth century is characterized by the retreat from and deconstruction of a stable concept of character. Modern drama deindividualizes, dehumanizes, and shifts interest away from sympathy for recognizable people and toward allegory or the nature of its own workings. If modern theater killed character, Cangiullo's bullet—at once dehumanized, allegorical, and metatheatrical—must be listed among the causes of death.

The play's transmogrification of character into pure action may seem an inherently anti-theatrical move. But *Detonation* can also be seen, with only slight exaggeration, as the logical terminus of Aristotle's insistence that the *sine qua non* of drama is the representation of an action: "the structure of events, the plot, is the soul of tragedy, and the soul is the greatest thing of all. Again: a tragedy cannot exist without a plot, but it can without characters..."[79] For that matter, in this play Cangiullo adheres, despite the tongue firmly in his cheek, to the classical unities of time, place, and action, and features a pivotal reversal, followed almost immediately as the curtain falls by recognition, not to mention frustration.

Detonation stands at a crossroads in the history of dramatic form. In one direction, it looks back to suggest the surprise dead end of both Aristotelian and well-made-play dramaturgy. Like the compression in other Futurist theater, this is not swift action itself, but a conversion of action into myth, into the idea of action.[80] Cangiullo's violent *fait-divers*, like the random attacks presented without context or explanation in *fait-divers* plays and *Grand Guignol*, translates incident into idea. This is the same process that lay behind Maeterlinck's evocative naturalism in *Interior*, which estranges the tragic revelation of the girl's death so that the play's climax becomes the idea of a climactic action. At the same time, looking forward, *Detonation* suggests possibilities for a whole range of atmospheric, antagonistic, and conceptual theater that would follow. The play's terse description of a barren setting—"Road at night. Cold. Deserted"—closely resembles the opening of *Waiting for Godot*: "A Country Road. A tree. / Evening."[81] As on the spare stages of Beckett, Pinter and others, the desertion of this empty space makes palpable the absence of traditional reassurances: morality, religion, context. The play's resistance to revealing its secrets—who shot the gun? at whom? for what reason?—sets a precedent for withholding vital information that a number of minimalist playwrights would continue. When in Beckett's *Endgame*, Hamm asks the anguished question, "What's happening, what's happening?" Clov's reply summarizes the minimal assurances of modern dramatic plotlines in this vein: "Something is taking its course."[82] The synthetic theater manifesto defends this sort of reticence as more true to reality. By this logic, *Detonation* may depict the way most people experience gunshots—as shocking and inexplicable interruptions—more realistically than it would if a story, a gun, or a motive were visible. Withholding explanations on stage recreates our general ignorance of causes and backgrounds as spectators in the world.

Crucially, the play both involves and antagonizes the audience. After the implied opening curtain rises on an empty stage, the audience's assumption that there will be something to see fuels their confusion and spurs their impatience. As already stated, the final surprise both satisfies and explodes expectations, and prompts the audience to hang a story on this sparest of plot points, imagining both crime and victim or admitting that they are the victim, whose tragic flaw was their expectation to get what they paid for: human characters, gradual exposition, denouement. In either case, the most important dramatic arc is the spectator's. A similar histrionic, violent opposition to one's audience characterized surrealism. *Detonation* resembles a radically controlled version of the act André Breton would later suggest as the archetypal surrealist action: "dashing down into the street, pistol in hand, and firing blindly, as fast as you can pull the trigger, into the crowd."[83] Cangiullo's theatrical hyperbole anticipates Breton's rhetorical hyperbole, and both cast the crowd as helpless victim of a surprise assault by an artist who hijacks their complacency.

In the early 1970s, during the height of another twentieth-century war, performance artist Chris Burden would, like Cangiullo, embrace the gunshot—icon of swift, mechanized violence—to stage a similar instantaneous assault on audience sensibilities that was even more self-destructive than *Detonation*. Burden's 1971 performance art piece, *Shoot*, started and ended when, before a small audience in Santa Ana, California, he was shot at close range in the left arm by a friend wielding a copper jacket .22 caliber long rifle. Like *Detonation*, Burden's violent experiment in performative concision asks whether a random act of violence may qualify as art, and just how short a work of art may be. Burden has claimed of the performance, "In this instant I was a sculpture."[84] But at which instant is the sculpture—or the performance—complete? When the gun goes off? When the bullet casing hits the ground? When Burden reacts? When someone views the recorded performance? Although Burden singles out the instant of the shot—and presumably the millisecond when the bullet pierces his flesh—as the operative moment, the video clip that records the performance is eight seconds long, and he eventually recorded a two-minute video in which he introduces and describes the performance. On the tape, the minute before the shot consists only of a sparse soundtrack of the final preparations with no video shown. Like Cangiullo's long empty opening minute, the minute of blank screen before Burden is shot builds considerable suspense as the spectator wonders what may be happening. So while Cangiullo and Burden were both attracted by the idea of a performance as instantaneous as a gunshot, in their final compositions, both cater (minimally) to an audience's desire for a period of rising tension before a climax. The similarity of *Detonation* to Burden's performance may suggest that Futurism is an ancestor to later performance art practices, but both theatrical explosions remain indebted to a minimal dramatic structure. Like *Detonation*, *Shoot* is at once a complete repudiation of traditional ideas of performance and an encapsulation of the obsession that fuels so much theatrical activity: the aura surrounding the moments just before an act of violence.

How Many Italians Does It Take to Screw in a Light Bulb?

Four years after he wrote *Detonation*, Cangiullo wrote another microdrama that uses a blank stage devoid of characters to orchestrate a drama of reception. Like so many Futurist shorts, *Lights!*, written in 1919 and published in revised form in 1922, is both an anti-theatrical joke mocking the audience's expectations and a hypertheatrical condensation fulfilling those expectations. Like *Detonation* before it, *Lights!* consists almost entirely of stage directions. This is the 1922 version:

> The curtain rises. The apron, stage, and auditorium of the theater are in darkness. Dark pause. Until someone shouts LIGHTS! (Still darkness.) Then two spectators shout LIGHTS! LIGHTS! (Still darkness.) Then four, then the impatient shout becomes magnified, contagious, and half the theater shouts: LIGHTS LIGHTS LIIIGHTSSS! The entire theater: LIIIIGHTSSS!!! Suddenly, the lights come up everywhere on the apron, stage, and in the auditorium. Four minutes of blazing fear. CURTAIN. And everything is clear. (*FP*, 255)

As in *Detonation*, the presentation begins harmlessly enough, with fading house lights and a rising curtain, but as the dark pause on the bare stage lengthens, confusion sets in. An early version of the piece specified that the pause should be three minutes long. This mute pause creates the first play I know of whose protagonist is its audience. The rising action of the piece is the *audience*'s frustration (stoked into an uproar by actors planted among them), and the Aristotelian reversal comes soon after their wish is granted, when, somewhere within those "four minutes of blazing fear," they realize the joke is on them. Later plays like Pirandello's *Six Characters in Search of an Author* and Peter Handke's *Offending the Audience* would implicate spectators in the performance, but few plays go so far in tipping the balance of action away from the stage and into the house.

Lights! attacks one of the most basic assumptions about playgoing since the introduction of electric lighting: when the lights go down in the house, they must come up on the stage. It displays nothing but an empty stage, it has no characters, it tells no story, and it manipulates and taunts the spectators for expecting to get what they paid for. With actors planted in the audience to model and encourage outrage, *Lights!* fulfills the claim from the synthetic theater manifesto that Futurists would "orchestrate the audience's sensibilities like a symphony, probing and reanimating the most sluggish depths of their being, by every possible means."[85] As in *Detonation*, the spectators are figured as victimized puppets, but here they are also the instruments that complete the symphony.

If *Lights!* succeeded in stoking uproar among the audience, it did so not only because it thoroughly offended their expectations but because it catered to a competing set of expectations. By the time the Futurists started writing *sintesi*, they had been staging soirées for several years and had come to relish their reputation for scandalizing audiences. But the Futurist reputation for provocation was so strong that by 1913 and 1914, audiences arrived at performances fully expecting to be appalled and looking forward to the enjoyable sense of control that came from ruining a production.[86] Critics complained that it was often very difficult to hear the action on stage over the rowdy crowds. As Futurist Francesco Pratella recalls in his autobiography, by a certain point, the "scuffles at the end of each show were almost preprogrammed."[87] A caricature by Filiberto Mateldi encapsulates the tenor of audience expectations before Futurist performances. A pair of policemen has stopped two men who are lugging a sack of vegetables into a theater. One officer asks, "What are you carrying there into the theater?" They reply, "The applause for the Futurists." When spectators

- Che portate li dentro?
— Portiamo gli applausi pei futuristi.

Fig. 4.—"What are you carrying there into the theater?"—"The applause for the Futurists." Caricature by Filiberto Mateldi. *Noi & Il Mondo*, 1 March 1921.

made a point of visiting the fruit stand before the show, little provocation was needed. Hecklers abused the performers and tossed produce almost regardless of what happened on stage. Futurist performances, like so much anti-bourgeois art, offered audiences pleasurable victimization. The gamble involved in a script like *Lights!*, which relies on the crowd being stirred into a frenzy on cue, arguably only pays off when the audience is primed to be shocked. The performance of provocation is completed by the audience's counter-performance of shock and outrage.

An audience rioting against a performance may seem like a textbook example of anti-theatrical behavior. But the dynamic of theater artist as provocateur and audience as willing co-conspirator in theatrical scandal was in fact characteristic of modern drama and underlines one of its major fault lines. In *Performing Opposition: Modern Theater and the Scandalized Audience*, Neil Blackadder argues that the phenomenon of the theatrical scandal recurred so frequently in the early twentieth century because the evolution of audience responses to Western non-musical theater had reached a trou-

Fig. 5. Umberto Boccioni, *Riot in the Gallery*, oil on canvas, 1910. Milan, Pinacoteca di Brera. (Photo Credit: Scala/Art Resource, NY.)

bled transitional phase. Until the mid-nineteenth century, playgoers had been freer to express their approbation or disgust during performances. By the mid-twentieth century, audiences would become fully accustomed to sitting silently in the dark for hours. But from around 1880 to 1930, audience members bristling against the still awkward convention of total passivity embraced and encouraged scandal as a pleasurable way to resist their loss of agency.[88] In this light, what seems like an attack on the audience in fact completes the performance experience they hope for. Berghaus speculates that the escalation of audience hooliganism led to the abandonment of the *serate* as a form around 1914 and to the restriction of theater spaces to more artistic (rather than political) activities, activities including synthetic theater. As a result, audiences of the *sintesi* met with a new shock: relatively conservative fare.

Unlike *Lights!*, the majority of theatrical syntheses in fact upset audience expectations not because they were unrecognizable as theater but because they were more recognizable than Italian audiences were expecting from the Futurists. Despite Futurism's self-professed radicalism, tour performances of synthetic theater demonstrated the surprising tenacity of theatrical and dramatic conventions.[89] The plays were generally performed in traditional theater buildings by established companies who employed stock scenery and demanded higher prices than previous Futurist events. Unlike the early theatrical evenings, where the Futurists themselves took the stage to read manifestos, declaim poetry, and provoke audiences, in the synthetic theater tours, the performers were primarily professional actors who practiced traditional acting techniques.[90] Armed with fruit-stand ammunition, crowds were rearing for a riot but found instead seemingly trivial plays performed against the backgrounds the companies used for their other commercial performances. In place of the Futurists, who in earlier performances had welcomed outrage and reciprocated attacks, the audience found professional actors unaccustomed to flying vegetables and prone to running off stage in the face of them. And instead of an accelerating gymnasium for the spirit, they found sluggish performances with overlong intermissions. From this perspective, both the long wait of *Lights!* and the frustration it sought to engender would have been anything but surprising to its audience.

IN SINTESI / IN SHORT

Focusing on dramatic form, and in particular on the kinds and uses of brevity in the synthetic theater, reveals a number of surprising contradictions at the heart of Futurist dramaturgy. A theater built for the future in fact seeks to capture a sense of the historical present and remains obsessed with the past. Shrunken plays aim to expand our view of life, random and illogical fragments offer familiar experiences of reality, and simultaneous scenes that promise everything at once rely on the successive rhythms of back-and-forth comparison. Compression meant to purify instead corrupts, and

plays built to conquer time highlight more than ever the weight and monotony of its passage. In the widest sense, Futurist manifestos and plays
expose the movement's conflicted relationship with theater. For the Futurists, theater was a stale set of conventions to be demystified, mocked, and
abandoned, and at the same time a privileged, invigorating, educational
forum for extraordinary activity. Both utterly nauseating and "an inexhaustible source of inspiration," theater, in the Futurist imagination, promised to rescue and enrich the present but only to the extent that it bore no
resemblance to theater (FST, 207).

Surveying these texts and performances, however, reveals theatricality
without theater to be a fantasy. Futurist theatricality is steeped in and predicated on dramatic tradition. Their anti-theatrical reforms depend upon a
deep respect for the power of theatrical activity to effect change in an audience and rely upon an invisible network of preconceptions about the shape
and time of theatrical experience. As a result, the Futurists running away
from the theater of their day stumble across its cornerstones. *Detonation*,
timed to self-destruct, reinforces the fundamental alternation of tension
and release that underlies all drama and highlights modern drama's instru-
ment of choice for triggering that release. Finally, anti-theatrical strategies
sabotage the predictable course of a theatrical evening, yet at the same time
create counter performances that succeed to the extent the plays fail. But
even such orchestrated failures—plays that never start or that race to their
own deaths—can fail in unpredictable ways when audiences find them either more entertaining, more sluggish, or less scandalous than they had
expected.

In all of these ways, Futurist *sintesi* make an excellent case study in the
avant-garde's tendency to ingest aspects of popular culture, to process it
into purified or distorted form, and to rebrand the result as shocking or
extraordinary. If the historical avant-garde in general undertakes a self-
conscious parody of modernity's intelligibility and order, as Matei Calinescu has argued,[91] Futurist synthetic theater is a half-conscious parody of
modern theater that captures both its destructive formal innovation and its
peculiar resistance to change. By the early twentieth century, an empty
stage like the one at the beginning of *Detonation* was not empty, but littered
with expectations, conventions, scenarios, and congealed habits of mind. It
was the three-dimensional equivalent of what in visual art we might call,
following Gilles Deleuze, the precluttered canvas.[92] As attempts to move
beyond theater that end up mired in it, Futurist plays represent a step along
the road to what Hans-Thies Lehmann calls postdramatic theater, an experimental strain of twentieth and twenty-first century theater that denies

the primacy of dramatic scripting but, in the process, necessarily highlights "deep structures that still inform the expectations of the majority of the audience when they come to the theater . . ."[93] The messier view of Futurism that emerges from this discussion resonates with Christine Poggi's persuasive recent account of the movement as an ambiguous, ironic, contradictory set of discourses and practices, rather than a boisterous and naïve embrace of modernity.[94]

Finally, and most important, the synthetic theater underscores a crucial lesson about the elusiveness of theatrical brevity. For all of their formal iconoclasm, the Futurists subscribe to a very narrow range of ideas about the effects of compression in performance. The lesson of *Waiting*, the idea that time might be radically non-shareable, is more nuanced than those of the manifestos, which tend to assume a unified audience and a rigid temporal dramaturgy in which faster equals more intense and performance has an immediate, contagious, homogenous effect on its audience. Even if we take the manifestos, the scripts, and the performances together as a collection of diverse innovations suggesting a more nuanced picture of Futurist aesthetics, their thinking about the range of possible reactions to short form remains limited.

In the next chapter, I turn to Samuel Beckett, whose increasingly delimited drama sought new and better ways to sabotage predictable theatrical and temporal experience. Despite Beckett's many differences from the Futurists, he shares with them an interest in the theatrical potential of inaction, an essentially parodic outlook, a deep love of vaudeville, and a penchant for implicit metatheatricality. He also inherited from the Futurists and others the modernist assumption that a writer can use scripts to harness and control an audience's experience of time. But as we shall see, Beckett's increasingly careful attempts to take hold of performance time ultimately register a deep skepticism about the ability to measure or account for time's passage, a skepticism that contrasts sharply with the Futurists' ideological optimism.

| The Shape of Time in
Beckett's Late Theater

In Samuel Beckett's play *Endgame*, as Clov fervently collects a few objects littering the ground, he says, in frustration, "I'm doing my best to create a little order."[1] Clov yearns to bring the single room that bounds his existence under control, to combat entropy with habit. Clov's statement is, on one level, the complaint of a weary domestic servant employing chores as consolation to make the space he tends for three other people more tolerable. But he is also a stage manager and property master who lifts the handkerchief from Hamm's face like a curtain, structures the passage of time with his alarm clock, and creates the little ordered movements that constitute a diurnal performance. In this role, Clov ventriloquizes Beckett, who could have summarized his career with Clov's line, "I'm doing my best to create a little order." Clov's words, written in 1956, seem to announce an aesthetic of reduction that would characterize Beckett's work over the following thirty years: "I'm going to clear everything away. . . . I love order. It's my dream. A world where all would be silent and still and each thing in its last place, under the last dust" (*DW*, 133).

Over the years, Beckett grew more and more interested in clearing everything away, in working with less material, in creating one "little order" after another. He moved from wandering and exhausting novels to the relative compression of dramatic form, and then worked to shrink theater to its vanishing point, crafting increasingly spare plays, some of which he called *dramaticules* or tiny dramas. As the amount of material in Beckett's pieces shrank, the specificity of their instructions and the degree of control they sought to exercise over performers and directors increased. The later plays are small worlds realized through minute commands, or if you prefer, they are little orders made possible by little orders.

At its most extreme, this tendency led to the thirty-five-second piece *Breath*, whose script consists entirely of instructions for a presentation in which light and sound replace actors and dialogue. The resulting play both distills theater and creates something closer to visual art or installation:

CURTAIN

1. Faint light on stage littered with miscellaneous rubbish. Hold about five seconds.
2. Faint brief cry and immediately inspiration and slow increase of light together reaching maximum together in about ten seconds. Silence and hold about five seconds.
3. Expiration and slow decrease of light together reaching minimum together (light as in 1) in about ten seconds and immediately cry as before. Silence and hold about five seconds.

CURTAIN (DW, 401)

On the surface, *Breath* seems like a joke. Beckett once referred to it as "a farce in five acts," ostensibly silence, inhalation, pause, exhalation, and silence. Beckett might seem to have little in common with the frantic Futurists, but this serious farce bears a strong resemblance to an earlier microdrama that makes light into a character, Cangiullo's *Lights!* But whereas Cangiullo's light show excites and manipulates the audience in order to poke fun at their assumptions, as we saw in chapter 3, Beckett has philosophical and eschatological ambitions. The production notes specify that the "brief cry" is an "instant of recorded vagitus," that is, the birth cry of a newborn: the play compresses a life into its central twenty-five seconds. It is the nonverbal equivalent of Pozzo's line from *Waiting for Godot*, "They give birth astride of a grave, the light gleams an instant, then it's night once more." (DW, 82)[2] The play's extraordinary brevity suggests the transience of a single life, echoing Psalm 144's sentiment, "Man is like a breath,"[3] but also evokes the transience of everything, from creation to apocalypse. The directions describe breath not as inhalation but "inspiration," winking at divine inspiration, a concept embedded in the Hebrew name for the holy spirit, *ruach elohim*, the wind or breath of God. Similarly, breathing out in this play is not exhalation, but "expiration," a terminal breath. The final dim silence presents five seconds that could be an eternity.[4] *Breath* is Beckett's most extreme expression of the minimalist conceit that brevity expands a piece's scope: all of time, in no time. It is not a strictly representative Beckett microdrama; each of his other shorts demands the presence of an actor's body, however residual. But other *dramaticules* share *Breath*'s methods, including the reduction of the theater event to one of its fundamental processes (here the rise and fall of lights), the uncanny tendency of that minimal theater to resemble other art forms (sculpture, dance, visual art installation, prose narrative), as well as an evident desire to orchestrate

stage time and space so as to call attention to time as such, and to use theater to suggest alternative ways of understanding it.

This chapter asks why theater, and especially brief theater, appealed to
Beckett and what conceptual work his short theater pieces might do. The
first section quickly surveys the extensive literature on Beckett's shorts,
outlines his debts to earlier dramatic traditions, and explores the popular,
if often underexamined, idea that brevity helped reduce theater to essential
properties. The reflexive tendencies of Beckett's shrinking drama should be
understood in the context of his lifelong preoccupation with taking up and
exhausting one medium after another, a preoccupation described elegantly
in Daniel Albright's monograph *Beckett and Aesthetics*.[5] From this perspective, Beckett's artistic life was an exploration of the perceived capacities
(and intransigence) of aesthetic forms and media: his novels draw attention
to the profound uncertainty of written narrative, his plays to theater's basic
materials (especially presence and time), his single film to a paranoid version of the filmic gaze, his radio pieces to the nature of audition, and so on.
In a trenchant recent essay on Beckett's historically specific understanding
of media, Martin Harries reminds critics to put pressure on Beckett's own
pronouncements about his work and especially to question his characteristically modernist assumption that art forms might have essential properties.[6] In what follows, I strive to follow this advice by revealing blind spots
in Beckett's conception of media as discrete arenas with inherent properties, while at the same time acknowledging the generative influence of that
assumption on his work. In order to build the case that Beckett's short theater must be understood in relation to his career as a whole and to his work
in other media, the chapter incorporates some material from Beckett's novels and his full-length plays, material that may at first glance seem unrelated to brief theater.

Crucially for my purposes, each stage of Beckett's serial colonization
and evacuation of art forms from the 1950s to the end of his career was
characterized by reduction. Limiting the amount of material in each piece
allowed closer attention to elements that might be considered fundamental to each medium, but in the process also made the bedrock of each
medium look threadbare and untrustworthy. So, as we began to see with
Breath, attempts to purify theater to an essence frequently threaten to reveal its debts to related arts: visual art, sculpture, dance, installation, music, or storytelling.[7] In the second section, I focus on a crucial step in this
career-long process—Beckett's turn from novel writing to playwriting—to show that theater promised a more concrete realization of an aes-

thetic of reduction that had always animated his work. Short theater in particular promised Beckett a new set of tests for the paradoxical axiom that restriction can expand a work's significance and that brevity is an aesthetic trade-off whose rewards not only outweigh its shortcomings but might even stem from them.

The third section shows that the turn to theater was also an attempt to reshape time more directly by turning to a medium in which the experience of time could be used to defamiliarize itself. Many of his plays feature clocks and discussions about time, but the later plays themselves become unusual clocks that measure time neither by the sun, by the hour, nor by dramatic convention. His brief stage worlds proceed slowly and deliberately, like the symbolist plays in chapter 2, forcing attention to mere duration and dramatizing empty or unmarked time as a source of anxiety. They take advantage of the oddity of theatrical time—tied to the clock yet frequently wriggling free of it—to dramatize human struggles to wrestle mere duration into more tolerable and sequential shapes, and to suggest that conventional understandings of time are themselves comforting constructions. Throughout the chapter, a theme recurs in which what seems like Beckett's obsessive control or dominance signals its opposite: the perpetual quest to distinguish and refine artistic forms underscores their muddled imbrication, the careful delineation of theatrical space overcompensates for a perceived lack of control in verbal expression, the delimited movement of actors affords them a counterintuitive sense of freedom, and precisely timed scripts and strict directions to actors about pacing begin to unravel a precise concept of time.

BECKETT AND BREVITY

For the roughly thirty years between *Happy Days* in 1960 and his death in 1989, Beckett wrote prose pieces, radio drama, stage plays, and teleplays, but nothing that could be called full-length without some radical rethinking of what we mean by that term. Among conspicuously brief plays in modern theater, Beckett's shorts are the best known and have generated an enormous volume of criticism. Multiple book-length studies and essays focus specifically on his output since 1965—the so-called later work.[8] Given the relative scarcity of scholarship on brevity in modern drama, what accounts for the abundance of interest in the little plays of a single author? The most obvious answers are that Beckett was well known before he turned to little forms, and that he did not return to longer ones. His novels

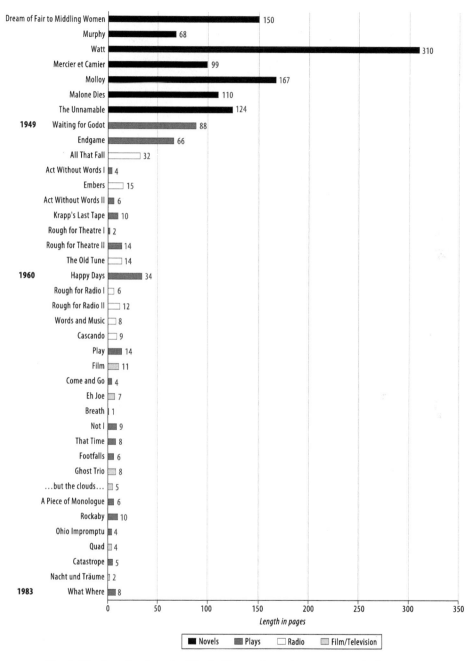

Work	Length
Dream of Fair to Middling Women	150
Murphy	68
Watt	310
Mercier et Camier	99
Molloy	167
Malone Dies	110
The Unnamable	124
1949 Waiting for Godot	88
Endgame	66
All That Fall	32
Act Without Words I	4
Embers	15
Act Without Words II	6
Krapp's Last Tape	10
Rough for Theatre I	2
Rough for Theatre II	14
The Old Tune	14
1960 Happy Days	34
Rough for Radio I	6
Rough for Radio II	12
Words and Music	8
Cascando	9
Play	14
Film	11
Come and Go	4
Eh Joe	7
Breath	1
Not I	9
That Time	8
Footfalls	6
Ghost Trio	8
…but the clouds…	5
A Piece of Monologue	6
Rockaby	10
Ohio Impromptu	4
Quad	4
Catastrope	5
Nacht und Träume	2
1983 What Where	8

Length in pages

■ Novels ▨ Plays ☐ Radio ▨ Film/Television

Fig. 6. The length of most of Beckett's works, using page counts from
the Grove Centenary Edition, in order of composition. The short prose
is omitted here for lack of space, but including it only strengthens the
overwhelming later preference for brevity.

attracted some attention and praise, *Waiting for Godot* catapulted him into the public eye, and the "full-length" plays that followed—*Endgame* and *Happy Days*—cemented his reputation as not only one of the greatest dramatists of the century, but one of its greatest writers. He won the Nobel Prize in 1969, although by that point it had been almost a decade since the composition of *Happy Days*, his last play with a running time over thirty minutes. As a result, anyone who paid attention to Beckett after the Nobel Prize would have had no choice but to attend to short form. That the trajectory of Beckett's career reverses familiar narratives of artistic development in which short juvenilia lead organically to later so-called complete or mature work has seemed to demand explanation, and has led to a number of narratives (mine included) that seek to uncover a logic behind Beckett's shrinking forms.

The volume of critical attention to the short plays by Beckett scholars rather than theater historians has tended to obscure Beckett's theatrical antecedents. Scholars seeking to explain a given example of Beckett's work most often compare it to his other work. Ruby Cohn, an exception, identifies the remnants of previous dramatic forms in Beckett's plays—"a residue of tragedy and comedy in *Godot* and *Endgame*, marriage farce in *Happy Days*, melodrama in *Play*, folk drama in *All That Fall*"[9]—but concludes that they remain essentially unique creations. When critics discuss precursors, they usually (rightly) place Beckett within a symbolist genealogy including Maeterlinck and especially Yeats, a fellow Irishman whose efforts to stage "a deep of the mind" foreshadow the "profounds of mind" in Beckett's later plays.[10] Many note Beckett's debts to vaudeville, but few use the fact to connect him to the Futurists, who were among the twentieth century's most explicit lovers of variety theater and whose short plays share surprising sympathies with Beckett's. Where Marinetti thought variety would jumpstart audiences, Beckett leverages vaudeville's simple scenarios, verbal banter, and comic outlook on pain to more nuanced effect. His use of repetition to underscore the monotony of relationships in *Waiting for Godot*, *Endgame*, and *Happy Days*—"All life long the same questions, the same answers"—resembles the evacuated banter of the bourgeois couple in the Futurist short *Passatismo* (Pastism) discussed in chapter 3, but by prolonging the incessant banter, Beckett explores subtler gradations of monotony (DW, 95). His parody sends up not the bourgeoisie, but everyone; it is parody without the implication that one could avoid the behavior being parodied. One might assume Beckett's excruciatingly slow theatrical worlds offer the opposite of Futurist acceleration, presentism, and self-promotion: his plays resist recognizable time and maintain a dignified distance from audiences and critics. But they share with Futurist shorts a reliance on the assumed building blocks of theater, an outsider's attraction to the stage that embraced the medium by dismantling it, and a fascination with dilated time. As a result, their microdramas often resemble each other to a remarkable degree. We saw above that *Breath* recalls Cangiullo's *Lights!* in a philosophical rather than political register. Beckett's second mime piece, *Act Without Words II*, is another close parallel. Like Mario Dessy's side-by-side portrait *Waiting*, it takes advantage of shared theatrical time to contrast the mental speeds of two men—A who is "slow, awkward . . . absent" and B who is "brisk, rapid, precise" —in order to suggest that one's mental pace can generate either comedy or tragedy (*DW*, 215).[11] Both sets of microdramas reveal the complexity of simple theater, but do so from different directions. The Futurists fled from traditional theater but tripped over its cornerstones; Beckett, as we will see, sought theater's foundation in the tangible space and felt time of live performance, but ultimately revealed the instability of theater, space, and time.

Refining and Redefining Theater: Acts without Words?

What accounts for Beckett's shrinking drama? Many explanations perpetuate conventional assumptions about his purported nihilism: these temporary, indigent spaces capture the impoverishment and futility of human existence.[12] Some make the equation more historically specific by connecting the defoliated futility of his plays to the precariousness of existence in a postatomic era. For others, the persistent fragmentation of subjects, bodies, and memories in these plays casts doubt on the unity of the human subject or the stability of memory.[13] Each of these approaches tells part of the story, but I am most sympathetic to the critical strain that reads Beckett's shorts as interrogations of the perceived capacities of theater.[14] His interest in theatrical compression coincided with his increased involvement directing productions and reveals his attempts to explore the limits of theater as he understood it. Even more insistently than Maeterlinck's shorts or Futurist *sintesi*, Beckett's shorts require a conventional mid-twentieth-century interior theatrical space and make little sense outside of one. From the wings and fly space of *Act Without Words I*, to the spotlights in *Play* and *Not I*, to the light and sound cues in *Breath*, or to the recorded voices in *Krapp's Last Tape*, *Rockaby*, and *That Time*, they assume a dark space, sealed from the world, in which light and recorded sound can be precisely manipulated in front of an audience who watch from one position. But unlike much metatheater, Beckett's works by implication. Instead of showing us the machinery, he isolates small pools of light on dark stages, setting up loose miniature frames within the frame of the proscenium.[15] If modern theater suspends alternate universes in the dark, Beckett's microdramas amplify that ontology by shrinking it. Beckett employs theater's isolation of time and space to make tacit philosophical or ontological arguments, but his inquiry proceeds from the assumption that problems like identity, memory, or the experience of time cannot be separated from questions of representation.

Simultaneously yoked to the stage and stripped of so much that makes theater familiar, these plays, like other microdramas, ask what if anything about theater might be irreducible. The one-person mime *Act Without Words I* offers Beckett's earliest and seemingly most straightforward proposal about the *sine qua non* of theater: mere presence in time before an observing gaze. Written in 1956 while Beckett was finishing *Endgame*, the twenty-minute piece was his first stab at short drama, apart from the unpublished parody *Le Kid* discussed in chapter 1. A figure called simply "the man" is thrown backwards on stage from the right wing and finds himself in a desert bathed in dazzling light. Taunted by an offstage whistle, he makes repeated attempts to relieve his desperate situation—exiting to either wing, seeking the shade of a tree, stacking blocks to reach a drink of water, lassoing the water, hanging himself, or doing himself harm with a pair of scissors—but each time the world refuses to cooperate and the man, stymied and left in the unforgiving light, "reflects" on his situation (*DW*, 191–94). The play's reversal comes when in response to the whistle, he does not move to reach for the carafe that "dangles and plays about his face," but simply lies on his side, facing the auditorium, and looks at his hands (*DW*, 191). The mime's allegory is more transparent than Beckett's later microdramas, but it shares several of their hallmarks, including a resistance to dramatic closure, a generic figure subjected to regard whose theatrical plight stands in for some aspect of human experience, and a denuded landscape that is both here and now and nowhere and never. Like naturalist, symbolist, and Futurist plays before it, the play is reduced to archetype. The trapped everyman could say, along with *Godot*'s Vladimir, "But at this place, at this moment of time, all mankind is us, whether we like it or not" (*DW*, 72). But this Tantalus or Sisyphus or Bartleby, unlike many of us, gains perspective on his appointed rounds and opts out of them. Albert Camus' 1942 essay, "The Myth of Sisyphus," suggests that in the fleeting interval of consciousness between his labors, Sisyphus comes to understand his condition and gains a perverse happiness.[16] Beckett's play, too, offers an origin myth for the moment of existential self-regard, but the happiness or despair of this man regarding his hands cannot be determined. A series of acts without words ends without action and without consolation.

Beckett's clearest statement of the medium specificity of *Act Without Words I* came when he defended it against screen adaptation. In a 1957 letter to his American publisher Barney Rossett, Beckett clarifies his desire to discriminate among what he calls genres (but which many today would call media):

> Now for my sins I have to go on and say that I can't agree with the idea of Act Without Words as a film. It is not a film, nor conceived in terms of cinema. If we can't keep our genres more or less distinct, or extricate them from the confusion that has them where they are, we might as well go home and lie down. Act Without Words is primitive theatre, or meant to be, and moreover, in some obscure way, a codicil to End-Game, and as such requires that this last extremity of human meat—or bones—be there, thinking and stumbling and sweating, under our noses, like Clov and Hamm, but gone from refuge.[17]

Waiting for Godot and *Endgame* had begun to suggest that the stage is an existential waiting room, but the "primitive theatre" of *Act Without Words I* removes nearly all distraction from theater's enabling condition: the observation of thinking meat "under our noses," "stumbling and sweating" in a continuous present tense. Beckett's letter could easily be confused with conventional arguments for theater based on co-presence and immediacy, such as Open Theater founder Joseph Chaikin's sentiment that theater is "a gathering of creatures who breathe together and are vibrantly alive and become an organized world."[18] Beckett would agree theater offers an organized world, but offers a far less romantic take, indeed a paranoid take, on shared presence, imagining presence before an observer as a kind of subjection.[19] This act without words more closely resembles a comic take on Maeterlinck's vision of little plays as experimental spaces in which "poor little trembling, elementary creatures" shiver for an instant and weep on the brink of a gulf.[20]

The notion that media might be discrete and have essential properties is, Martin Harries reminds us, both characteristically modernist and worth questioning.[21] As the letter above attests, it is an idea Beckett took seriously at least as an enabling fiction. But his various attempts at distillation often demonstrate a strange alchemy in which reducing theater to an ostensible base—a body observed, a wait for conclusive action, organized light and sound, an escape from everyday time—weakens and warps the proposed

foundation. Beckett's account of *Act Without Words I* as fundamental theater may seem like a final word, but it gives at best a partial picture of the
operations of the play and of the complexity that results from Beckett's re-
ductive impulses. The piece relies on intimate proximity, and yet a body
present before our eyes cannot keep the man's identity and personality
from dissolving into abstraction. As in the naturalist and symbolist plays
discussed in chapter 2, the paucity of material reality converts objects and
figures into symbols. The man is right there, under our noses, and nevertheless "gone": gone from refuge, gone from identification, and to a large
extent gone from the immediate circumstances of audience members. He is
separated from them on the far side of what Maeterlinck called a gulf. Creating a pool of "dazzling light" in a presumed dark auditorium, the play
capitalizes on the imagined ontological distance between modern stage
and audience, to offer what Beckett would later call *"un univers à part* [a
separate universe]."[22] This distance heightens the illusion of temporal autonomy that has always been possible on stage, but which is easier to establish with controlled lighting. The man's stumbling and sweating unfolds in
the present, but it is also happening at no time in particular. As we will see
later in the chapter, Beckett magnifies the tension in all theater between
presentness and timelessness until the distinction breaks down.

Insisting on *Act Without Word*'s paradigmatic theatricality also obscures
its proximity to other media. As a set of movement instructions for an un-
speaking body, it approaches dance.[23] The play's portrayal of a mute figure
struggling in vain against an intransigent world owes such a debt to Buster
Keaton, whom Beckett greatly admired, that with little or no adaption it
could be the scenario for an early silent film—despite Beckett's objections
to the contrary. *Act Without Words I* also reflects Beckett's reading in behav-
ioral psychology in the 1930s, especially Wolfgang Köhler's book *The Men-
tality of Apes*, which describes experiments in which apes in Tenerife stacked
cubes to reach a banana.[24] Through Köhler's lens, having a so-called "primitive" creature under one's nose is less essentially theatrical than essentially
experimental. And just as in a laboratory, the experimental subject's body
must be present, but their identity is irrelevant.

Beckett's other shorts further complicate a tidy sense of theater's core,
suggesting a variety of overlapping answers to what if any essence it might
have. Like *Act Without Words I*, *Waiting for Godot* and *Play* imply that theater
is purgatorial observation. *Come and Go* and *What Where* cast the stage as a
round robin of entrances and exits. *Breath* abandons language and implies
that theater is at base the manipulation of light and space over time. But
most of his later shorts, including *Not I*, *That Time*, *Footfalls*, *A Piece of Mono-*

logue, *Rockaby*, and *Ohio Impromptu*, dramatize the desperate attachment of one or more figures to a repetitive narrative that bears close but imperfect relation to the situation represented. By setting into opposition two image-generating elements of theater, language and *mise en scène*, these shorts suggest that a fundamental riddle of theater for Beckett was the perpetual tension between a world generated by words and a world whose actions and settings speak for themselves.[25] Taken together, these varied accounts of theater's essence suggest a vision of modern theater as a form defined by the friction among its constitutive parts. The plays are short and relatively static, but teem with ambiguous negotiations among light, sound, space, bodies, voice, and story.

Daniel Albright's *Beckett and Aesthetics* situates Beckett's reflexive investigation of theater within a series of representational stress tests dismantling by turns prose fiction, theater, radio, and television. This cycle proceeds, it seems to me, like occasional intentional molting: one form is gradually desiccated and its dissolution feeds a naive leap into a new one, which is later abandoned in turn for another. In this tendency, Beckett resembles his character Molloy, who says "in me there have always been two fools, among others, one asking nothing better than to stay where he is and the other imaging that life might be slightly less horrible a little further on" (M, 43–44). While one might mistake this cycle for progress, its spirit is closer to variation as a coping mechanism: "And if all muck is the same muck that doesn't matter, it's good to have a change of muck, to move from one heap to another a little further on, from time to time . . ." (37). So what seems at any point like an obsession with a given medium is better understood as the latest episode in an ongoing inquiry into representation itself. In this respect, Beckett's career holds lessons similar to those we might find by examining the historical succession of new and newer media, in which each new medium prompts an investigation into the powers and limitations of representation itself.[26]

The remainder of this chapter focuses on two aspects of this career-long churn of formal experimentation: first, Beckett's move from novel to theater in the late '40s; and second, that move's temporal ramifications, which become clearest in his plays from the 1970s and '80s. One could easily extend the discussion into Beckett's work in recorded media (radio, film, and television), which amplified and in some cases even surpassed the capacities that originally led him to theater: immediacy, directed attention, and tight framing. But since my subject is short theater and its peculiar temporal operations, I restrict myself to Beckett's work for the stage.

Central to my argument is the sense that Beckett's vision of reduced theater relied on his assumption that theater was already, compared to prose fiction, a reduced and simplified medium. This reading puts pressure on a line of Beckett criticism that interprets his theatrical strictures as a manifestation of a particularly modernist desire for authorial control. Martin Puchner's excellent chapter on Beckett in *Stage Fright* exemplifies the assumption that the progressive confinement of action and the persistent use of narrative and description in his plays constitutes a bid to dominate the uncontrollable actor's body. According to Puchner, the "descriptive and narrative strategies" in Beckett's plays "participate in a modernist anti-theatricalism that is primarily directed against the integrity of actors and their freedom of movement."[27] Dehumanized, fragmented into gestures, and trapped in poses of reception, the figures in Beckett's late plays are subjected to and subordinated to the unfolding of narrative, either their own or other people's. Puchner's argument implies that for Beckett, as for other modernist writers, narrative promised the secure footing of formal control, while theater necessarily threatened that mastery by requiring that the author surrender his work to the whims of performers, producers, and directors. Beckett's plays certainly place severe limits on movement and on the latitude of performers or directors to interpret the work. But reading them as the triumph of narrative over theater requires that we ignore Beckett's deep mistrust of narrative and his lifelong interest in the aesthetic potential of failure and impotence. By considering Beckett's experiments in theater as a response to difficulties he explored in prose fiction, the next section offers one explanation for why Beckett might have pushed theater to do as little as possible, and suggests that his microdramas are not only laboratories for theater but places of refuge from fiction that nevertheless cannot escape its influence.

A WORLD LESS ILL CONTRIVED: FROM NOVEL TO DRAMA

> Less seen and seeing when with words than when not.
> —*Worstward Ho*[28]

In order to understand the final period of Beckett's playwriting career, we must remember why it began. Beckett's decision to begin writing plays at all stemmed from his sense that theater offered more, not less, control over his output. Like Chekhov, Shaw, Pirandello, and Genet, he had a substantial career as a fiction writer before writing drama. By early 1947 when he wrote his first complete play, *Eleuthéria*, he had already written four novels.[29] He began *Waiting for Godot* late in the following year after having written two more novels, *Molloy* and *Malone Dies*, and just before writing the third novel in the trilogy, *The Unnamable*. That Beckett began writing for the stage during the two-year period (1947–49) of his most sustained and prolific novel-writing helps explain why he described the move to theater as a solution to a problem prompted by writing novels: "When I was working on *Watt*, I felt the need to create for a smaller space, one in which I had some control of where people stood or moved, above all of a certain light. I wrote *Waiting for Godot*."[30] Contrary to the conventional wisdom that playwriting strips writers of control by requiring that they surrender to the vagaries of production, Beckett chose the theater because its "smaller space" — tangible and limited — promised the artist more direct control over an image's shape and time's passage than does the space of the page.

Beckett's statement that theater offers "some control" over the disposition of bodies and light implies that fiction may in fact offer little direct control over these elements. Consider Beckett's protracted description over several pages of Molloy's elaborate ritual of sucking sixteen stones in a particular order.[31] Molloy's problem is essentially Beckett's: how to keep track of so many moving parts within a system that leaves so many things out of sight and uncertain. One can hear echoes of Beckett's frustration (and the reader's) in Molloy's admission three quarters of the way through a paragraph that stretches for eighty pages: "I was beginning to lose all sense of measure, after all this wrestling and wrangling, and to say, All for nothing." (65). Molloy's eventual solution — "to throw away all the stones but one" (69) — anticipates Beckett's: drastically reduce the number of variables and locations in order to be sure, or at least less unsure, what you are dealing with.

If all fiction offers itself to the imagination, Beckett's speakers surrender before they have finished speaking. These are narratives troubled by a pervasive impatience with the potential instability of narrative, haunted by the fear that all storytelling is a lie, that as the speaker of *Molloy* reminds us, "every time I say, 'I said this,' or 'I said that' . . . , I am merely complying with the convention that demands you either lie or hold your peace. For what really happened was quite different" (82). Beckett's considerable linguistic skepticism infects his speakers, whose narratives have a tendency, like Malone's notes, to "to annihilate all they purport to record,"[32] pretending to decompose even as they compose: "It is midnight. The rain is beating on the windows. It was not midnight. It was not raining" (MD, 170). The final voice in the prose trilogy, Worm, who is said to have "no voice" and yet "must speak" (301), has been so thoroughly stripped of traditional markers of subjectivity that what remains is like a message from the thread-bare medium itself: "I'm neither one side nor the other, I'm in the middle, I'm the partition, I've two surfaces and no thickness. . . . I'm the tympanum, on the one hand the mind, on the other the world, I don't belong to either" (376). *The Unnamable* imagines language attenuated from a world-building device to a membrane—thinner than the paper on which it's printed—that can evoke little more than the ultimate insubstantiality of identity, communication, or knowledge.

Of course, most printed words are not significantly more or less substantial than others. Although many critics characterize the trilogy's attenuation as an aesthetic of linguistic failure or impotence, borrowing Beckett's own language in interviews and in "Three Dialogues with George Duthuit," I prefer Audrey Wasser's careful correction: that no carefully crafted linguistic object positing a coherent theory can properly be said to fail, and that Beckett's novels rather use formal devices successfully to render sensible their own inability to reach an implied ideal.[33] Chief among these devices is a rhythmic technique Bruno Clément identifies as "epanorthosis," that is, a returning to a previous statement to correct, weaken, retract, or amplify it.[34] The rhythm of compulsive return, of multiple attempts, of starting over again better to express what one has already expressed not only characterizes the novels but also helps explain why Beckett turned from them to a new medium. His plays return again and again to figures and themes that populate the novels: immobilized anonymous tramps make their way through muck in unspecified times and places and fill time by inventing and reinventing stories that bear suspicious resemblance to their situations but yet remain ambiguously distinct from them. But as in rhetorical epanorthosis, Beckett's retracing of familiar ground in new forms from the late 1940s on was also a bid to correct, to surpass, and to clarify previous expressions. In particular, theater promised to render space and time sensible in a way the novel could not.

The stage, always tied to particular spaces and times, yet estranged from quotidian time, seemed an ideal venue in which to use duration and space as the means of their own defamiliarization. Beckett's comments about the attractions of theater are suffused with a sense of the medium as simultaneously grounded and distant. During rehearsals for a production of *Endgame* in Berlin, Michael Haerdter asked Beckett about the relationship between the stage world and the world outside the windows of Hamm and Clov's room. At first, Beckett said he would rather not talk about it. But then he continued,

Can one call what we make novels? It's something different; we don't write novels any longer. I don't like to talk about it, but it's a work of imagination . . . it's a matter of imagination; of the attempt to escape from the tangle [of things]. There are so many things; the eye is as incapable of comprehending them as the mind of grasping them . . . So a person creates his own world, *un univers à part*, to withdraw when one gets tired. . . . In order to get away from the chaos into a simpler world . . . Yes, Clov too has this need for order . . . I have progressively simplified situations and persons, *toujours plus simples*."[35]

Beckett found that theater, like other forms of play, converts a part of the world into a world apart. It aims to escape from the tangle of things by focusing attention on a very small number of visible things. When asked to explain *Endgame* after its American premiere, he insisted that the only answers would be found in the "extreme simplicity of dramatic situation and issue."[36] The dramatic situation itself—which could just as easily be described, even in its simplest forms, as a dense interplay among actor, character, spectacle, spectator, audience, and story—is, from the perspective of a novelist frustrated with the multiplying ontological confusions of narrative prose, a kind of extreme simplicity: "For me theater is first of all relaxation from work on fiction. We are dealing with a definite space and with people in this space. That's relaxing."[37] One might expect that the collaborative medium of theater would provoke anxiety for a modernist author with a "need for order"; indeed, that is roughly Puchner's argument. But for Beckett, theater felt relaxing because it promised to speak for itself, yoking ideas to the phenomenological givenness of the stage and mining the material world for its conceptual richness.

To be sure, Beckett's stage worlds often seem as prone to disintegration, dissolution, and obstruction as the fiction. But his plays use performance to lay hold of deteriorating language and vanishing time, the more clearly to mark their passing. Compared to the narrator's dilemma that "you either lie or hold your peace" (*M*, 82), theater was relaxing because it promised a third alternative: a space where you can hold your peace and yet allow a body or a stage image to exist and persist through time or (as more often happens on Beckett's stages) where an image can be put into tension with the fabrications of language, and the relation between the two modes can become the essential signifier. Beckett put this very complaint about language into the mouth of *Endgame*'s onstage raconteur, Hamm, who expresses a wish for reprieve from the stories he cannot stop telling: "If I can hold my peace and sit quiet, it will be all over with sound, and motion, all over and done with" (145). *Endgame's* closing moment, in which Hamm *"remains motionless"* as if embalmed beneath his soiled handkerchief while Clov stands *"impassive and motionless"* on the threshold of the door, frozen between dependency and departure, begins to realize the dream of a peace that can be held, of time that becomes palpable in suspense. The last words of the script call for a "brief tableau" (*DW*, 154). Ending a play with a tableau vivant might seem to place Beckett in the lineage of melodrama, but where melodrama's climactic tableaux typically literalize the very process of narrative resolution by stopping time at the most opportune moment, *Endgame* pauses at the threshold between the irresolute and resolution.

Theater may have provided relief from work on fiction, but Beckett envisioned that relief not as a suspension of thinking but as a different form of thinking. When his first literary agent, the poet George Reavey, wrote to ask that he offer the reader some relief in the novel *Murphy*, he responded, "There is no time and no space in such a book for mere relief. The relief has also to do work and reinforce that from which it relieves."[38] The plays bear out a similar pattern. Their time and space offer relief but not mere relief. Physical bodies promised perceptual and temporal stability, but the material world in these plays continually offers stumbling blocks parallel to those that beset language. Characters cannot move, or they trip and fall. They struggle to discern the hour, and like audiences find themselves unable to do so. The world of bodies and moments, like that of language, fails to cooperate. The stage does offer relief, illustrating the world's shoddiness more immediately and observing the unbearable passage of time more directly, but this brand of relief also reinforces the sense of absence and timelessness from which it offers relief. I return to this theme below in the discussion of Beckett's reshaped time. But it will be helpful first to elaborate and put pressure on the assumption, clear in Beckett's reply to Michael Haerdter, that "progressively simplified situations and persons" might allow one more fully to comprehend the tangle of reality.

Greater Smallness

> Know minimum.
> —*Worstward Ho*[39]

Both Beckett's turn to theater and his later attempts to reduce its elements are deeply indebted to the idea that restricting the amount of material or time under consideration might allow more complete knowledge. This counterintuitive notion—which I call Beckett's epistemology of limitation—is a recurring theme in the novels, but it became a driving force behind his work in theater, a medium whose inherent limits promised to test the thesis more directly. One may take issue with the contention that minimal art is necessarily more knowable or pure or clarifying than its longer or more complex counterparts, but it is worth exploring why Beckett embraced the idea and whether his short work bears it out.

From the beginning, Beckett's imaginative worlds are governed by the assumption that limitation might be a virtue. He wrote these lines in *Watt* in the early '40s:

> I was very fond of fences, of wire fences, very fond indeed; not of walls, nor palisades, nor opacious hedges, no; but to all that limited motion, without limiting vision, to the ditch, the dyke, the barred window, the bog, the quicksand, the paling. I was deeply attached, at that time, deeply deeply attached.[40]

Beckett shares this attraction to obstructions that permit visibility. The title character of *Malone Dies* learns that you do not truly know what you have until it's gone: "Now that I have lost my stick I realize what it is I have lost and all it meant to me. And thence ascend, painfully, to an understanding of the Stick, shorn of all its accidents, such as I had never dreamt of. What a broadening of the mind" (247). This notion would come to animate Beckett's career: to restrict characters and viewers to less input isolates thin bands of existence and reveals their inherent complexity. Moran, the speaker of the second half of *Molloy*, has a minor epiphany that encapsulates Beckett's aesthetic of minor epiphanies:

> I was not long either in making the following addition to the sum of my knowledge, that when of the innumerable attitudes adopted unthinkingly by the normal man all are precluded but two or three, then these are enhanced. . . . Yes, when you can neither stand nor sit with comfort, you take refuge in the horizontal, like a child in its mother's lap. You explore it as never before and find it possessed of unsuspected delights. In short it becomes infinite. . . . Such are the advantages of local and painless paralysis. . . . To be literally incapable of motion at last, that must be something! My mind swoons when I think of it. And mute into the bargain! And perhaps as deaf as a post! and who knows as blind as a bat! And as likely as not your

memory a blank! And just enough brain intact to allow you to exult!
(*M*, 134–35)

Moran articulates with remarkable prescience—and characteristic self-mockery—Beckett's epistemology of limitation as it would develop over his career. If, as Beckett suggests, knowledge is a sum, perhaps we can add to it by subtracting. Restricting attention to a narrow range provides an intensified view of the remainder, which expands to fill the frame and the imagination.

The move to theater promised to ground this epistemology of limitation in the bodies and circumstances of the stage, converting one of theater's fundamental difficulties into an advantage. When Émile Zola wondered in 1881 why naturalism had not taken hold on the stage, he complained that, unlike the novelist who is "absolute master of his medium," the dramatist "is enclosed in a rigid frame; he must obey all kinds of necessities. He moves only in the milieu of obstacles."[41] Beckett could hardly have agreed more, but he welcomed and embraced the milieu for its obstacles and added new barriers whenever possible. Hemming in situations and figures provided characters, actors, and audiences rare opportunities to contemplate what remains. Moran's hyperbolic wish—to be "literally incapable of motion at last"—would be made literal again and again in the positions of Beckett's stage figures, from the mute protagonist trapped on stage in *Act Without Words I*, to Nagg and Nell stuck in their ashbins or the blind Hamm unable to stand and Clov unable to sit in *Endgame*, to *Play*'s urn-bound trio, to the speaker of *A Piece of Monologue* who stares "as if unable to move again" at the blank spaces on the wall where his memories were (*DW*, 267), or to W in *Rockaby* who we presume has just enough brain intact to register the end of her rocking at long last. These plays propose not merely that "There always remains something," as Winnie insists in *Happy Days* while buried up to her neck in a scorched mound,[42] but also that the meager remainder of a plot, of a person, or of a dramatic tradition might be preferable to its undiminished counterpart.[43]

One reason Beckett preferred a meager remainder is that it seemed the only amount one might presume to understand. In rehearsals for a 1975 production of *Endgame* in Berlin, Beckett was uncharacteristically straightforward about the post-Enlightenment philosophy that fueled his interest in theater:

The crisis started with the end of the seventeenth century, after Galileo. . . . The Encyclopedist wanted to know everything . . . But that direct relation between the self and—as the Italians say *lo scibile*, the knowable, was already broken . . . Leonardo da Vinci still had everything in his head, still knew everything. But now! . . . Now it's no longer possible to know everything, the tie between the self and things no longer exists . . . one must make a world of one's own in order to satisfy one's need to know, to understand, one's need for order. There for me, lies the value of the theatre. One turns out *a small world with its own laws*, conducts the action as if upon a chessboard . . . Yes, even the game of chess is still too complex.[44]

Here, Beckett imagines theater in general and in particular his play named after the final moves in a chess game, *Fin de partie*, as a kind of necessary game. Theater appealed because, like any game space, it offered local and temporary coherence. Johan Huizinga's foundational 1938 study of "the play element" of culture identifies local coherence as a central motivation for all play, using language that closely resembles Beckett's above: "Here we come across another very positive feature of play: It creates order, is order. Into an imperfect world and the confusion of life it brings a temporary, limited perfection."[45] For Huizinga and for Beckett, play appeals because it organizes the chaos of life into little alternative orders in limited space and time.

Beckett's minimalism was, among other things, a strategy to escape the shadow of Proust and James Joyce, those masters of encyclopedic excess who seemed to know everything and to have arranged it all into interconnected and comprehensive systems in *À la recherche du temps perdu* and *Ulysses*.[46] Beckett's quip that "Joyce was a synthesizer, I am an analyzer," distinguishes him from encyclopedic modernism by stressing the minimalist residue that *analysis* retains from its Greek root: the act of dividing or dissolving something into its constituent parts so as better to understand it.[47] Beckett allied himself instead with a tradition that valued loss as a kind of gain. Herbert Blau recalls a conversation in which Beckett began to sketch this genealogy: "But the theme again was impotency, which led him to say, however, that there is in some—a Goethe or Yeats, of course—the discovery of other powers out of a sense of loss . . ."[48]

The idea that "limited perfection" might be the best one can hope for is precisely the lesson of Nagg's joke in *Endgame* about the tailor, a parable that both describes and instantiates Beckett's minimalist aesthetic. A man rushes to the tailor to get a pair of striped trousers for New Year's. The customer returns numerous times to pick them up, but each time the tailor complains that he's ruined another part of the pants, and demands more time. By spring, still without a finished product, the customer erupts,

God damn you to hell, Sir, no, it's indecent, there are limits! In six
days, do you hear me, six days, god made the world. Yes Sir, no
less Sir, the WORLD! And you are not bloody well capable of
making me a pair of trousers in three months!"
(*Tailor's voice, scandalized.*)
"But my dear Sir, my dear Sir, look—
(*disdainful gesture, disgustedly*)
—at the world—
(*pause*)
and look—
(*loving gesture, proudly*)
—at my TROUSERS! (*DW*, 107)

Set against the limited perfection of a single pair of pants painstakingly
crafted, the wide world looks like a slipshod disaster. Nagg's joke hinges
on the surprising revelation that a small, laboriously made object may surpass the entropic mess of the world. The tailor, like Beckett, would agree
with the customer that there are and must be "limits." But to his mind, if
we have any chance of producing something worthwhile, we must embrace limitation and restrict our scope to the creation of modest objects.
Like so many of Beckett's raconteurs, Nagg has told this story many times
and has honed it to such rhythmic perfection—with rolling lines like "Yes
Sir, no less Sir, the WORLD" and symmetries like "look—at the world—
and look—at my TROUSERS"—that it has become an exquisite example of
its own thesis. For Nagg, for the tailor, and for Beckett, we cling in an imperfect world to the local and transient delights of form. And yet, like the
tailor, Nagg is continually dissatisfied with the story: "I never told it worse
. . . I tell this story worse and worse" (*DW*, 107). Nagg shares with Beckett
and the tailor the humility of the perfectionist, the shame of the experienced craftsman, whose stubbornness derives from the certainty that his
work is never quite good enough.[49]

The notion that holding more tightly to the material world might loose
us from it parallels the experiences of some of his actors. Although some
actors accused Beckett of making them "disembodied puppets of his
will," those who worked with him extensively often found to the contrary
that the intense rigor his productions required granted them an ascetic
brand of freedom.[50] For Brenda Bynum, who starred as the disembodied
mouth in *Not I* and as Winnie buried up to her neck in *Happy Days*, "Beckett puts you in a strait jacket as he does with the text. He makes your body
and your senses cut off" but nevertheless "the rules give you freedom. In

the most restricted circumstance, if you accept those restrictions, it is like a world in a grain of sand; you get inside those parameters and you find so much, a new universe."[51] Jack MacGowran, similarly, argued that Beckett "creates a freedom in working which actors do not often enjoy in the theatre today, and this freedom is always the bedfellow of true discipline."[52] These actors speak like devotees of a benevolent deity or of a martial arts master. But their words have uncanny resonance with Beckett's, who imagined theater as a small world opening onto a separate universe. And the smaller the world, the better. In a postscript to a letter to Alan Schneider in 1957, Beckett wrote: "I quite agree that my work is for the small theatre. The Royal Court is not big, but 'Fin de Partie' gains unquestionably in the greater smallness of the Studio."[53] We can guess why he preferred the smaller theater: a confined space would emphasize the claustrophobia of the basement room, would enclose the audience in closer proximity to Clov and Hamm's sweating subjected bodies, would allow his carefully arranged tableaux to be seen clearly, and would heighten the dissonance between the present stage and the distant imagined refuge. But whatever the rational, Beckett winks here at the perverse appeal of "greater smallness."

At Least

The same, but less.
—*Ill Seen Ill Said*[54]

. . . just the necessary time for hope to be born, grow, languish and die, say five minutes.
—*The Unnamable, DW* 356.

Moving to theater at all involved restriction. But Beckett's continued efforts to make theater minimal along all sorts of dimensions—in time, in space, in action, in progress, in visibility—aimed to push it into a reverse sublimity.[55] The late plays approach nothingness asymptotically; they limn the edge of perception. The women's voices in *Come and Go* are "as low as compatible with audibility," and the auditor's movements in *Not I* lessen until "scarcely perceptible" (*DW*, 388, 405). Somewhere between the pallet in *A Piece of Monologue* that is "barely visible" and the door in *Ghost Trio* "imperceptibly ajar" lies the thin promised land of the minimally perceptible (*DW*, 453, 436). Like *Molloy*'s Moran who learns to "take refuge in the horizontal" and finds that it "becomes infinite" and "possessed of unsuspected delights" (135), these plays uncover unsuspected rewards lurking in the thin but surprisingly flexible territory "next to none," the land between a little and nothing, and between a little time and no time (*DW*, 454). If the broad outlines of this minimalist project were visible from the middle of Beckett's career in the idea of failing better and in his admission that his "little exploration is that whole zone of being that has always been set aside by artists as something unusable,"[56] his late plays give form and movement to the theory, testing it against an audience's actual perception of light, sound, and time. Although Beckett stopped writing criticism, bits of his late prose clarify this philosophy of the minimum (even as they exemplify it). In *Worstward Ho* (1981–82), he writes,

> Naught not best worse. Less best worse. No. Least. Least best worse. Least never to be naught. Never to naught be brought. Never by naught be nulled. Unnullable least. Say that best worse . . . Unlessenable least best worse.[57]

Like the concept they describe, these nearly verbless koans play along the border between significance and sound. But they make an elegantly mimetic case: nothing cannot be an ideal because it nullifies and cancels itself—it's simply not there—but the superlative "least," which can be neither voided nor reduced, attains distinction. Here, at last, is a version of successful failure that might escape from paradox or come very close to doing so: one can theoretically succeed at capturing the quality of light or speech or representation just at the threshold of its failure.

RESHAPING TIME

The move from prose fiction to theater promised to translate Beckett's visions not only into visible space but also into perceptible time. Authors often wield punctuation to break up, to delay, or to arrest—for instance—the reader's pace, or may use the lack of dots and commas and lines to keep the pace moving at a brisk clip until at last arriving at a thought. But in the end, every author surrenders the time of the text to the reader or performer. In the twentieth century, some playwrights began to write scripts that exerted more control over timing. They continued to arrange words carefully to suggest rhythms but increasingly employed stage directions not just to indicate entrances and exits but to mandate the rhythms of line readings, to script pauses, and to suggest the pace of delivery. For Beckett, who had always been interested in rhythm and whose scripts grew exceedingly explicit about

timing, the stage promised a space in which to wrestle duration into awareness. In the novel *Molloy*, the difficulty of measuring time is tied up with the
limitations of narrative itself. As Molloy describes the slow journey dragging
himself along towards his mother in the gloom, he starts to say that from
time to time he came upon a crossroads. But he trips on the phrase "from
time to time," and interrupts the narrative to inspect its surface and exhume
the dead metaphors that structure accounts of time's passage:

> But from time to time. From time to time. What tenderness in these
> little words, what savagery. But from time to time I came upon a
> kind of crossroads, you know, a star, or circus, of the kind to be
> found in even the most unexplored of forests. (M, 77)

The phrase "from time to time" imagines moments as locations, as places
we might travel between. The regular iambic beat of these little words,
"from time to time," is tender because it converts the uncertainty of the
intermittent into a steady pace. But by replacing uncertainty with a false
rhythm, the phrase reminds the self-conscious Beckettian speaker just how
often narrative casually but savagely misrepresents temporal experience.
In saying "from time to time," we must admit to misrepresenting time.
Molloy here catches himself making the mistake that so irritated Henri
Bergson—imagining time as a series of discrete locations in space—and,
like Bergson, associates this mistake with language, which requires that we
separate the flow of experience into divisible words.

A similar fascination with time and tension between clock time and narrative animates the page-long description in Beckett's late prose piece,
Company, of a second hand and its shadow as they move around a clock.
The speaker describes a prone man who stares at an analog clock until he
finds a different rhythm within its revolutions, so that

> instead of reading the hour of night they [his eyes] follow round and
> round the second hand now followed and now preceded by its
> shadow. Hours later it seems to you as follows. At 60 seconds and 30
> seconds shadow hidden by hand. From 60 to 30 seconds shadow
> precedes ahead at a distance increasing from zero at 60 to maximum
> at 15 and thence decreasing to new zero at 30.[58]

As the speaker's focus shrinks to the clock face, the clock expands to fill all
attention and becomes a local cosmos, a set of bodies following a predictable but novel cycle in which the shadow waxes and wanes every thirty

seconds. As in Beckett's time-obsessed theater pieces, close attention makes clock time an abstraction, a compulsory dance between the steady flow of time and its shadow creeping ahead or lingering behind. The speaker discovers, within the pedestrian rounds of the second hand, a dramatic arc tucked inside every half minute, a recurring miniature drama tied to the clock but superseding it. For Beckett, clock time is always threatening to become something unfamiliar, but prose narrative cannot reveal this process as directly as theater can. The play *Breath*, written ten years before *Company*, represents a remarkably similar half-minute drama that rises to "maximum" and back to a new zero within twenty-five seconds. But in doing so, it strives to do for the audience in less than a minute what hours of attention did to the figure in *Company*: to make the experience of time the means of its own defamiliarization. *Breath* presents an alternative clock that evokes the natural rhythm of breathing and relies on precisely timed seconds but uses both to establish its own temporal universe.

Theater did not alleviate the difficulties of representing time; it highlighted them. *Waiting for Godot* is renowned for magnifying theater's capacity to make time palpable in suspense. "All theatre is waiting," as Beckett once told James Knowlson.[59] But how quickly or slowly the wait passes, Beckett thought, is largely in the hands of the playwright. His plays' punctilious orchestrations of stage time dramatize the inevitable, but ultimately insufficient, attempts of their figures to impose shape on the mere succession of experiences, to make flux more tolerable by giving it form. After Pozzo and Lucky depart in the first act, Didi is pleased to have had company:

> VLADIMIR. That passed the time.
> ESTRAGON. It would have passed in any case.
> VLADIMIR. Yes, but not so rapidly.[60]

On Beckett's stages, as in the pages of his novels, the business of life is largely the struggle to give a tolerable shape to duration, to punctuate the unrelieved elapse of events by imposing beginnings or endings, and this struggle is waged more directly in the beats and pauses of theatrical performance than in a series of written words.

Beckett's plays depart from measurable time in a number of mutually reinforcing ways. First, they are wedded to an exacting and measured pace in performance yet unmoored from calendrical and natural time. Second, the plays imagine time as a divisible, accumulating substance, both impossible to ignore and impossible to reckon. To imagine time as a succession of identical grains helps undermine the logic that would make any collection of moments cohere into a whole, posing a fundamental challenge to conventional theatrical assumptions. Third, Beckett's alternative timepieces exfoliate duration to its fundamental emptiness and dramatize habitual if ultimately illusory struggles to fill it.[61]

All dramatists use time to represent time. What sets Beckett apart is his tendency to use the oddity of theatrical time—yoked to the present yet able to represent any time—to pry time away both from the clock and from nature. Beckett's early plays are deeply concerned with time and likely to have timepieces on stage. In the first act of *Waiting for Godot*, Pozzo checks his watch, a relic from his grandfather, but by the second act, he has lost it. The world of *Endgame* is further divorced from timekeeping but retains a pivotal alarm clock. In *Act Without Words II*, figure B compulsively consults and winds a "large watch" (*DW*, 216). Krapp's first action in *Krapp's Last Tape* is to sigh and look at a "heavy silver watch" (*DW*, 221). But the presence of clocks only magnifies the sense that time in these spaces cannot be measured using traditional means. Despite Beckett's extraordinary, exacting attention to the pace of performance—an attention that grew more intense as the plays themselves grew leaner—the time represented could hardly be more ambiguous. These are precisely paced non-times.[62] The year is irrelevant, the date unclear. It's impossible to discern whether it is day or night. Characters struggle to pin their moments to any natural or calendrical anchor. Vladimir exclaims, "Time has stopped!" (*DW*, 30). He has a hunch it's Saturday, but Gogo is unsure: "But what Saturday? And is it Saturday? Is it not rather Sunday? (*Pause.*) Or Monday? (*Pause.*) Or Friday?" (*DW*, 9). Regard the grim indeterminate light that illuminates these stages and you often come to the same conclusion as figure B in *Rough for Theatre I*: "Day . . . Night . . . (*Looks.*) It seems to me sometimes the earth must have got stuck, one sunless day, in the heart of winter, in the grey of evening" (*DW*, 238). *Happy Days* unfolds in a belated world where "the old style" of measuring time has become obsolete, replaced by the arbitrary bells for waking and for sleep and by Winnie's machinations to pass the time (*DW*, 280). The plays complete the project alluded to in one of Malone's stories, when Macmann "has come to that stage of his instant when to live is to wander the last of the living in the depths of an instant without bounds, where the light never changes and the wrecks look all alike" (*M*, 226).

Although the later plays feature no clocks on stage, the plays themselves have become alternative timepieces.[63] In addition to eluding natural, historical, and calendrical markers, they withdraw from ordinary time by enforcing a slower than conventional pace and by decelerating action over the course of a play. Like symbolist shorts, Beckett's microdramas impose slug-gish pacing and move entropically toward stasis in order to decelerate per-ception. They offer figures mulling fragments of memory, and force specta-tors to ruminate over the fragments they see. The slight, slow, mechanical rocking of the chair in *Rockaby* creaks like a sluggish metronome, and three times comes to a stop after the line "time she stopped," as if time were stop-ping along with the chair (*DW*, 462). The "rapid tempo" of *Play* and machine gun ejaculations of the Mouth in *Not I* are rare exceptions to the slow pace of Beckett's shorts, but these tempi are no less measured; and both plays use repetition to emphasize the insufferable monotony of breakneck speed (*DW*, 355). Ruby Cohn enumerates several of Beckett's strategies for dilating the perceived length of time: constant lighting and scene, lots of dialogue about time, solo pieces like Lucky's speech in *Waiting for Godot*, and the rep-etition of speech and action.[64] But Beckett's most radical method of stretch-ing time's passage is a trick he borrowed from Chekhov: marking time with minimal activity that seems to effect little or no forward momentum. The-ater, film, and television audiences are so accustomed to plots that compress more activity than usual into a brief span that they find pieces whose rhythms are closer to those of a lazy afternoon surprisingly ponderous. We have seen that Beckett turned to theater to locate manageable worlds out-side of the chaos of experience that would "satisfy one's need to know, to understand, one's need for order."[65] An essential part of knowing, these plays suggest, is revealing the complexities and impositions of the mysteri-ous process we tend, too easily, to describe as time's passage.

Staging Granular Time

The speaker of *The Unnamable* voices an axiom of Beckett's physics: that time accretes.

> . . . time doesn't pass, don't pass from you, why it piles up all about you, instant on instant, on all sides, deeper and deeper, thicker and thicker, your time, other's time, the time of the ancient dead and the dead yet unborn, why it buries you grain by grain neither dead nor alive, with no memory of anything, no hope of anything, no knowl-edge of anything, no history and no prospects, buried under the sec-onds, saying any old thing, your mouth full of sand . . .[66]

In this elegant description of time as a mounting heap of sand rather than a Bergsonian flux, repetition, parallelism, and punctuation contribute to a vision of time as something that accumulates with unwearying, even oppressive weight. Clov's opening lines in *Endgame*, written ten years later, show Beckett translating the same conception of granular time into a temporal medium—theatrical performance—that can more directly divide and inhabit each instant:

> CLOV (*fixed gaze, tonelessly*)
> Finished, it's finished, nearly finished, it must be nearly finished.
> (*Pause.*)
> Grain upon grain, one by one, and one day, suddenly, there's a heap, a little heap, the impossible heap.
> (*Pause.*)
> I can't be punished any more.
> (*Pause.*)
> I'll go now to my kitchen, ten feet by ten feet by ten feet, and wait for him to whistle to me.
> (*Pause.*)
> Nice dimensions, nice proportions, I'll lean on the table, and look at the wall, and wait for him to whistle me.
> (*He remains a moment motionless, then goes out . . .*) (*DW*, 92)

Commas that break the stream of language into grains are accompanied here by the more insistent punctuation of mandated pauses. Punished by time's mounting weight, Clov finds solace in the dimensions of an actual space, but the description of a space with nice proportions ("ten feet by ten feet by ten feet") occurs in nicely proportioned time. The tempo set by the opening lines continues throughout *Endgame* as short phrases accumulate at a sluggish, measured pace suggested by recurring rests and made more noticeable by how often the characters talk about time:

> HAMM
> (*Pause.*)
> I'll say to myself, He'll come back.
> (*Pause.*)
> And then?
> (*Pause.*)
> And then?
> (*Pause.*)
> He couldn't, he has gone too far.
> (*Pause.*)

And then?

(*Pause. Very agitated.*)

All kinds of fantasies! That I'm being watched! A rat! Steps! Breath held and then . . .

(*He breathes out.*)

Then babble, babble, words, like the solitary child who turns himself into children, two, three, so as to be together, and whisper together, in the dark.

(*Pause.*)

Moment upon moment, pattering down, like the millet grains of . . .

(*he hesitates*)

. . . that old Greek, and all life long you wait for that to mount up to a life.

(*Pause. He opens his mouth to continue, renounces.*)

Ah let's get it over! (*DW*, 142–43)

Imagining time as a substance might seem to suggest that it is easy to grasp, but by atomizing duration, these plays more often suggest its tendency to slip through our fingers, to frustrate attempts at measurement.

Hamm's talk of grains mounting up to a life and Clov's reference to the "impossible heap" both evoke the sophist Eubulides of Miletus, who like Zeno argued that a heap of sand is a logical impossibility. This argument, which has come to be known as the sorites paradox after the Greek *soros* (heap), holds that a single grain is not a heap and the addition of another grain is never sufficient to convert the group into a heap.[67] Beckett's notes from his extensive reading in pre-Socratic philosophy in the 1930s reveal his early attraction to this line of thinking: "Euclid's adherents Eubulides and Alexinus were famous for a series of such catches, among which the Heap (which kernel of grain by being added makes the heap?) and the Baldhead (which hair falling out makes the head bald?) were fundamental thought far back to Zeno, who used it to argue that the *composition of magnitudes out of small parts is impossible.*"[68] This line of reasoning is best known from Zeno's more famous paradox about the impossibility of movement—since a flying arrow is at any given instant caught in one place, how can its instants of stasis ever add up to motion?—and Aristotle's response (in the *Physics*, 239). As redeployed by Hamm, the question becomes personal: At what point does a series of instants amount to a life? Hamm and Clov struggle to mark each moment as it falls, but their grains lack an hourglass to measure against, so they remain unsure if they are making progress. "What time is it?" Hamm asks, and Clov replies, "The same as usual" (*DW*, 94). Some twenty years after Beckett took careful notes on the pre-Socratics, Alan Schneider wrote to ask him about "that Old Greek." His reply reinforces *Endgame*'s contention that no logic will convert a series of moments into a temporal whole: "One purpose of the image throughout the play is to suggest the impossibility logically, i.e. eristically, of the 'thing' ever coming to an end. . . . In other words the impossibility of catastrophe. Ended at its inception, and at every subsequent instant, it continues, ergo can never end."[69] Taking this contention seriously explodes Aristotelian assumptions about the possibility of a unified dramatic whole that fits together as organically as the body of an animal.

Following Zeno and Eubulides, Beckett's microdramas question the logic by which small parts or small moments ever become wholes. For Beckett, dividing time into grains underscores the arbitrariness of distinguishing one event from another. For the speaker of *The Unnamable*, time's grains pile up without generating history or narrative: ". . . when you have nothing left to say you talk of time, seconds of time, there are some people add them together to make a life, I can't, each one is the first, no the second, or the third . . ." (388). Like the paradox, Beckett's inquiry into the question of parts and wholes proceeds from a fascination with ambiguity and especially with the vagueness of language, which requires that one carve up the world into referents. His characters' strenuous efforts to distinguish middles from endings, or one moment from the next, work in two directions: they register a desire to pin down temporal categories (an event, a scene, a play) but also reveal Beckett's hunch that dividing time is like sifting the sand or slicing a river. The atomization of time preempts the fiction of a single cohesive unit—the novel or the organically whole play—with an accumulation of little bits, both within works like *Endgame* and in the succession of short plays and prose texts he produced from the '60s through the '80s, each of which is a sort of little heap, a gathering of grains. More than most authors, his pieces really deserve the name; they are bits of a series, whose names often reinforce their presumed incompleteness: *Texts for Nothing, Rough for Theatre, Fizzles, Breath, A Piece of Monologue*. Strictly speaking *Endgame* does finally end, as do each of Beckett's shorts, but the logic of their theatrical conceits is not formal but eristic, offering elegant temporal arguments that impress even if they fail under strict scrutiny.

The most common temporal argument put forward by the late plays is a twist on the "little heap." The heap paradox is additive, but its focus on the vagueness of definitions connects it to the subtractive question about baldness: at what point does reduction push something over the border from one category into another? How much can one remove from a play and still have a play? Does the systematic removal of elements promise to refine one's understanding of the thing or simply reveal its underlying arbitrariness? *Happy Days* (1960) marks Beckett's most explicit departure from "the old style" of time into a realm where the bell for waking and the bell for sleep come at arbitrary moments, but the play itself retains a conventional structure: two acts with an intermission. Every play he wrote after *Happy Days* lasts less than a half hour in a typical performance, and, more important, begins and ends at points chosen as if by chance along a vast continuum. Whereas classical plays and most modernist shorts begin relatively close to a moment of crisis, Beckett's later plays fade up on a process or situation long underway and, in almost every case, far from conclusion. They are excerpts from eternity. Even as the house lights go down before *Not I*, the play's sole speaker, Mouth, is already muttering unintelligibly behind the curtain. The ad-libbed muttering continues as the curtain rises and does not transition into the play's first lines until the curtain is up and the audience's attention is "sufficient" (*DW*, 405). When some ten minutes later the curtain begins to fall again, the mouth is still talking and continues behind the curtain again until the house lights come up. Both the play's inciting incident and its ending are defined not by particular actions but rather by the threshold between unintelligibility and intelligibility. We need only about twelve minutes and three or four repetitions of Mouth's ravings to understand that her condition is interminable. A brief window of time suggests an unending experience. This is a temporal variant of greater smallness: under the right circumstances, less playing time can expand the horizon of expectation we assume for the creatures on stage. The late plays last just long enough to establish a strong sense of the endlessness of their repetitive series. In this respect, they resemble contemporaneous minimalist music by John Cage or Morton Feldman that strained against traditional musical development over time and resisted the imposition of beginnings or endings.[70] Feldman, whose work often explored extremes of duration, met Beckett at the Schiller Theater in Berlin in 1976 while the latter was overseeing rehearsals of *Footfalls* and *That Time*. They became friends and went on to collaborate on settings for the prose pieces *Neither* and *Cascando*, and the radio piece, *Words and Music*. An even closer musical analog—in spirit if not in letter—might be the 1893 musical composition *Vexations* by the proto-minimalist composer Erik Satie; its one-page score instructs that an 80-second sequence be played 840 times. When

Vexations was first performed—by Cage in 1963 at the Pocket Theatre in New York—the performance lasted for 18 hours.[71] One imagines the audience of Satie's piece got the point after about ten minutes. Beckett preferred to script only enough time to imply perpetual motion (or perpetual immobility) and to let the imagination fill in the repeats ad infinitum. A major reason not to extend the repetitions, I think, is that they might become too comfortable and slip from strangeness into familiarity.

The Pacing of Footfalls

A picture of Beckett as a minimalist composer of time emerges clearly from his 1975 play *Footfalls*, whose temporal motifs—brief yet slow, precise yet immeasurable—exemplify the tendencies the chapter has been tracking. The script calls for a single strip of light, "length nine steps, width one metre," and dictates that a disheveled female figure, May, walk with "clearly audible rhythmic tread" nine steps in one direction and nine in the other, starting on a specific foot in each direction.[72]

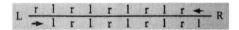

Fig. 7. Beckett's diagram for the shape of M's pacing in the script of *Footfalls*, in *DW*, 427.

The light, "strongest at floor level, less on body, least on head," directs attention to the movement of feet much as Marinetti's play *Feet* had done by lifting a curtain only to waist height. But whereas Marinetti's podiatric slice of life uses framing to defamiliarize a typical bustling café scene, the minimalist world of *Footfalls* makes a single pair of feet the center of attention and of gravity, and converts them into the basis for a controlled experiment in pacing as such. May's rhythmic movement frequently comes to a halt, and in these breaks, she and an offstage voice she refers to as Mother converse and take turns reciting monologues in voices "low and slow throughout" (*DW*, 427). The outlines of a story emerge and tempt the viewer to understand the narratives as elaborations on what we see: an antisocial girl shuffles to and fro on a carpet she has worn bare, "revolving it all" "in her poor mind" until, decayed into middle age and worn away like the carpet under her feet, she does little more than pace and offer injections to her ailing mother (*DW*, 428, 429). *Footfalls* crystallizes into a stage sequence the philosophical ruminations of Stephen Dedalus walking along the strand in Joyce's *Ulysses*: "I am, a stride at a time. A very short space of time through very short times of space. Five, six: the *Nacheinander*."[73] The German, *nacheinander*, "one after another," refers to Lessing's distinction in the *Laocoön* between subjects appropriate for poetry, in which elements unfold "one after another" over time, and subjects appropriate for the visual arts, in which elements work "side by side in space."[74] May's pacing confutes Lessing's distinction by fusing temporal and visual art. The steps come one after another, but the action is so repetitive and ritualistic that the overriding impression is not development but stasis.

In the Berlin rehearsals for *Footfalls*, Beckett as director was much more concerned with the piece's rhythm than its content. Even more than the directions in his scripts, directing offered him immediate control over the time of performance. He read lines with a pronounced lilt, in a very particular rhythm, and did not shy away from offering line readings to his actors, as if communicating the pace of the score in his head. He told his actors, "It is about pacing. Nine steps one way. Nine steps the other. The fall of feet. The sound of feet walking on the ground, as on a tomb."[75] May's existence is constituted and measured by the clearly audible tread of footsteps, the fundamental unit of human movement, and the derivation of all pacing. Her footfalls are the audible equivalent of Clov's grains of time, minimal markers that reinforce a sense of time shuffling along with what *Texts for Nothing* calls "little heavy irrevocable steps."[76]

Beckett's notebooks for the 1976 premiere at the Royal Court Theatre outline the exacting precision of his conception. For a section in which V speaks over May's pacing, he drew horizontal lines on graph paper to represent each length of May's course, and along those lines marked precisely when V's lines would fall. Mapping each line of dialogue onto specific steps in May's rhythmic course, the notebook becomes a choreographic score in which action is mapped along a temporal axis in counterpoint to the steady shuffling percussion of May's steps. This is closer to Labanotation than scriptwriting.[77] The oddity of the play's sense of time is encoded in the diagram, which lacks a single temporal axis: its time snakes sluggishly forward only by retracing its steps. Moreover, the clarity of May's position on the timeline fades as the light dies out between point F and G.

Beckett's assistant Walter Asmus recorded Beckett's precise attention to pacing in his rehearsal notes: "The walking should be like a metronome; one length must be measured in exactly nine seconds."[78] But as the play unfolds, its rhythms are more erratic and punctuated than a typical metronome. May frequently halts to speak, so conversation and narrative replace her rhythmic tread even as they perpetuate its shuffling rhythms. During

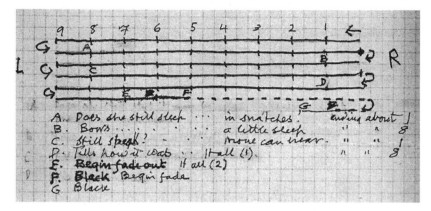

Fig. 8. Diagram of the end of the second section of *Footfalls* in Beckett's production notebook from 1976 Royal Court Theatre production. (University of Reading Samuel Beckett Archive, MS 1976.)

one such pause, her words describe a pause like the one they fill: "Some nights she would halt, as one frozen by some shudder of the mind, and stand stark still till she could move again" (*DW*, 430). In addition to the pauses, every five minutes or so, the light fades out, the steps stop, and a faint chime rings. Four such chimes, each fainter than the last, divide the play into four sections: three of about five minutes each, and a final coda in which ten seconds of minimal light on the bare strip betrays "No trace of May" (*DW*, 432).

Taken together, the written, drawn, and spoken instructions for *Footfalls* all cast Beckett as a watchmaker intent on making the play an experimental timepiece that counts in a self-consciously odd manner and winds down to stasis. *Footfalls'* pacing is not just counter-clockwise but counter clock: its fundamental cycle is base nine rather than base sixty; its chimes divide time into arbitrary spans; and within those spans, its metronome keeps time only intermittently as steps, words, and pauses take turns or overlap. The reduced conditions of May's existence make her so evacuated that one imagines her not just as not all there, but, like the girl she describes, "as though never there" (430). The play's odd pace represents human attempts to establish timing and sequence—through pacing, through narrative accounts, through habitual injections—as gambits with similarly dubious claims on reality. A metronome is meant to measure time as it passes, but the regular monotony of May's footsteps arguably makes time harder to measure as it dilates. When May asks V, "Can I inject you again?" the response, "Yes but it is too soon," reveals how boredom has warped May's sense of time. Measured by monotony, May's forty-odd years feel like an eternity:

> M: What age am I now?
> V: In your forties
> M: So little? (*DW*, 428)

Footfalls' alternative clock reveals attempts to impose time as falsifying. Experiential time dilates not despite but as a result of our struggles to measure it. A similar distension occurs for the audience: the play unfolds in three five-minute sections, but to me they feel longer. A spectator told at the end of the piece that only fifteen minutes had passed might echo May's skepticism, "So little?"

The pace is not only slow but growing slower, suggesting an entropic loss of momentum over time. Beckett read widely in physics, and his stage worlds often dramatize the second law of thermodynamics, which describes how random differences of speed and location in a closed system will tend toward inert equilibrium.[79] So, the voice in *Rockaby* grows "gradually softer," and the chair eventually comes to a stop. Each time we hear the chime in *Footfalls*, it is "a little fainter" and the light on the strip is "a little less," until the final bare strip of light, lit by "even a little less still," is just above the threshold of perception (*DW*, 429, 432). Over its fifteen-minute course, *Footfalls* shrinks from dialogue and action between two characters, to narrative description by V, then to autocommentary by May, and finally to light on a bare stage. As the play's clock winds down, its chime can barely be heard, and footsteps, its smallest rhythmic units, are present, if at all, only as echoes in the audience's imagination, memories of a reassuring pace that has vanished, as if never there.

It is tempting to read the deliberate and measured rhythms of Beckett's microdramas as means of escape from the perceived pace of the twentieth century, but to do so obscures Beckett's actual motivations. Richard Eyre, the director of the film version of *Rockaby*, understands the deliberate pace of the play's rocking chair—and its final refusal to rock—as a repudiation of "the rhythms of MTV."[80] Jonathan Kalb too imagines Beckett's plays as antidotes to the pace of commercial entertainment: "His drama has been, for many, an oasis in that desert—its spareness and quietude, its wit's-end, last-ditch humanism were blessed refreshments in the face of media-swarm and rampant cynicism. . . . He now represents a dream of emancipation from the relentless demands of the fast-paced entertainment world."[81] Beckett's stages certainly resist familiar ways of measuring time, replacing Winnie's "old style" of predictable hours and days with a style of time shorn of markers and made sluggish, tangible, and unfamiliar. These strategies distinguish his plays from the frantic pace of much of the century's entertainment, but to my mind, this distinction is a byproduct of a more fundamental project to reveal conventional conceptions of time as reassuring fictions. To interpret Beckett's time-spaces as sanctuaries ignores how unsettling their visions of unmarked duration are both for characters and audiences. Theater allowed Beckett to place figures and audiences in a precarious position, inside duration but outside of conventional time, forcing both to invent new temporal measures. From this perspective, measured time is more mirage than oasis.

The Habit of Time

> May one still speak of time?
> —Winnie, *Happy Days*

As early as the 1930 essay on *Proust*, Beckett describes life as long stretches of comfortable habitual existence punctuated by perilous "periods of transition" between one reality and another, precarious instants during which habit falters, leaving us "for a moment free" to experience the unadulterated and intolerable "spectacle of reality" that habit obscures.[82] Beckett's stage worlds, where the passage of time becomes palpable and oppressive precisely because its typical rhythms and indicators are missing, are artificial periods of radical transition, ruptures in habitual time, and in conventional dramatic time, that focus attention on the fallacy of standard temporal measurements.

The ultimate implication of *Footfalls* and other shorts dramatizing the failure to package duration is that the concept of objective time—as an Aristotelian line running from past to future—is a construction. In life, as in storytelling and drama, we tend to imagine experiences within a complete and coherent sequence including moments in their appointed places, but in both the actual and the imagined worlds, the sense of time as the bedrock of experience is an extrapolation from incomplete information. This perspective puts Beckett very close to the thinking of philosopher Bastiaan Van Fraassen, who posits that time is an illusion fabricated from the mutual relations among events. For Van Fraassen, time in the world is "not different in essential character from the constitution of time by the reader in his construction of the narrated world as he reads the text."[83] There is, strictly speaking, "no such thing as time"; rather time is "a logical space" for events just as the color spectrum is an invented logical space for color.[84] In lives, in texts, and—I would add—on stages, things happen one after the other, and we use clues to order them on an imagined timeline. Listening to *Footfalls*, one cannot help but stitch the scraps of memory together into the life experiences of a person, however provisional. This is a lesson not just in theatrical spectatorship, but in our instinctive temporal habits. Van Fraassen's conclusion about time echoes one suggested by the play: we must accept "the same imminent vagueness for the order of real events, underdetermined by the facts, as we do for the order of narrated events, underdetermined by the text. In both cases, the world is conceived of as determinate, but the necessity in how things are to be conceived does not engender a necessity in how they must be" (34). In other words, that we conceive of time as fixed does not guarantee that it is so.

We have seen how Beckett's fictional prose exaggerates the immanent vagueness of narrative, the inability of linguistic clues to determine a spatiotemporal world or a stable sequence:

> I say that now, but after all what do I know now about then, now when the icy words hail down upon me, the icy meanings, and the world dies too, foully named. All I know is what the words know, and the dead things, and that makes a handsome little sum, with a beginning, a middle and an end as in the well-built phrase and the long sonata of the dead. And truly it little matters what I say, this or that or any other thing. Saying is inventing. (M, 27)

The difficulty of representing time and space in fiction certainly fueled his interest in theater, as I have argued, but in the end, the plays use a temporal medium to reiterate a stronger version of the same skeptical thesis: not only is saying inventing, but ordering lived experience is inventing, too. In *Endgame*, Nagg resigns himself to living in time, "One must live with the times . . ." (DW, 132). But when Alan Schneider asked Beckett what this line meant, his reply underlined his conviction that living in time is impossible: "Typical illogism. Life is an asking for and a promising of what both asker and promiser know does not exist."[85] Pozzo's tirade against time, and against Didi's servile addiction to it, makes a similar point:

POZZO (*suddenly furious*) Have you not done tormenting me with
your accursed time! It's abominable! When! When! One day, is
that not enough for you, one day he went dumb, one day I went
blind, one day we'll go deaf, one day we were born, one day we
shall die, the same day, the same second, is that not enough for
you? (*DW*, 82)

The warped clocks of Beckett's late plays amplify the challenge of identifying and ordering time, prompting the spectator to impose sequence but simultaneously suggesting that one moment or one day is the same as any
other ("one day we shall die, the same day, the same second"), and that any
moment might be enough, or even too much.

The rhythms within individual plays often reinforce this cycle of
reassuring habit, especially habitual narrating, interrupted by moments of unbearable confrontation with the passage of time. Pauses in
the volley of conversation in *Endgame* cause Hamm to request relief
("This is slow work. [*Pause.*] Is it not time for my pain-killer?" *DW*, 99)
as if the immeasurable elapse of time is the pain that needs killing. Similarly in *Rockaby*, each time the chair's rocking and the accompanying
refrain come to a stop, there follows a long still pause before W, as if
unable to bear unmarked stasis, demands "More" and the rocking and
the lullaby resume (*DW*, 462, 464, 465, 467). A similar series of pauses
breaks up the stream of speech in *Not I*; during each, the silent auditor
gives a gesture of "helpless compassion" (*DW*, 405). For May, too, the
moments when she stops pacing find her "frozen by some shudder of
the mind" (*DW*, 430).

The cycle in which habit is suddenly ruptured, then provisionally re-
paired, only to be unsettled again occurs frequently in the plays; it is also
imposed on audiences by the plays. A typical spectator thrown into *Play*'s
"hellish half-light" and confronted with the "largely unintelligible" mut-
terings of its trio of heads can at first scarcely make out the words, much
less piece together the scrambled melodramatic plot they relate (*DW*, 361,
355). The *da capo* repeat of the seven- or eight-minute sequence provides a
second exposure to the story. By the time the repeat draws to a close with
the line "we were not long together" some fifteen minutes after the play
started, one has almost grown accustomed to the tempo and rules of this
universe, and might almost have a handle on the series of events it dangles
out of reach (*DW*, 366). But the lights blink out before oddity congeals into
habit. Beckett's microdramas explore the half-life of the unfamiliar. They

end before their strangeness can degrade but continue decomposing and recomposing in the spectator's mind. The distaste for congealed habit also animated his career-long churn of aesthetic forms, a series of dogged attempts to wrestle free from habit, which Vladimir calls "a great deadener," in favor of perpetually renewed perspectives alive to the strangeness and unaccountability of our lives and times (*DW*, 83).

The agonizing unaccountability of duration as such is perhaps most acute in *That Time,* completed the same year as *Footfalls* (1975) and premiering together with it at the Royal Court Theater in 1976. Light fades up on an old white face, the Listener, illuminated in a dark void ten feet off the stage, with white hair splayed around it. The setting estranges conventional stage orientation by ninety degrees, giving the audience the impression of floating over a supine figure "as if seen from above," observed perhaps in the moments before sleep or death but also in the nowhere and non-time of recollection (*DW*, 417). For most of the piece, he listens with eyes closed to an unbroken "general flow" of three alternating recorded voices, all "moments of one and the same voice," his own, as each narrates memories in unpunctuated streams. The "slow and regular" breathing of the listener sets a somnolent pace for his memories and provides a counterpoint to their flow:

A that time you went back that last time to look was the ruin still there where you hid as a child when was that (*eyes close*) grey day took the eleven to the end of the line and on from there no no trams then all gone long ago that time you went back to look was the ruin still there where you hid as a child that last time not a tram left in the place only the rails when was that

C when you went in out of the rain always winter then always raining that time in the Portrait Gallery in off the street out of the cold and rain slipped in when no one was looking and through the rooms shivering and dripping till you found a seat marble slab and sat down to rest and dry off and on to hell out of there when was that

B on the stone together in the sun on the stone at the edge of the little wood and as far as eye could see the wheat turning yellow vowing every now and then you loved each other just a murmur not touching or anything of that nature you one end of the stone she the other long low stone like millstone no looks just there on the stone in the sun with the little wood behind gazing at the

wheat or eyes closed all still no sign of life not a soul abroad no
sound (*DW*, 417–18)

These intercalated memories recollected in tranquility—spots of time,
even—look back to earlier moments of stillness and quiet, past interruptions in the stream of activity, drawn into mutual relation by echoes: a ruin,
a slab, a stone. Each recalls a past moment when the passage of time—and
its occasional imbrication—became most acute. Voice A above remembers
a time long ago in adult life when he visited for the last time a place where
as a child he had invented stories in a ruin. We hear a fading memory (was
there a tram?) of a time when he remembered youth, a youth spent hiding
in ruins even before memory made a ruin of it. But at three roughly equi-
distant moments in the typically twenty-minute piece, the stream of memories of silence gives way to ten long seconds of near silence in the theater,
measured only by the listener's breath and intensified by an increase of
lights from half strength to maximum. During each extended pause, the
listener's eyes open after several seconds, as if unsettled by the emptiness
of the present, and stare ahead in the unrelenting light. Spectators and
readers often pay more attention to the flowing words than to the pauses.
But Beckett told the production crew in Berlin that the fundamental unit of
time in *That Time* was ten seconds, suggesting that the most vital microdrama is the one unfolding during the very brief window when blank time
imposes itself. When the voices resume, the eyes close after a few seconds,
the lights dim again to half, and the face rests until the next rupture.[86] These
memories are a fugue not only musically, as an alternating series from multiple voices on a single theme, but etymologically, a flight or fleeing from
the present moment.

   The play imagines memory as a form of habitual storytelling that pack-
ages flux. To specify a portion of experience as "that time" is to imagine a
stretch of time as a stable object one might point to. The three voices strive
to carve memory into slices, but struggle to distinguish them: "that time
altogether on the stone in the sun or that time together on the towpath or
that time together in the sand that time that time making it up from there
as best you could always together somewhere in the sun . . . was that the
time or was that another time another place another time" (*DW*, 420, 423).
To say "that time" builds an implicit pact between the speaker and another
who can decode the demonstrative determiner *that*. When the speaker and
the listener are the same, the pact promises to unify the speaking self with
a past self who could verify the remembered order of events. Voice C re-

calls the attraction of turning points, moments of reversal that imagine time changing course—"turning-point that was a great word with you before they dried up altogether always having turning-points and never but the one the first and last that time curled up worm in slime when they lugged you out . . ." —but now concedes that the only verifiable turn is birth, the first rude awakening into the harsh realities of duration (*DW*, 420). The events in *That Time* are shuffled and out of order, stymying attempts to distinguish this time from that, but the struggle is not different in kind from any attempt to give order to events. No clock or memory can verify time's objective reality. *That Time* returns to a conclusion that Malone had suspected long before in *Malone Dies*: "There's no use indicting words, they are no shoddier than what they peddle" (189). Words may fail to capture the experience of time, but that experience itself is remarkably patchy and immeasurable.

That Time, like so many Beckett works, represents storytelling ("making it up that way to keep it going") and dramatic discourse ("making it up now one voice now another") as defensive gambits to stave off the pressure of empty duration, which carries with it a suggestion of the emptiness at the core of consciousness: "making yourself all up again for the millionth time" (*DW*, 422, 419, 423). Theater offered Beckett a space where his earlier conviction in *Proust*—that "the creation of the world did not take place once and for all time, but takes place every day"[87]—was an unavoidable default condition. The ten-second breaks enact what the stage directions call "solution of continuity," an antiquated medical term for the unnatural separation from each other of normally continuous body parts, bones broken or tissue torn.[88] In these pauses, in other words, the self threatens to come apart, as if temporal breaks might break us down, and unorganized time might cause one to melt, thaw, and resolve into a dew. Making oneself up with sequential stories promises to stitch the self back together again but creates an artificial construct, a Frankenstein's creature cobbled together from patches of memory.

To the extent the speakers resemble Beckett, forever making up one voice after another that "all sounded the same," the play is a portrait of an artist whose work begins as a defense against unmarked time (419). The last installment of the second voice, B, tells of a time when the "tales to keep the void from pouring in" falter, and into the space left behind pours an awareness of unrelieved time, the harbinger of mortality: "tried and tried and couldn't any more no words left to keep it out so gave it up . . . gave up for good and let it in and nothing the worse a great shroud billowing in all over you on top of you" (424). The B voice has been remembering times together with a lover, but here he is alone. His words recreate the assault of empty time ("not another sound hour after hour hour after hour not a sound . . ."), but they capture its force less directly than the considerably more evacuated time that unfolds in each ten-second break.

The play counterbalances the voices' ruminations with only the slightest visual information: the listener's face, eyes shut but for a few alert caesura. The onstage action is so minimal that Beckett told James Knowlson that *That Time* lay "on the very edge of what was possible in the theatre."[89] The play is like a radical distillation of *Krapp's Last Tape*—his earlier masterpiece featuring an old man attending to recorded memories—that aims to realize Krapp's dream of a final rest in which memory supplants the present and promises living reincarnation. On the last tape Krapp listens to, an earlier Krapp dreams of a time when memory would be the only recording he needs:

> Go on with this drivel in the morning. Or leave it at that. (*Pause.*) Leave it at that. (*Pause*) Lie propped up in the dark—and wander. Be again in the dingle on a Christmas Eve, gathering holly, the red-berried. (*Pause.*) Be again on Croghan on a Sunday morning, in the haze, with the bitch, stop and listen to the bells. (*Pause.*) And so on. (*Pause.*) Once wasn't enough for you. (*DW*, 229)

As for Krapp, once is not enough for the listener, whose mind flees to the past. Both plays imply that attempts to "Be again" are pipe dreams; one can only ever simply be. Once was also evidently not enough for Beckett, who reincarnated *Krapp* in reduced form. During composition, he struggled to decide whether the pared-down image would drown against the deluge of words but ultimately placed his bet again on greater smallness: "To the objection visual component small, out of all proportion with aural, answer: make it smaller on the principle that less is more."[90] More than one critic has nevertheless considered *That Time* theatrically untenable. James Knowlson finds the disproportion "surely too great for a resounding success in the theatre."[91] And reviewer Robert Cushman agreed: "Not this time. . . . High on the list of things which I can live, even die, without would be, had I ever thought of it, Mr. Magee in three-track stereo. . . . the substance is only a re-run of *Krapp's Last Tape* without the props: a process of refinement but not necessarily enrichment."[92] Does this impoverishment enrich? The play certainly tests the border between theater and radio drama and falls flat for some in the process. But by giving the audience only the most minimal anchor in the present moment, it dramatizes the uncanny insufferable resilience of presence. The face serves as a perpetual reminder of a concept the voices skirt: "this time," the time of performance, and of self-invention. Like the speaker in *Not I* who cannot bear the first person, the voices in *That Time* resist the present tense. But the play suggests, along with Augustine, that the present is all there is. One may wish to escape from this time into "that time," to find reprieve from mere duration, but that face staring at us in the light refuses to let us run from the problem of being here and now.

In the final shred of memory heard in *That Time*, one of the voices recalls finding shelter from the rain in a silent library surrounded by old tomes. Suddenly, the room filled with a cloud of dust, and the dust seemed to whisper a message:

> not a sound only the old breath and the leaves turning and then suddenly this dust whole place suddenly full of dust when you opened your eyes from floor to ceiling nothing only dust and not a sound only what was it it said come and gone was that it something like that come and gone come and gone no one come and gone in no time gone in no time. (424)

The library, a monument to recorded memory and history, is for a moment obscured, even shrouded, in dust that seems to say to the speaker, "come and gone in no time." This miniature drama staged by motes in sunlight lasts only as long as it takes for the dust to rise and settle again. The suspension interrupts the natural cycle of "the old breath" as well as the naturalized but unstable turning points of storytelling, figured as book pages that turn like leaves dying on a tree. The disturbance is "gone in no time," but to the speaker it whispers the terms of an allegory suggesting the brevity of human life ("dust thou art, and unto dust shalt thou return," becoming "no one") and also implies a deeper mystery about time. The moment of suspended animation, in which time is forced to be itself, is gone "in no time," not merely because it ends soon but because all time is no time. Our comings and goings, like the motes of dust, are ultimately uncountable. However convincing this idea may be philosophically, Beckett's depiction of it relies on carefully counted time. Although "gone in no time" are the play's last spoken words, there follows a silence crafted by one of Beckett's most temporally precise stage directions:

Silence 10 seconds. Breath audible. After 3 seconds eyes open. After 5 seconds smile, toothless for preference. Hold 5 seconds till fade out and curtain. (DW, 424)

Much as Beckett used words to unwrite themselves, here he uses a precise duration to unravel the experience of duration. The orchestration of seconds drives home the insufficiency of the second hand as an account of time. The listener's face fades into darkness, and his impending freedom from presence may be the strongest motivation for his ridiculous, ambiguous smile. But even when visible, he was "gone in no time," lost in the careful construction of little dramas that marked time, but whose turning points remained arbitrary, and whose consolations always failed to last.

FIVE

Long Shorts

Contemporary Micro-marathons

We want the mega and we want the micro, the super-
size-me and the sushi—all at the same time.
—Mark Ravenhill, 2008

The house lights fade and the audience settles before the show. A rectangle of white LED lights frames the proscenium's four edges, creating the illusion that a sheet of darkness hangs between them and the stage, a virtual fourth wall. As the lighted border blinks off, stage lights reveal the interior of a bright white cube, its five visible sides lined like enormous sheets of graph paper, unbroken by any opening that might facilitate entrance or exit. A conversation is already in progress between two people, one begging for the other to reveal a secret.

> Please please tell me
> no
> please because I'll never
> don't ask don't ask
> I'll never tell
> no
> no matter what
> it's not
> I'd die before I told[1]

Like many plays that begin in medias res, this scene from the New York Theater Workshop's US premiere production of Caryl Churchill's 2012 *Love and Information* tantalizes the audience, provoking curiosity by holding knowledge just out of reach. After about a minute of continued pressure from the interlocutor, the secret holder relents and whispers in the other's ear. In response, disbelief:

No
yes
no
I warned you
but that's
yes
oh no that's
yes
how could you
I did.
Now what? Now what? Now what? (5)

The lights cut out, and the LED frame flicks on for a moment. Seconds later, the frame flicks off and the stage lights blink on to reveal, astonishingly quickly, an unrelated conversation between a new set of figures who bear no obvious relation to the first pair. The rhythm of brief scenes punctuated by blackouts continues.

Churchill's *Love and Information* includes more than sixty discrete micro-dramas featuring over one hundred figures. Its kaleidoscope of scenes offers a rapid-fire series of meditations on knowing and feeling in contemporary culture, presented in a format designed to test one's capacity for information overload. The script's scenes range in length from two words to several pages, each written in the spare style seen above without character prefixes, with minimal punctuation, and with almost no stage directions. Churchill calls the pieces in *Love and Information* "scenes," "items," or "things," and refers to the miscellaneous addenda as "random items," but since each presents a distinct story or situation and since no characters repeat across the scenes, I consider each of these pieces a microdrama. One could also call them *faits-divers*, or variations on a theme: each grapples in some way with the play's organizing terms, information and love, often explored through subject matter from popular science: memory palaces, MRI studies of animal learning, the speed of light. The pieces are organized by loose thematic affinity into seven sections, followed by an appendix. Churchill specifies that the sections should be played in their published order, but that the scenes within each section can be performed in any order. The appendix includes ten scenes about depression, each less than one sentence long, that are "essential" to the play but can happen in any section, as well as nineteen optional fragments, including *Cold* (*Someone sneezes.*) and *Google* ("There's a train at 4.22 gets in at half-past eight.") (74, 77). In any combination, the result is a collection that skips quickly from

Fig. 9. Phillip James Brannon, left, and Jennifer Ikeda in *Secret, Love and Information*, New York Theater Workshop, set design Miriam Buether. (Credit: Sara Krulwich, The New York Times.)

one thing to another and leaves little time for viewers to digest or consider each piece before it disappears. At the end of the play described above, titled *Secret*, the audience's curiosity is piqued but not sated. In place of the satisfactions of conclusion, *Love and Information* substitutes the momentum of variety and variation.

The previous chapters have largely focused on microdramas as individual units, asking how the fifteen minutes of Maeterlinck's *Interior*, for instance, or the single minute of Canguillo's *Detonation*, or the twenty minutes of Beckett's *Footfalls* might inflect an audience's experience of time and distill lessons about theatrical activity. But as we have learned, microdramas are almost never performed in isolation; playwrights, directors, and producers tend to compile plays into a program or an evening substantial enough to convince audiences to travel to a theater and pay for a seat. As a result, a full account of brevity in theater should consider not only of the minutes of a given play but also the rhythms of the theatrical evening as a whole and, more generally, the aesthetics of compilation, seriality, and variety. This chapter takes up these questions by exploring a recent trend that makes structural rhythm unavoidable: marathon compilations of very short plays, with particular focus on Churchill's *Love and Information* and Suzan-Lori Parks's even more extreme compilation, *365 Days/365 Plays*. Parks's project, which began in 2002 as a personal challenge to herself to write a play a day for a year and culminated in a yearlong international collaborative performance festival in 2006 including more than 800 theaters, offers in its literary and theatrical manifestations a sustained, self-conscious interrogation of both the limits of dramatic form and the challenges of serial variety.

I call these conspicuous accumulations of shorts *microthons*, but I am not interested in defining a genre. A two- or three-hour evening of twenty-minute one-act plays is unlikely to earn the designation microthon—not least because such standard formats reinforce assumptions about length rather than challenging them—but the Neo-Futurists' hour-long race to complete thirty original plays in sixty minutes qualifies despite its relative brevity. I am interested in works that exaggerate to conspicuous extremes the rhythms of variety, rhythms popularized in music halls and cabarets in the nineteenth century, later embraced by the Italian Futurists, and increasingly prevalent in a contemporary popular culture characterized by 24/7 streams of news, social updates, and entertainment.

This chapter's two sections develop separate but related arguments about recent microthons. The first argument is historical: microthons have gained popularity and prominence because they reflect and recreate the information overload that characterizes contemporary experience. The practice of performing multiple plays back to back is as old as theater, but recent microthons, and especially those like Churchill's and Parks's that were written as collections, register an encyclopedic urge stoked by the pace and promise of the digital, an urge simultaneously to break the world into comprehensible bits and to make everything available at once. In the process, microthons often put even more pressure on the concept of the play than other microdramas do because they stretch dramatic form to accommodate both the smallest possible incident as well as the gargantuan collection. Microthons are animated by the tension between the idea of a play as an autonomous entity and the logic of juxtaposition or accumulation. Churchill's and Parks's microthons in particular highlight a paradox in the temporal authority of the dramatic script after Beckett: both Parks and Churchill seem to offer their scripts as generous and open-ended invitations to production teams, but their texts nevertheless exert considerable influence over the nature and timing of performances, both within individual plays and through the pace created by their compilation.

The second set of arguments is aesthetic. Microthons illuminate valuable lessons about the operation of serial variety. How should we describe or account for a succession of short plays? What does it feel like to watch Churchill's fifty-seven unrelated microdramas back to back in an uninterrupted two-hour sitting? Like all short plays, the individual pieces in a microthon put pressure on theater's affective machinery, prompting pointed versions of questions raised by many microdramas: How quickly can we come to care about a new situation, and as the plays accrue, how does the accumulation of variety tend to affect an audience's emotional investments? While it is difficult to generalize, I suggest that extreme compilation tends to militate against certain slow feelings, including empathy with the figures in a given play, even as the frenetic pace of a microthon can generate a sense of familiarity. I argued in the introduction that a viewer's experience of any theatrical performance sets in motion a number of timers running concurrently, each measuring a different scale or facet of time. Watching a microthon highlights certain of these timers and adds the additional layer of tracking the relationship among numerous parts. Increasing the ratio between total event time and the running time of a given piece calls attention to what I call structural rhythm. Strictly speaking, rhythm and pace are always structural, but I use the term to refer to the rhythm established among the constituent sections of a performance—scenes or acts or episodes—and also to the overall pace of a theatrical evening. Microthons like Parks's 365 and Churchill's *Love and Information* suggest that while audiences are less likely to feel strongly about a given character, one can identify instead with the frustration born from one's inability to connect deeply with stories that pass by quickly. In this way, a microthon can feel deeply familiar and charged even when, or especially when, we feel little connection to its characters. This kind of strategic frustration is a subset of a phenomenon we might call rhythmic identification: our familiarity not with a human figure but with a particular pace.

THE THEATER OF INFORMATION OVERLOAD: A SURVEY

One factor contributing to very long sets of very short plays is the popularity and pervasiveness of short attention span theaters in a sound bite culture. Contemporary audiences have become accustomed to long successions of shorts: Sit-coms, soap operas, and long-form television shows offer near-endless dramas diced into forty-four- or twenty-two-minute episodes, and further subdivided into typically eight-minute sections, most of which contain one or more miniature arcs of suspense and revelation. In the twenty-first century, online video has exploded in popularity and threatens to become the predominant short entertainment form of the future. As televisual and digital cultures have produced new spectatorial rhythms, they have in turn produced new kinds of playwriting. Kenneth Koch—whose provocatively titled microthon *One Thousand Avant-Garde Plays* (1988) contains 112 plays, most only a page long—cites television as one of the primary inspirations for the brevity of his plays: "I can switch from one channel to another and be in the middle of three different movies and in 30 seconds I could be laughing or crying at what I saw . . . And I wanted to get that part of drama, that part of theatre, on stage—or at least into these texts."[2] Of course, television did not create the ability to absorb a complicated scenario in an instant, but the pace of electronic entertainment and of the drama written in its wake has cultivated our ability to ingest scenarios quickly and to switch among them at a rapid pace. Jon Jory, one of those responsible for institutionalizing the ten-minute play festival at the Actors Theatre of Louisville, cites television as one of the factors contributing to the popularity of the ten-minute play:

> After . . . decades of the television sit-com, problem drama, and social commentary of the week, we've developed an emotional shorthand which these plays suit perfectly. Bam! A page to set the situation. Crash! A few character details. Wham! The obstacle. And Shazam, the resolution.[3]

Jory's explanation obscures important institutional motivations behind the creation of the ten-minute play festival at the Actors Theatre, which invented the form to deal with script overload in their literary department, but nonetheless helps explain why ten-minute play festivals—and their shorter cousins, three- and one-minute play festivals—have been so popular over the past thirty years.[4] A public accustomed to the rhythms of television, Internet surfing, and online or streaming video arguably has both a higher capacity for absorbing information quickly and a higher capacity for extended consumption.

From this perspective, microthons represent an instance of what new media critics call remediation.[5] Instead of withdrawing from contemporary excess as Beckett's shorts did, these works embrace and/or parody it. Just as the advent of modernist shorts was in part a reflection of the faster pace of encounters in urban life, contemporary marathons of shorts reflect not only the even faster perceived pace of life in a digital world but also the holistic, all-encompassing perspective of a global information age. The remainder of this section surveys a range of microthons produced since the 1980s in order to underscore their popularity, their diversity, and their debt to the idea that contemporary life is disorientating and encyclopedic.

The Reduced Shakespeare Company has, since the 1980s, produced a series of microthons that poke fun at the kind of dilettantism encouraged by information overload. For nearly twenty years, the three-person troupe has made a career taking "long, serious subjects" and reducing them "to short, sharp comedies."[6] The title of their signature show, *The Compleat Works of Wllm Shkspr (abridged)*, reveals their shared love of comprehensiveness and compression, and realizes an ideal of distillation suggested by Marinetti in the 1915 Variety Theater manifesto: "Reduce the whole of Shakespeare to a single act."[7] Reduced Shakespeare both mocks and caters to audience members who assume they no longer have time for great plays or great books, playgoers who, in the words of the troupe's slogan, want "a little culture. Very little."[8] A performance that offers Shakespeare's thirty-seven plays all in one go promises to satisfy one's urge to ingest vast stores of information quickly: to have it all, all at once.

Ten-minute play marathons, like the variety shows and little theaters of the modernist era, offer commercially viable forums for very short performance. Over the past twenty years, short play festivals have emerged all over the world, their diversity limited only by the marketing savvy of managing directors.[9] Now that ten-minute play festivals are well established, some micro-festivals call for even shorter pieces; there are three-minute play festivals (the Spaghetti Club's Three Minute Warning in London), one-page play festivals (the Lamia Ink! International One-Page Play Competition), and even the One-Minute Play Festival (OMPF), a New York-based theater company that partners with theaters and local artists across the country to produce evenings of one-minute plays, typically ninety plays in ninety minutes.[10]

As of 2016, the longest-running show in Chicago was a microthon called *Too Much Light Makes the Baby Go Blind*, the original signature show of a troupe called the Neo-Futurists. *Too Much Light* began as a late-night underground stunt in Chicago in 1988 and became a twenty-eight-year phenomenon, spawning sister Neo-Futurist troupes in New York and San Francisco. *Too Much Light* is not a play; it's a set of instructions for compilation designed never to produce the same results and to perpetually refresh itself. At each performance of *Too Much Light*, the troupe attempted to perform thirty original plays in sixty minutes under the insistent countdown of an onstage darkroom timer. Since the audience determined the order in which the thirty plays were performed, and since the troupe added between two and twelve new plays each week (based on the roll of two dice), each production of *Too Much Light* was unique and irreproducible. To date, the Neo-Futurarium in Chicago has produced nearly 10,000 two-minute plays for *Too Much Light* and more than sixty longer plays or site-specific theatrical events. The New York branch of the troupe celebrated their ten-year anniversary in 2014 by performing a twenty-four-hour marathon of *Too Much Light*, including some 600 plays. In early 2017, the Neo-Futurists lost the trademark license to *Too Much Light*, but all three troupes continue to perform an ongoing compilation of two-minute plays under the title *The Infinite Wrench*.

The Neo-Futurists share with their namesakes, the Italian Futurists, an irreverent, playful, and provocative attitude; a penchant for manifestos; a love of simultaneity; and an unapologetic embrace of the possibilities of short performance. Founder Greg Allen explains that the Neo-Futurists borrowed from the Futurists the conviction that "you can, in fact, write a two-minute play with just as much depth and humor and poignancy as something that takes five acts, twenty characters, fifteen set changes, and two hours and ten minutes to complete."[11] In particular, they rely on the tendency of extraordinarily brief performances to disrupt the suspension of disbelief. The Neo-Futurists aim to create "a world in the theater which has no pretense or illusion," that is "a fusion of sport, poetry, and living newspaper."[12] Extreme brevity enforced by a ticking clock reinforces this goal by reminding the audience of theater's immersion in the present moment.

At their best, Neo-Futurist shorts take advantage of the tendency of microthons to call attention to themselves, exploring what remains in theatrical performance when the cornerstones of traditional dramatic content—plot, character, mimesis, context—have been removed. At the beginning of *George Spelvin is Alive and Well*, the actor Tim Reinhard is alone on a dark stage. A spotlight fades up and moves gradually over and around him while he speaks the following text:

> Gradually, very gradually, more and more of his face becomes visible, until at last, it is clear that he is none other than who he appears to be. He is exactly himself. A man, illuminated by a single lamp, speaking into the darkness, he is all the image of an actor, on stage during the climactic soliloquy in which the twisted inner workings of his character are revealed. But for this man there is no character. There is no plot. There is no intention. There is no larger context within which he is to be seen. There is no identity for him to get caught up in. No ego to confuse him. There is no history. No habits.

No expectations, and he is pleased by simple things, like unre-
hearsed gestures, knowing they mean nothing and are merely expressions of his being. He is content in his freedom, for he knows
that tomorrow he will once more be cast in the role of the sales clerk,
and will once more be asked to play the part of the boyfriend, and
the family member. So he holds on for a moment longer, and savors
the silence and basks in the joy of being himself . . . alone in the spotlight.

CURTAIN[13]

The figure alone in the spotlight is not George Spelvin of the title, or not
exactly. George Spelvin, like his counterparts Georgette and Georgina
Spelvin, is a traditional pseudonym in the American theater for an actor
who wishes not to be named in the program or for a character that never
appears on stage.[14] The title invokes Spelvin to underline the absence of
character in the play. We are asked to recognize in place of George the presence of the actor as nothing other than himself. Here is theater aspiring toward presence emancipated from identity, story, or time itself. The present-
tense narration aims to describe nothing more or less than what is
happening at each moment. The man onstage aims to escape not only from
theatrical narrative but also from the roleplaying of everyday life into a
sanctuary of emptiness, a reprieve from theater through theater. The play's
happy ending hinges on its gambit to preserve the mystery of theatrical
attention unadulterated by content.

The Neo-Futurists have a reputation for insisting that a tiny collection
of moments can constitute a play, so it is fitting that the New York branch
of the group spearheaded Twitter Plays, an initiative that applies the
twenty-first century's most of-the-moment technology, Twitter, to playwriting. Since the inception of the micro-blogging service in 2007, theater
professionals and aficionados around the world have embraced Twitter as
a free publicity engine, as a platform for networking on the fly, and as a
soapbox for amateur short-form dramatic criticism. Tweets have become
the decentralized *faits-divers* of the early twenty-first century. There have
been Twitter poems, Twitter fiction, Twitter film scripts, and, thanks in part
to the Neo-Futurists, there are now Twitter plays.[15] Beginning in March
2009, the New York Neos began asking their fans to post, in response to a
weekly challenge, plays the length of a single tweet. The response has been
enthusiastic; by March 2012, the site had published more than 4,150 minuscule dramas by over 800 authors.[16]

Microthons have only grown in popularity since the early 2000s. In 2007, inspired by Parks's play-a-day commitment, British playwright Mark Ravenhill—best known for his in-yer-face diagnosis of the consumer age, *Shopping and Fucking* (1996)—wrote a new play to be performed each day of that summer's Edinburgh Festival Fringe. The result was *Shoot/Get Treasure/Repeat*, a set of seventeen short plays exploring the ramifications of the war on terror. In 2011, choreographer Bill T. Jones's and Arnie Zane's dance company produced the multimedia work *Story/Time*, in which Jones read in random order seventy stories in seventy minutes as dancers performed in circles around him, challenging audiences to find meaning in a haphazard succession of elements.[17] In 2014, the playwright Michael Frayn—who had previously written a collection of eight playlets about the distractions of modern life called *Alarms and Excursions* (1998)—published *Matchbox Theater: Thirty Short Entertainments*, a set of closet dramas inspired as much by vaudeville as by contemporary culture. That same year, the Chicago troupe the Hypocrites premiered Sean Graney's *All Our Tragic*, a marathon adaptation of all thirty-two surviving Greek tragedies into a twelve-hour epic of irreverent shrunken plays, each about fifteen minutes long. A number of durational performance pieces also take the form of microthons: in 2008, Forced Entertainment staged *Quizoola!*, in which three actors in clown makeup selected one question after another from a list of two thousand and improvised answers to them over a six-hour span. For Jonathan Kalb, who writes about the production in his study of marathon theater, the piece's capacious scope reflects and critiques postmodern society's "information swarm."[18] More recently, the troupe staged *12am: Awake & Looking Down* (2014), a "narrative kaleidoscope" in which five silent performers use a stack of cardboard signs and a collection of clothing to reinvent themselves again and again and again over a running time of six to eleven hours.[19] In a nod to these productions' implicit engagement with the exhausting serial pace of contemporary culture, the troupe has livestreamed recent performance events on its website. When Forced Entertainment restaged *Quizoola!* at the Barbican in 2013, they invited spectators to contribute to a real-time Twitter feed using the hashtag #quizoola24. Similarly, they hosted a live stream of 12am and solicited live feedback at the Twitter feed #12amLIVE.[20]

What are we to make of the recent proliferation of microthons? Have playwrights, theaters, and audiences sacrificed contemplation, depth of appreciation, or fullness of experience in the search for the latest fix of entertainment, a conveyor belt of performative aperitifs delivered on demand? In a recent essay, playwright Richard Foreman eloquently described what is at stake:

> I come from a tradition of Western culture, in which the ideal (my
> ideal) was the complex, dense and "cathedral-like" structure of the
> highly educated and articulate personality—a man or woman who
> carried inside themselves a personally constructed and unique ver-
> sion of the entire heritage of the West. [But now] I see within us all
> (myself included) the replacement of complex inner density with a
> new kind of self—evolving under the pressure of information over-
> load and the technology of the "instantly available."[21]

As we are drained of our "inner repertory of dense cultural inheritance,"
Foreman concludes, we risk turning into "'pancake people'—spread wide
and thin as we connect with that vast network of information accessed by
the mere touch of a button."[22] Are microthons pancake drama? My readings of Parks and Churchill suggest that the creators of contemporary microthons do register the attenuated flatness of contemporary culture, even
as they offer positive alternatives to the cathedral for an increasingly networked world: inclusive, interconnected constellations of moments that
reveal the breadth and complexity hidden in the seemingly thin stream of
mediated contemporary experience.

Eons in an Instant: Suzan-Lori Parks's 365 Days/365 Plays

> It all took eons to happen and it all happened in an instant.
> —Parks, *Abraham Lincoln at 89*[23]

Suzan-Lori Parks's mammoth project, *365 Days/365 Plays* began with an
arbitrary limit, not on running time but on composition. Starting in November 2002, just after winning the Pulitzer Prize for *Topdog/Underdog*,
Parks challenged herself to compose a play a day for a year. She compared
this solo test of creative stamina to "running a marathon without the crowd
cheering you on."[24] Parks approached the marathon with near religious
dedication and, a year later, completed a long, heterogeneous collection of
very short plays, ranging in length from a few sentences to a few pages.
After the more or less naturalistic *Topdog/Underdog*, Parks found in the private rigor of *365* a daily method to revisit, reclaim, and re-explore modes of
formal experimentation that fueled her early plays. The daily challenge of
writing intensified her already highly self-conscious style, making the
writer a spectator of herself and of theatrical form. Even without knowing
that Parks did not originally intend to publish or stage the plays, one could
easily classify the collection as closet drama. The extreme brevity of the

plays, their many impossible stage directions, and the daunting scale of the cycle as a whole all resist performance.[25] Like Gertrude Stein's and Beckett's idiosyncratic plays, both of which influenced Parks, the cycle largely operates according to its own intimate rhythms and its own hypotheses about what might constitute a play.[26]

The cycle remained in Parks's drawer until 2006, when she and her longtime friend, producer Bonnie Metzgar, devised an ambitious plan to turn her private ritual outward: the 365 Festival. The festival divided the country into sixteen regional networks and a university network, each of which organized a complete run of the cycle by finding fifty-two theaters or other groups each willing to perform a week of plays, in whatever way they saw fit. On November 13, 2006, four years after the first play was written, the Festival kicked off a year-long marathon of simultaneous performance that has been dubbed "the largest theatrical collaboration in U.S. History."[27] The same day, Parks published the series as a book. When Metzgar convinced Parks to turn "intimacy . . . outward" and uncloset the plays,[28] their idiosyncrasy and difficulty became something akin to the productive anti-theatricality that Martin Puchner identifies in modernist closet drama.[29] The cycle's radical departures from traditional theater were absorbed into the mainstream theater community and became the basis for its temporary reorganization.

So *365 Days/365 Plays* refers to two distinct microthons: a private compositional journey exploring dramatic form and a public experiment testing theatrical possibility. *365* exemplifies the microthon impulse on every level: as a performance festival that straddled the global and local, as a one-time compositional challenge that created a potentially endless recurring cycle, as a very long book yoking hundreds of tiny mostly unrelated pieces, as a national epic composed largely of personal anecdotes, and as a home to plays that frustrate designations like long or short by attempting to be both at once. Superlatives cling to the project. Some of the cycle's plays challenge the record for the shortest play ever and imply that a moment or a thought can be a play, but as a whole, the nearly 400-page book is among the longest and most heterogeneous collection of scripts ever published. Parks wrote so many plays that *Variety*'s Mark Blankenship could reasonably claim, with a wink, that only six years into the twenty-first century she was already on track to becoming "the century's most prolific playwright."[30]

The 365 project shares some general similarities with the contemporary microthons surveyed above, but demands sustained attention because of its formal inventiveness and because of its aim to use what she calls "radical inclusion" to redefine both dramatic form and the geography of contemporary theater. Critics, including Philip Kolin, Rebecca Rugg, and Kathryn Walat, have argued that Parks's democratic embrace of radical inclusion, collaboration, and flexibility has expanded and leveled the map of American theater.[31] In what follows, I acknowledge these virtues while calling attention to opposing forces that generate productive tensions in the project: exclusion, privacy, limitation, formal rigor, and temporal constraint. Like Churchill's *Love and Information*, to which I return later in the chapter, Parks's microthon poses as a generous and open-ended gift to the reader or production team, but nevertheless playfully directs the timing of its performances.

The plays in *365* cannot escape their dates of composition, which are printed just before each title, but they routinely evade everyday time. Parks appreciates what Rebecca Schneider calls time's theatricality, its playful citation of the past and anticipation of the future. Since the beginning of her career, Parks's plays have routinely subverted linear time, allowing the historical past and the future to coexist and mingle in Augustinian present moments that conflate "yesterday today next summer tomorrow" and "just uh moment ago."[32] "I do play with time," she has said, "but it's because it's all happening right at once for me. Everything that ever happened, it's all happening right now."[33] In *365* Parks pushes this view of time folded in on itself to extremes. Parks's dramaturgy imagines time as infinitely flexible but remains committed to the idea that it is under the playwright's control. Her temporal manipulations in *365* both reinforce traditional dramaturgy by exaggerating the ways theater has always warped time (excerpting, eliding, dilating, or juxtaposing moments) and push against theater's temporal limitations by borrowing time signatures from other media, including film, art installations, and visual art in order to freeze time, to accelerate it beyond the limits of live actors, or to loop it endlessly.

The plays of *365* provide a hyperbolic catalog of the ways theater distorts time. Some plays drastically accelerate standard theatrical compression. The 3rd Foreign Dignitary in *Abraham Lincoln at 89* does a "beautiful and complicated" narrative dance relating a national epic. The stage direction that follows describes the central paradox of Parks's cycle: "It all took eons to happen and it all happened in an instant" (38). A number of plays in the collection last forever despite being only a few lines long; these "forever plays" are simultaneously among the shortest and the longest ever written. *The 2nd Constant* is one of a trio of pieces Parks invites anyone performing any part of *365* to insert into their production wherever they please. The play reads:

> Someone standing still. They could be dressed in mourning.
> The sound of wind or whales forever. (x)

With *The 2nd Constant*, Parks exemplifies Maurice Maeterlinck's notion in "The Tragedy of Everyday Life" that tragedy can consist in nothing other than someone waiting patiently and giving ear to the eternal. On its face, the play gives the reader or production team considerable freedom. It can be inserted anywhere in the production or not performed at all. The someone standing still could be anyone: a man or a woman, young or old, of any race. They "could be" dressed in mourning, or by implication, could be dressed otherwise. The sound could be wind, or it could be whales. Either choice puts the figure outside, anywhere accessible to the wind. The word "forever" may seem like the most rigid possible stage direction, but its very impossibility liberates a director to invent their own imaginative solution.

But Parks tucks considerable information into her indeterminate directions. To say "they could be dressed in mourning," replaces a direction with an interpretation. It unfolds a story behind the inaction that necessarily inflects it. A reader or director understands, whether the actor is dressed in mourning or not, that the atmosphere of emptiness and loss must be palpable. The phrase, "Someone standing still" follows Beckett in capitalizing on the ambiguity of the word "still," a word that, like this play, is simultaneously frozen (to stand still) and continuous (to remain standing). As a result, it is arguably incumbent upon director and actor to communicate that the figure has been in the position for some time and is *still* in it. Similarly, the alliterative respiration of the words "wind or whales" connects the whales and the wind, and suggests that we register the sound of *both* wind and whales together, a connection I think inevitably places the figure by an imagined seaside. The script calls to mind, at least to my mind, a narrative of someone pining for a lover lost at sea.

Most often, Parks bends linear time into cyclical patterns. The circularity of time has long been a central hypothesis in her dramaturgical physics. In her essay "Elements of Style" (1994), she writes,

> I walk around with my head full of lay-person ideas about the universe. Here's one of them: "Time has a circular shape." Could Time be tricky like the world once was—looking flat from our place on it—and through looking at things beyond the world we found it round? Somehow I think Time could be like this too. Not that I'm planning to write a science book—the goofy idea just helps me NOT

to take established shapes for granted. Keeps me awing it. Attaches the idea of Rep & Rev to a larger shape.[34]

If Parks has always seen the moment of performance as a fusion of past, present, and future, some plays from *365* replace repetition and revision with a form of strict repetition borrowed from film installations: the infinite loop. *Father Comes Home from the Wars (Part 11: His Eternal Return—A Play for My Father)* is a "never-ending loop of action" in which an unending series of five returning husbands twirl their wives and greet their children (368). The play is a gift to Parks's military father, who left and returned many times in her youth, as well as a gesture of impossible faith that the world's fathers will return home from their wars in perpetuity. In other plays, Parks applies repetition and revision to the play as a whole, so that they recreate themselves but with slight variations. The end of *Dragon Keeper*, for example, moves through apocalypse to a rebirth that is a revised beginning:

> Fires and Armageddon. Eons pass within an instant.
> God blinks the Great Eye and, as the world is born anew
> and creation rapidly surges forward,
> evolution happens double-triple time. We're all caught up to
> where we were just before this play started, but this time,
> instead of burning, we'll continue to sleep,
> unaware of our power. (150)

The tension between linear and cyclical time in plays like this one reflects a parallel tension animating the project as a whole. On the one hand, Parks set a goal and marched resolutely forward toward its finale, including everything she could along the way to shore up a sense of comprehensive finality. On the other hand, *365* remains insistently a cycle shaped by the rhythms of daily practice and annual renewal. Each day asked Parks to oversee the birth of another world only to abandon it, blink, and start over again the next day. The project as a whole ends where it began on November 12, and the promise of performance means the plays will be continually reinvented by new production teams.

From one perspective, the forever plays are provocative hyperbole, playful winks to readers and directors that invite creative solutions.[35] As Rebecca Rugg describes, Parks's "open time signature" in *365* liberates the plays and represents a tacit admission that all stagings will be approximate and provisional.[36] But from another angle, Parks may be serious when she claims that the plays last forever. Even before they are performed, Parks insists, "plays are complete—they just exist in another realm."[37] This neo-Platonic definition keeps open the possibility of an ideal play that lasts forever in the mind, while inviting performers and directors to drag the idea into being in whatever way they may. On this account, the accidents of performance make do in time, but the plays themselves refuse to be bound by any time but their own.

"A New Geography . . . in the Internet Age"

The 365 Festival production team intentionally set out "to create a new geography for artistic productions in the Internet age," and the resulting festival shows what theater might look like reimagined for a networked culture.[38] Using the Internet to coordinate geographically-specific and idiosyncratic performances around the world, the festival unsettled distinctions between mass-produced global media and live performance event. Collectively, the festival was a yearlong global durational theater event. But its 800 troupes each created local, often site-specific performances within regional networks that fostered limited community. The festival offered the best realization yet of Philip Auslander's provocative idea that "live performances can be mass-produced."[39] To support his suggestion, Auslander cites an earlier experiment in decentralized American theater, the WPA Federal Theater's 1936 production of *It Can't Happen Here*, which opened simultaneously in eighteen American cities. A play with eighteen premieres may not qualify as mass-production, but an event with seventeen distinct premieres of 379 plays surely does.[40] Parks's yearlong festival of shorts was digitally enabled theater, a performance predicated on the dual contention that the live need not be local and that the global need not be televisual.

On its face, Parks's generosity appears to cede control almost entirely to others. Her name for the project's capacious hyper-democratic impulse is "radical inclusion."[41] With regard to the festival, radical inclusion meant inviting any theater in the world to participate by producing a week of the cycle anywhere they want, any way they want, for only a dollar a day in licensing fees. They were performed on streets and subway platforms, in temples and in bathrooms, in department store windows and private homes, on sidewalks and ice rinks, and in regional theaters. The week of plays could be performed together or separately. They could be staged readings, happenings, or fully produced spectacles; one company performed its plays as a conference call radio drama.[42] Theaters were forbidden from charging admission, so the audience could include anyone, at least in principle. Radical inclusion also meant dismantling the traditional hierarchies and divisions regulating commercial theatrical output by giving well-heeled theaters and rogue troupes of disorganized thespians equal access to the productions in order, however temporarily, to reorganize the map of the American theater to reflect an increasingly decentralized world. Campbell Robertson of *The New York Times* took this rhetoric to heart, claiming that the festival "created a sort of theatrical Internet, which was the idea; ideally a tiny theater in, say, Denver that is presenting a certain week will trade ideas with a theater presenting the same week thousands of miles away."[43] The project's ambitious goal was, in the words of producer Bonnie Metzgar, "to have the largest shared premiere ever in the history of anything. And possibly the largest art collaboration of any kind."[44] As self-declared "hosts" of the festival, Parks and Metzgar were fond of saying: everyone's invited to the table, and "there's pie for everyone."[45]

The Internet enabled Parks's rhetoric of radical inclusion by promising a digital table large enough in theory to accommodate anyone, but in practice, the radicalism and range of the 365 Festival remained limited. Parks and the producers clearly attempted to be as inclusive as current digital and theatrical networks would allow, but just how radically inclusive was the festival in the end? Despite the festival's sincere rhetoric about democracy and leveling, the "grassroots" festival would never have gained momentum without Parks, a Pulitzer Prize-winning celebrity powerhouse of the American theater, as its central authorizing figure. The 365 Festival was organized before the plays were published, so it asked hundreds of artistic directors—including those at venerable institutions like the Public Theater in New York and the Goodman Theatre in Chicago—to agree in advance to stage seven plays they had never read. Parks may be right that the 365 Festival offers pie for everyone, or at least *petit fours*, but the primary reason theaters were willing to commit time, energy, and attention to these miniature recipes is that Parks has proven in the past that she can make excellent pie, and producers and audiences trusted that at least some of the same ingredients would appear in the plays. While Parks's project contends that the merest gesture can constitute a play, it does not abandon the author function. On the contrary, a universe of theaters only became a constellation when connected by Parks's often naval-gazing text. Audiences too were by and large more traditional than radical. Anyone in the world was free to perform the plays, and all performances were open to the public without charge, but the overwhelming majority of those exposed to the project were already theatergoers or theater students in the United States and in a handful of other countries.[46]

The same tension between inclusion and limitation that animated the festival also runs through the collection itself. On its face, the book offers a testament to theatrical flexibility and capaciousness, something like the opposite of Beckettian restriction. The collection's heterogeneity suggests that anything can be a play, its minimalism leaves considerable room for interpretation by readers and production teams, its stage directions often present multiple possibilities or playfully assume that theater is capable of staging anything, and Parks's rhetoric describes playwriting as a selfless gift. But closer attention to Parks's text reveals her significant investment in authorial control over the disposition and timing of her plays, and so betrays a continued commitment to the idea that scripts can dictate the rhythm of a play for both readers and audiences.

Inclusion and Its Limits

A year of writing a new play every day, Parks has said, required opening a passageway to "the river of the collective unconscious," and letting everything in. No subject matter was too quotidian, no form too outlandish or minimal to be included. As she put it, one needs "to dismiss the bouncer who works the door of your creative mind. All ideas are welcome. All ideas are worthy for play-making."[47] The collection flouts any temporal or spatial limit one might propose for a play, comprehending the momentary and the infinite, the quotidian and the cosmic.

The radical dramaturgical hospitality of 365 aims to include even those plays the collection could not accommodate. In *Outtakes*, a writer and an editor are surprised as the stage fills, paradoxically, with a crowd of theatrical outtakes from the cycle: "some characters, some plays that werent even fully formed enough to get titles, like little almost-birds who fall out of the nest." The editor takes pity on them and announces, "We'll call the play 'Outtakes.' They'll be welcome here" (309). An even more poignant expression of the theme is *Too Close*, written when Parks had only two months in her year of daily writing. A Writer Woman holds a clear plastic bag, blows her nose, balls up the tissue, and drops it in the bag. She coughs into a napkin, examines the phlegm, balls it up, and adds it to the bag. She empties her pockets of countless tiny folded slips of paper covered with words, reads some, and carefully places each in the bag. Her brief monologue is a eulogy for the author's unnumbered thoughts that will never grow into brainchildren:

> You start thinking after awhile about the ones that got away. Not the ones you wrote. But the ones you didnt write. Like the eggs that passed out of yr body without becoming babies. Or sperm, if yr a guy. Imagine if each one became somebody. Time is limited, I know, even in a work of this length. So Ive jotted down the un-included ones and put them in this plastic bag. (309)

Like the tomb of the unknown soldier, the bag of unknown characters is, along with its play, a placeholder, an anonymous memorial. Parks tries to preserve every scrap of mental detritus, and yet, even plays like *Outtakes* and *Too Close* that purport to include the lost, serve as reminders of the impossibility of total inclusion and the inevitability of loss. These gestures underline Parks's rigid temporal limitations even as they resist them. Even in the longest of works, time and space are limited. Like all art, plays rely on selection, and in this sense, theater of any length remains impoverished.

Parks's love of encyclopedic diversity closely resembles that of an earlier American artist who also contains multitudes, Walt Whitman, for whom "nothing is too close, nothing is too far off" to be included.[48] Just as Whitman's ecstatic embrace in *Leaves of Grass* aims to include everyone from the slave, to the corpse, to the prostitute, Parks's epic is a microcosm that would exclude no creed, no color, and no class. The multicultural catalog of anecdotes in *365* updates *Leaves of Grass* for the twenty-first-century metropolis. Whitman could not resist adding to *Leaves of Grass* as the years went by. Similarly, Parks labored to admit everything from the microscopic to the telescopic as her yearlong American drama accumulated. Both authors strain against the limits of their medium. Whitman yearns to collapse the distance between art object and viewer. "This is no book," he wrote in the 1860 edition of *Leaves of Grass*,

> Who touches this, touches a man
> (Is it night? Are you alone?)
> It is I you hold, and who holds you,
> I spring from the pages into your arms.[49]

Parks shares Whitman's love of the capacious embrace that spills off the page and touches the world. The stage directions that comprise Parks's *Something for Mom* reach beyond the bounds of the play (or any play) and express her hope that a modest gesture, whether a play or a hug, can have a contagious, enormous effect:

A Kid (you could even cast an actual child),
holding a bunch of flowers, runs toward Mother.
Mother is surprised and happy. Kid presents flowers.
Mother admires the flowers. Then, lifting Kid,
Mother showers love.
This happens several times, with other Mothers and other Kids.
And "Mothers" and "Kids" are mutating and expanding to
include all of us, filling the stage, the theater, and the world,
as the action continues and repeats forever.
Even during peacetime. (163)

The simplicity of the gesture and the lack of dialogue or conflict make this a minimal drama, but the closing stage directions ask it to expand to impossibly large proportions, becoming a microthon of its own. In this case, Parks bypasses the spatiotemporal bounds of live performance by borrowing the split-screen conventions of video. This is stage direction as wartime wish fulfillment, as a gesture of faith, not only in a production team to execute the instructions but also in the world to enact them. It is an experiment in viral love, a play conceived as an endless gift that might trump time and space by virtue of its hopefulness. However saccharine the play may be, the 365 Festival at least partially brought *Something for Mom*'s impossible instructions to fruition in late March of 2007, when at least seventeen different sets of Mothers and Kids populated far-flung stages during the same week. A play that asks to include "all of us" underscores the impossibility of total inclusion, but the simultaneity and global reach of the 365 Festival offered a possible model for a "mutating and expanding" action that expands to fill the world and repeats again and again.

The Window of Opportunity, written in the first week of the cycle, is another diminutive parable that nevertheless aims to include everything, mean everything, and contain all time. Like the Great Hole of History in Parks's best known work, *The America Play*, the window in *The Window of Opportunity* uses the space of the stage to resuscitate a dead metaphor and invest it with significance. Onstage, window curtains cover an ordinary window. A uniformed figure, the Window Meister, enters to perform his official duty. Like many of the figures in Parks's cycle, the Window Meister is a metaphysical functionary, an idea—here time or fate—personified and made mundane, functional, blue-collar. He checks his watch, checks the wind, then takes a deep breath. He draws the curtains, opens the window "with a great flourish," stands at attention, and announces, "The Window of Opportunity is now open!" At first, nothing happens. Then the curtains start to flutter in the breeze, and continue as the Window Meister announces the passage of absolutely everything to date in a dizzyingly abbreviated paragraph:

> WINDOW MEISTER: Ellipses. Ellipses. Before. The Dawn of Time. The Creation of the Universe. Ellipses. The fish crawls out of the sea. Ellipses. Olduvai Gorge. Ellipses. Homo Erectus in God's image. Ellipses. Gods, Gods and more Gods. The Rise. The Fall. Ellipses. Ellipses. Ellipses. Confucius and the Buddha. Ellipses. Jesus. Ellipses. Ellipses. United States version: Mayflower and Indians and Slavery; Washington Crossing the Delaware. Ellipses. Civil War. Ellipses. The War to End All Wars. Ellipses. Ellipses. All universal events of great significance up to and including the Present Day. (9)

The Window Meister announces that the Window is closed, and a moment later, someone enters running but has arrived just a moment too late. The Meister offers a word of encouragement, "Look at it this way: Yr 'The One Who Got Away' . . . Maybe next time" (10). The Window Meister, pulling back the curtain ("perhaps a gorgeous portion of purple velvet drapery"), is also a stage manager. The opening and closing of the window mark the beginning and end of a play within the play, a microdrama the length of a paragraph that nevertheless represents a macrodrama whose beginning stretches to before the dawn of time itself.

The Window Meister's words, "Maybe next time," are small consolation to the figure, who leaves with a heavy heart, but the play itself represents some consolation. Parks is obsessed with the absences and holes in history—everything elided by the many ellipses in the Window Meister's speech—and thinks of her plays as parallel histories that make space for those who got away from traditional narratives and conventional conceptions of "events of great significance":

> theater, for me, is the perfect place to "make" history—that is because so much of African-American history has been unrecorded, dismembered, washed out, one of my tasks as playwright is to . . . locate the ancestral burial ground, dig for bones, find bones, hear the bones sing, write it down. . . . I'm re-membering and staging historical events which, through their happening on stage, are ripe for inclusion in the canon of history.[50]

Fig. 10. The One Who Got Away (Rachael Holmes) and Window Meister (Joan MacIntosh) in *The Window of Opportunity*. The Public Theater. Directed by Michael Greif. (Photo © Michal Daniel, 2006.)

Like other authors of microdramas, Parks understands theater's capacity to render its contents meaningful and so deploys her theatrical frame to redefine what events qualify as worthy of notice. In this case, she restages the holey whole of history in less than a minute, and makes the tragic protagonist a representative for those history forgot. But *The Window of Opportunity* is not just a parable about African-American or other subaltern history; it is also an expression of the futile race against fate, as well as a parable about the theater, and a reflexive commentary on *365*. As the title suggests, any play is a window of opportunity, a structure that invites us to view a world through a small frame for a limited time. That the figure's name, The One Who Got Away, is the same name Parks uses in *Too Close* to describe the ideas she couldn't record ("you start thinking about the ones that got away") reveals a personal thrust to the metaphor (309). When she wrote this fourth play in the series, Parks had just begun a race against time, a race to add something to the history of everything by seizing an opportunity to let in all of those who tend to get away.

The Window of Opportunity is a play about capacious inclusion, but its own significance is constrained. The play's title renders its metaphor more or less as transparent as its window. *Window* remains provocative despite its straightforwardness, but Parks's tendency to build plays around a single gesture or metaphor can also lead to facile reduction. In the past, Parks has resisted decoding the blueprints her plays provide, and has looked down on plays based on a single transparent idea:

> I think that the playwright provides the map. But I think a bad play only has a one-way road. Yes, I think the bad play has one road; one idea, one message, one way of doing it. It's so much about one thing. And everybody walks out of the theater going, "Yeah, homelessness is bad," for example.[51]

But the constraints of the marathon writing project frequently led Parks to pen plays that realize a single idea. In *1 and 2*, a man enters stage left walking backward two steps, forward one step, backward two steps, and so on until he collapses from exhaustion and sobs. Similarly, in *Almost Perfect*, a character whose sign reads "Almost Perfect" is profoundly disappointed when he meets another whose sign reads "Perfect" (363). Parks's habit of announcing the tenor of her single-serving allegories, ostensibly another gesture of hospitality, weakens this play and others in *365* by leaving the spectator with little work to do. Parks's signposting indicates, somewhat ironically, her lack of faith in the meaning-generating capacity of theater, or at least her awareness that building an allegory quickly is difficult. Beckett's shorts, by contrast, almost never announce the terms of their metaphors, and they are all the more remarkable for it.

The Open Closure of Minimalism in Parks and Churchill

Like *365*'s maximalism, its minimalism might seem to offer temporal freedom by making space for readers and production teams to answer crucial questions. The play *Empty* ruminates on the freedom afforded by an empty apartment, a blank canvas, or an empty stage, and its refusal to specify a context makes it a reflexive commentary on the flexibility afforded by an empty script.

> *Two speakers.*

> Its empty.
> Yeah.
> Its—really—very—

Empty.
Yes.
I told you it was.
I had to see for myself.

One speaker, familiar with the space, has brought another who is skeptical at first, but soon understands that emptiness provides its own immensity:

Anything could happen here because—
Because nothing's happening here right now?
Yr sort of getting the hang of it. How do you feel?
Less empty. Or—empty but ok.
Yr gonna go far. I can tell.
You think?
I'm betting on it.
Gee.
Yeah.
(Rest)
Tell me something. Whered everything go, you think?
Good question. Dunno.
Cool. (90)

One person's emptiness is another's possibility. Parks winks at her own provocative reticence. Providing less direction liberates directors, producers, and readers to discover their own meanings and time signatures in the spare landscapes of *365*. The lack of identifying features in Parks's minimal parables can add metaphysical resonance. Like Beckett, Parks takes advantage of spare or unmarked theatrical spaces to create ontological parables compressing moral or spiritual insights into an apparently simple story.[52]

I argued in earlier chapters that miniatures are implicitly metatheatrical; when drama is stripped to essentials, those elements bear increasing weight. Many of the microdramas in *365* bear out this tendency, interrogating assumptions about the minimum requirements for playmaking: that there must be characters (*This is Probably Not a Play, 1 and 2*; *The Blank Before the World*; and others), that something should happen (*The Second Constant: Action in Inaction*; *Does it Matter What You Do?*, *Less and Less*; and *Shine*), that there should be a beginning, middle, and end in that order (*Beginning, Middle, and End*), or that someone should care enough to watch it (*Look and This Is Shit*). The struggle of these pieces to qualify as plays is one of the leitmotifs of the often reflexive cycle. *Less and Less*, for instance, ruminates laconically on its own minimalism. In the first act, reproduced below in its entirety, two unnamed speakers wonder where all the content went:

1: I dunno.
2: You don't have to.

End of scene.

1: What happened?
2: To what?
1: To all the—
2: People?

(Rest)

1: Yeah.
2: I dunno.

Intermission. (180)

With its duo exchanging terse questions in an undefined landscape, the play resembles an even more drastically reduced and denuded *Waiting for Godot* that ends almost as soon as its premise is announced. Parks could have called it *Waiting for a Play.* In the second act, as in *Godot*, the poverty of the landscape generates conflict. Much like Parks, who asks reader or viewer to accept less material than they expected, Speaker 1 makes a consolatory offering to Speaker 2, but 1 soon grows impatient with the idea that such an offering could be enough:

1: Here.
2: Thanks.
1: No Sweat.

(Rest)

That all?
2: That's all.

1

2

1

2

1: There used to be more.

2: Yeah.

1: There used to be more and more.

(Rest)

And now theres less and less and less.

2: What do you want?!?

(Rest)

1. More. I want more. Like there used to be. More and more. More
   overflowing. (180)

The frustration leads to a conclusion, however provisional: speaker 2 heads off to "go get more." Speaker 1 reminds 2 that only a little more would do—"It doesnt have to be much more"—but both agree on the need for "more." For all the reader knows, the characters could be talking about anything in short supply, and a production team could assign a specific referent. But to do so would obscure the play's meta-minimalism: its use of emptiness to limn theater's minimum. The play's departure from expectations is its central dramatic conflict, and its most interesting lesson might be the extent to which self-critical and self-canceling plays often fail to fail. Like the Futurist *sintesi Negative Act*, the more a play convinces us it has nothing to tell us, the more clearly it transmits its intended message. Plays can rarely shrink small enough to divest themselves of the vestiges of human interest, character, and conflict.

At the end of her compositional odyssey, fifty-one weeks after writing *The Window of Opportunity*, Parks demonstrated that a play containing only wind and light moving through an empty stage can generate a story:

THE BLANK BEFORE THE WORLD

A very slow light cue, as slow as possible,
from deep black to white-hot zoom.
The light reveals the stage, which is completely blank.
(Is this possible?)

> The light cue is accompanied by a sound of wind—
> the wind which brought most of us here to this country
> or this planet. Then, the wind reveals itself to be
> an enormously elongated single breath.
> When the light cue has reached its maximum
> and the breath has expired—the lights bump out quickly. (376)

This penultimate play in the cycle restages Beckett's 30-second play, *Breath*, with key revisions that convert a pessimistic parable into a hymn to theatrical possibility. Like *Breath*, it has no characters and no dialogue, and consists in a single light cue, up and down, coordinated with the sound of a slow, single breath. But instead of a stage full of trash, we see a blank stage full of potential. Like *Breath*, this script is all stage direction, but where Beckett's directions exert control through mannered technical instructions, Parks's stage direction is a free verse poem with strategic line breaks that encode meaning somewhat more cryptically. Putting the parenthetical, "Is this possible?" on its own line makes it not only a question about whether a stage can ever truly be blank but also a wink at her own audacity: Is this play possible? Similarly, the line break that separates "the wind which brought most of us here to this country" from the next line, "or this planet," registers hesitation between a story about migration and American possibility, and a story about the creation of the world. Crucially, where Beckett's light rises and falls together with breath, Parks's version gives us one long sunrise. As the human breath gives out, hot light illuminates a blank stage. Beckett's play witnesses the end of the world; *The Blank Before the World* oversees its birth. Like Beckett, Parks understands the way theater encourages our natural tendency to organize even blank light and empty time into a story. Both playwrights capitalize on the human instinct to mythologize, to read the rhythms of the natural world—sunrise and sunset, inhalation and exhalation—as signs laden with metaphysical import. For Paul Ricoeur, "Time becomes human to the extent that it is organized after the manner of narrative."[53] While it might seem to have no story to tell, *The Blank Before the World* has a clear beginning, middle, and ending. It organizes time after the manner of narrative so as to render even a very short period of time, without any visible human presence, manifestly hopeful. What may seem like a rebuke to dramatic convention testifies to the tenacious conventions that structure our always-dramatizing imaginations.

Parks's open-ended stage directions occlude the ways her texts often

direct the reader or performer more insistently than other dramatic writing. She embeds directions about the length, timing, and tone of performances textually through the use of bold face, line breaks, alternating fonts,
white space, and vernacular dialect. Liz Diamond, director of the world
premiere of *The America Play*, has said that Parks's plays are characterized
by "poetry, the radical condensation of meaning in form."[54] Parks has gone
so far as to claim that ninety-five percent of the action in her plays can be
found in the line of text.[55] Her lyrical and complex stage directions—
liberated from parentheses, right-justified to stand apart from the dialogue,
and infused with narrative and poetic energies of their own—constitute a
parallel text that demands attention as often as it directs action. Many of
the stage directions in *365* are playfully open-ended:

> The Man sits and whistles something that sounds like the lonesome
> wind, or he bursts into tears. (17)

> The Reader is pushed forward, richly or poorly dressed, with a
> Servant at her elbow, or in chains and led by a master. (36)

Rebecca Rugg calls such stage directions "Parks's gift to those embodying
her words."[56] Greg Miller too characterizes the looseness of Parks's stage
directions as an act of generosity. These directions are indeed gifts, but they
nevertheless offer two defined options, both of which are Parks's more
than a production team's.

The most distinctive examples of Parks's penchant for condensing
meaning are her signature "spells," instants of heightened silence built into
scripts using character prefixes followed by no dialogue. Beckett often
mandates pauses; Parks scripts their development and assigns them to one
or more characters. Insisting that charged silences are the places "where
the figures experience their pure true simple state," she displays her faith,
along with Maeterlinck and Beckett, that character's essence can be distilled in a silent moment.[57] Consider the following scene from Parks's *Venus*, in which South African Saartjie Baartman finds herself on display in an
early nineteenth-century freak show:

THE MOTHER-SHOWMAN
Ladies and Gents:
The Hottentots best angle.
. . .

THE CHORUS OF THE SPECTATORS

THE VENUS

THE MOTHER-SHOWMAN

THE CHORUS OF THE SPECTATORS

THE VENUS

THE MOTHER-SHOWMAN

(Rest)

(The Chorus erupts in wild laughter)

THE CHORUS OF THE SPECTATORS

HAHAHAHAHAHAHAHAHAHAHAHAHAHAHAHAHAHAHAHA-
HAHAHAHAHAHAHAHAHAHAHAHAHAHAHAHAHAHAHA-
HAHAHAHAHAHAHAHAHAHAHAHAHAHAHAHAHAHAHA-
HAHAHAHAHAHAHAHA

THE VENUS

THE VENUS

THE VENUS[58]

The script suggests to reader or director that the pause after the Mother Showman's announcement is a tense negotiation among the Mother Showman, her subject and the audience; that the chorus's laugh is hyperbolic, stylized and protracted; and that the pause after the laugh is distinct—it is Venus's alone. Parks shares Beckett's conviction that the playwright can and should sculpt empty time, and her "architectural" spells underscore her prerogative to assign stretches of silent time to particular characters, to organize the passage of even silent time after the manner of narrative.[59]

Caryl Churchill's 2012 microthon *Love and Information* provides a compelling counterpoint to *365*. Like *365*, *Love and Information* atomizes theatrical form to create an encyclopedic picture of contemporary life that contains multitudes and that develops ideas by variation, iteration, and surveying rather than by protracted exfoliation. Both pieces direct attention away from individual plays and toward the novelty of their structural conceit. Just as Parks's celebrity greased the wheels of the 365 Festival, Churchill's reputation helped *Love and Information* secure a high-profile premiere with a world-class production team, despite the slightness of many of its plays. One reviewer was direct, "if anyone other than Caryl Churchill had written this play, it would have been cut dramatically if it ever even made it to this stage of production."[60] Both microthons are charged by the tension between the part and the whole, asking one to imagine each play operating independently but never allowing us to forget the ecosystem within which they exist. Both scripts often present dialogues shorn of context that leave room for the imagination, and that prompt actors, directors, and audiences to do a considerable amount of the world building. Both are open-ended and demanding by turns, riven by the tension between control and release.

But most important for my purposes is their shared commitment to serial variety. Apart from its overall shape, almost everything about *Love and Information* is remarkably conventional for Churchill: each scene offers a bit of realist dialogue suggesting unremarkable present-day British citizens. But as one would expect from Churchill, who has made a career warping theatrical form to craft deeply topical plays, *Love and Information* engages contemporary culture most significantly through form. By recreating a pace familiar from televisual and especially digital culture, the play does not just thematize information overload, it produces it structurally.[61] The plays ask how the pace of information affects our ability to feel, and their performance tests that question. As each new microdrama materializes, one is reminded not just of a camera shutter—which the set designer for London and New York, Miriam Buether, cited as an influence—but also of a television, film, or computer screen, a bright square capable of flashing from one scene to another instantly.

Churchill's script is even more remarkably spare than Parks's; it lacks character prefixes and contains only nine minimal stage directions. Here, for instance, is *Sleep* in its entirety:

SLEEP

I can't sleep.
Hot milk.
I hate it now.
Book?
I haven't got the one I like.
Just lie there and breathe.
My head's too full of stuff. Are you asleep?
No no, what, it's fine. You can't sleep?
I think I'll get up and go on Facebook.[62]

This miniature conversation offers a sketch, a remarkably thin slice of life. People who speak with the easy familiarity of intimates share a bed. One has difficulty sleeping, not for the first time, because of information overload, but the solution—to go on Facebook—promises to perpetuate the problem. The play, like many in the collection, offers the barest bones of a simple idea in a way that feels familiar if not profound: uneasy lies the head that surfs the web. Who are these characters? What is their history? What country are we in?

On the surface, *Love and Information*'s final form appears to depend to a remarkable degree on choices made by a production team, on the ways they choose to coax its information into performance.[63] A host of seemingly vital choices are left to the director: how many actors to cast, the age and sex of the actors, the setting of each play, which of the random items to include if any, and what order the plays will appear within each section. To date, *Love and Information* has had two high-profile runs, the world premiere at London's Royal Court Theater in 2012 directed by James Macdonald, and a restaging by Macdonald with New York Theater Workshop in 2014. Macdonald's production left out some optional pieces, so it included fifty-eight scenes lasting less than two hours and featuring 132 characters.

In both the London and New York productions, Miriam Buether's clinical white box of a set emphasizes the script's lack of context, abstracting each scene from particularities, and suggests a scientific slant to the play's isolation of action. Its anonymous characters pop into existence as if they were theorems or hypotheses made flesh, experiments that convert Churchill's bits of information into embodied people and, conversely, consider the extent to which human identity and experience can be reduced to information. Even more than most stages, *Love and Information*'s empty box of sketches-made-flesh presents specimens of humanity, twenty-first century slices of life. So one is not surprised when, in the penultimate play, *Virtual*, someone challenges another who is in love with a computer program, a simulated woman. In response to the charge that the beloved is just information, the lover argues that we are all information, strings of genetic data. The promotional material for the Royal Court production described the evening, accurately, as a concatenation of *situations* happening to "someone": "Someone sneezes. Someone can't get a signal. Someone shares a secret. Someone won't answer the door. Someone put an elephant on the stairs. Someone's not ready to talk. Someone is her brother's mother. Someone hates irrational numbers. Someone told the police. Someone got a message from the traffic light. Someone's never felt like this before." The play has more than a hundred characters, and yet arguably does not contain any characters as such. In this respect, the scenes resemble reenactments of the plates from Eadweard Muybridge's Animal Locomotion series, attempts to abstract from everyday life a rationalized picture of behavior that otherwise moves too fast to register, and to scrutinize quotidian and microtemporal behavior for its hidden

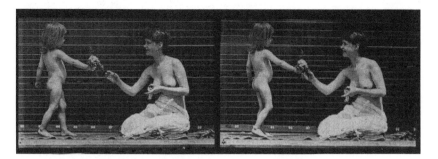

Fig. 11. Eadweard Muybridge, Animal Locomotion, 1887, Plate 465. Nude child bringing a bouquet to a semi-nude woman, detail. (Rare Books and Manuscripts Collection, USC Digital Library, University of Southern California.)

secrets. Accumulating like the hundreds of plates in Muybridge's study, Churchill's scenes are everyday chronophotography for a digital age.

Within each scene, Macdonald's production used realistic contemporary costumes and minimal settings—a patch of grass for a yard, a couch for a living room, a traffic cone for a construction zone—to suggest generic locations for the scenes, but these choices rarely shifted the significance of the plays in important ways. That the dialogues are almost immune to casting, that the lines could be put in almost any mouth in any setting, underscores the play's sense of the anonymity of contemporary life, its sense that the identity theft we should worry most about is the supplanting of identity by information. Here again, Churchill's reticence obscures her pervasive influence in shaping the script. *Sleep*, above, presents a vision of theater as nothing more than dialogue. By offering verbal exchanges shorn of character, location, and, in all but a few cases, stage directions, the reticent script makes a tacit argument for conversation (literally, a turning together) as the *sine qua non* of theater, rather than, say, action, observation, or framed time. In the process, she allows language, and dialogue in particular, to take pride of place as the fundamental force governing the production. As in Parks's *365*, Churchill's direction that the plays in each section can be played in any order might seem to cede control to directors, but it retains the assumption that the script is the ultimate arbiter of the play's arrangement and produces productions whose unpredictability, variety, and heterogeneity will, in each case, exemplify the play's implicit argument about the structure of contemporary experience.

SLOW FEELINGS AND FAST FEELINGS: THE PACE OF EMPATHY

Imagine an audience watching one of the plays in the 365 Festival, *Paper Tomatoes*, which stages a brief attack on a carnival strongman. This is the script in its entirety:

> A Strongman strides in. Sits on a crate.
> Immediately People come in and throw wads of paper at him.
> This goes on for quite some time. Then they leave.
> He sits there.

STRONGMAN

STRONGMAN

(Rest)

> He uses all his strength to hold back his tears.[64]

Paper Tomatoes revisits one of Parks's cardinal themes, the cruelty of spectatorship, through a theatrical lens at its most microscopic. Many traditional dramatic elements are here in miniature: inciting incident, rising action, conflict, and a final reversal. But how likely is catharsis? The answer could depend on production decisions: Just how long does the attack go on? How does the strongman react? How captivating is the performance? But in any production, is the spectacle of a public symbol of strength revealing weakness enough to move an audience in anything like the way the Strongman is moved? Placing a mute, nonviolent victim center stage and dramatizing his breakdown, the play asks spectators to feel for the Strongman, but in the absence of context, it will struggle, I think, to elicit empathy for him, despite going on for "quite some time." Does he deserve this punishment? What provoked it? *Paper Tomatoes* works best on paper or if the narration is read aloud. Without the stage direction, "He uses all his strength to hold back his tears," spectators are likely to miss the play's central turn, its play on "strength" that revises our understanding of the label, "Strongman." Resisting tears, in this case, is the true feat of strength. *Paper Tomatoes* reminds the viewer that the strong can also be vulnerable, but it does so whether we empathize with the Strongman or not.

Horace famously advised performers in *The Art of Poetry*, "Smiles are contagious; so are tears; to see / Another sobbing, brings a sob from me."[65]

Certainly many plays do not follow this formula, but Parks's seems to solicit a sympathetic reaction. The Strongman teeters on the verge of tears; what about the viewer? How often will a spectator develop intensities of feeling for the Strongman that approach what one might feel several hours into a tragedy watching Lear cradle the corpse of the daughter he helped undo? While shock or recognition or fear might occur in no time at all, does brevity militate against a familiar set of feelings characterized by deep absorption and shared understanding?

The second half of this chapter—which pivots away from theater history and literary analysis and toward aesthetics—argues that while Parks's and Churchill's projects illustrate the capacious flexibility of theatrical form and generate interest along many axes, their experiments also suggest that short plays are unlikely to produce certain emotional responses, including absorption in general and empathy in particular. I elaborate this argument through Parks because she has insisted in the past that her plays "beg for feeling," and through Churchill because her microthon is obviously interested in the relationship between the pace of information and one's emotional experiences, between information and love. But the tension between brevity and empathy I diagnose here surfaces in many microdramas, and provides one of the strongest justifications for scholars to attend to short form.

An examination of the pace of empathy helps lay the groundwork for an emotional poetics of theatrical brevity. Performance can encourage identification more quickly than written argument or abstract conversation because it puts individual human faces on abstract issues and places those individuals in the same space and time as the audience. But does the very abridgment and exaggeration that can make performances powerful and memorable tend to reduce an audience's capacity to empathize with their figures or issues? Watching *Paper Tomatoes*, one wonders why short plays so often convert pathos into bathos. Is it simply a coincidence or an accident of convention that there are countless short comic sketches and so few five-minute tragedies? Or is the horizon of emotional possibility tied to duration, however loosely? Understanding why shorts can feel insufficient might help explain what puts the full in full-length.

A close look at microdramas suggests genuine empathy—as opposed to automatic or sympathetic reactions—requires time to develop in audiences, and that the temporal demands of empathy pose a particular challenge for short performances that appeal to the emotions. The experience that interests me involves not only cursory identification or fellow feeling but also a substantial understanding of another's position, story, or experience. I use the term *empathy* to refer to experiences of this sort, while acknowledging the conflicting semantic baggage the term has accumulated. I focus here on the reception of a performance by an audience as opposed to the development of feeling among performers, a performer's empathy for his or her character, or the accretion of feeling in staff or crew during rehearsal. The recurring rhythm of rehearsal often encourages deep and abiding emotional engagement with the material and with one's collaborators, regardless of the length of the piece. But I am interested in situations that represent more challenging tests of theater's emotional machinery: cases in which spectators observe a performance for the first time about characters or situations with which they are at least partially unfamiliar.

If we assume that any performance makes possible a diversity of reactions from unmoved to overwhelmed, how might the length of an aesthetic encounter inflect the range of likely empathic responses for a given viewer? The idea that an object or body can provoke emotional responses in a viewer almost instantaneously is very old, although it has enjoyed a resurgence on the heels of neurophysiologic studies of perception. Robert Vischer first proposed an aesthetic theory of empathy (*Einfülung*, or "feeling into") in his 1873 essay *On the Optical Sense of Form: A Contribution to Aesthetics*. For Vischer, *Einfülung* described a form of engagement with a work of art or an object in nature in which we are "mysteriously transplanted and magically transformed into this other."[66] He distinguished between immediate sensory input and the subsequent kinesthetic reactions registered in the body but described both as if they were automatic and nearly instantaneous. In the 1930s, modern dance critic John Martin made the "inherent contagion of bodily movement"—the way in which another's yawn begets our own, for instance—the basis for a theory of dance spectatorship based on "inner mimicry."[67] Watching a dancer's body, the viewer's motor responses automatically "awaken appropriate emotional associations akin to those which have animated the dancer in the first place."[68] Our muscles tense when a weightlifter heaves, we jump when someone is surprised, and the vocal cords of professional opera singers tire just from watching operas they know well. Performance theorist Susan Leigh Foster places movement's contagion at the center of her genealogy of "kinesthetic empathy," an experience in which one body comes to understand another by registering its position, bearing, or movement.[69] Foster is careful to note that the "conditions under which viewers connect to what they see" change over historical time, but in each of the cases she discusses—an eighteenth-century tightrope walker; a twentieth-century modern dancer; and a collection of twenty-first-century 9/11 victims, cell phone interlocutors, and break dancers—an instant of reception lights the spark for a momentary phenomenon that she dubs "the empathetic moment."[70]

Although kinesthetic reactions may inform empathic responses, I reserve the term *empathy* for a more gradual and complex set of emotional reactions. In this approach, I follow David Krasner, who suggests that the range of audience experiences that contemporary viewers describe using the term *empathy*—identification with a character, moral compassion, sympathy (here defined as an urge to help a character after feeling their pain), and understanding (which may not involve agreement or sympathy)—all share fundamental similarities. In each, spectators, having established "some substantial understanding" of the situation or character and "a grasp of the narrative (even if the narrative is disjointed, fragmented, or illogical)," rely on intuition, imagination, or memory to enter into the action of the play imaginatively.[71] Spectators do not confuse themselves and the object of empathy but nevertheless associate feelings and observations with their personal experience.[72] Disagreeing with Brecht, Krasner argues that empathy does not preclude intellectual involvement but is a distinct form of intellectual involvement and a precondition for altruistic feelings and actions. For me, as for Krasner, empathy builds a substantial bridge between the viewer and another, and bridges of this sort can rarely be built in an instant.

Those plays in 365 that solicit an emotional response highlight a tension between estrangement and identification running through Parks's dramaturgy. On the one hand, Parks, a self-professed formalist and a fan of metatheater and Brecht, frequently calls attention to the theatrical frame. At the same time, she envisions her plays as emotional conduits. She explained in a 2011 interview, "I don't get to my plays through ideas. I think writing them would be easier if I did. Because ideas and thought, they're verbal, and I think my plays are preverbal. From my guts."[73] Her primary goal in crafting a play's language is to find the form that will tell an actor "how to shoot that energy through to the audience night after night, so they can ride that wave of language. . . . Read the words, and *feel*. My plays *beg* for feeling. They *beg* for the gut response. Let the stomach-brain, let the heart-brain, inform your head-brain, and not always the other way around."[74] Parks imagines her formal and theatrical estrangements as innovations that enhance the machinery of feeling.

If Parks imagines herself as a technician of emotional transfer, the miniature plays of 365 posed severe challenges to the mechanisms to which she had become accustomed. More than her other work, the plays in 365 tend to appeal to the head-brain more than the heart-brain. They may ask one to recognize or appreciate a problem, but they rarely depend on emotional identification with the characters and their struggles. Indeed, the fact that so few of the plays in the cycle seem to *"beg* for feeling" may represent the best evidence that, while very short drama can do many things, it struggles to generate deep emotional connections. That does not, however, stop Parks from trying. Plays in the collection that do seem to beg for feeling like *Paper Tomatoes*, become useful test cases exposing the emotional constraints of short form. Some intense affective reactions blindside us with their swiftness—the gasp of surprise, the unforeseen welling in the eyes, the gooseflesh of vicarious fear. But to envision empathy as an instantaneous event risks oversimplifying the emotional experience of spectatorship and downplaying one of the cardinal attractions of watching many full-length performances: the complex and gradual experience of engagement with a virtual world and the emotional lives of its figures.

We cannot fully empathize with Parks's Strongman until we know why he is the object of derision. This process becomes more difficult in short performances, in part because shortcuts take the place of gradual characterization. We learned in chapter 1 that as plays shrink, their characters tend to become less individual and more like terms in a parable or allegory. Viewing the Strongman in *Paper Tomatoes*, we arguably understand his mental life no more nor less than we would that of any figure with hypertrophic muscles and a leopard-print singlet. Our minds register the terms of a parable quickly, but how deeply can we feel for its figures?

The answer often depends on how familiar we are with the story before it begins. Prior beliefs and exposure to similar people or situations—factors that Marvin Carlson calls ghosts and Susan Feagin calls "conditioners"[75]— can lay the foundation for empathic bridges and speed their construction. For instance, when Parks's play *9–11* opens with two mothers sipping tea, recalling the attacks on the World Trade Center, and watching their boys play war games, a few broad strokes can quickly evoke a rich store of emotional memory because the play assumes an audience who share similar experiences:

> 1ST MOTHER: I sat there watching it on the tv and, you know, when those poor people were hanging out the windows waiting for the firemen to come. And I was talking to the tv, telling the people: "Dont worry, the firemen will come for you and youll be safe."

2ND MOTHER: Me too.

1ST MOTHER: Like they could hear me.

2ND MOTHER: I was doing the same thing.

1ST MOTHER: And then they started jumping. And then when they
    fell—

2ND MOTHER: Yeah.

MOTHERS

CHILDREN

MOTHERS[76]

The first mother need not finish her description because collective memory of remote trauma fills in the mother's narrative and gives shape to the silence that lingers after the second mother commiserates. The first mother tells a story of automatic sympathy for televised bodies trapped between fire and falling. Our empathy with the mother may not be as automatic as hers was for the victims, but it will be more likely to develop in those who, like the second mother, remember seeing footage of the same trapped figures and so can say along with her "I was doing the same thing." In cases like this, empathy may feel nearly instantaneous, but it represents the culmination of a process that has been at work over some time. Whether or not one names this experience empathy or uses some other term, brevity often complicates or forestalls a common form of emotional engagement in which exposure to the details of another's situation and history leads to a shared sense of the texture of a character's emotional life.

The Limits of Parks's Microdramaturgy

On the scale of the cycle as a whole and its democratic performance marathon, Parks's capacious embrace was both admirable and effective. But when she crystallizes the ethic of radical inclusion into single moments, her efforts to include everyone can lead to an obliteration of difference that solicits feeling but likely falls short of empathy. Parks's encyclopedic microthon is a strange hybrid: everyone and everything is included but none fully fleshed out; the scope is epic, but there's no hero (other than Parks) and no quest or direction. 365 is a union of atoms, a Whitmanesque epic composed of glimpses, a scrapbook history.

In *Pilgrims' Progress (for Thanksgiving)*, for example, a throng of pilgrims cross the stage deliberately and painstakingly. The stage directions call for pilgrims of every imaginable stripe—from Mayflower to Mecca, Canterbury to Varanasi, Western Wall to Mount Kailash—and demand, "All kinds of pilgrims. Accommodate as many as you can. Dont intentionally exclude anybody."[77] Those lines could have been a mantra for Parks, whose cycle juxtaposes as many kinds of history as possible: geopolitical and local, national and African-American, mythic and quotidian, private and theatrical. *365* reprocesses Parks's own history as a playwright by digging up themes from her earlier work—Abraham Lincoln and other dead presidents, holes and digging, race relations, absent fathers—and refreshes theatrical tradition by re-imagining classic works of theater, from *The Tempest* to *The Seagull*, in her own idiom. The exchange that concludes *Pilgrims' Progress* shrinks an impressive diversity of pilgrims to a pat capsule:

SOMEONE: All Pilgrims
SOMEONE ELSE: So different!
SOMEONE: But all going to the same place.

Smiles all around. (33)

Pilgrims' Progress asks for radical religious and cultural pluralism: this Thanksgiving, we should give thanks for seekers of all backgrounds. The play visually explodes assumptions about the word "pilgrim." But to what extent does it rely on empathy to make its point? The question may turn on decisions made by a director rather than Parks. How deliberately do the pilgrims move? Just how painstaking is their progress? While the text is brief, a production could extend the pilgrimage, allowing viewers to share long stretches of silent time with one or more pilgrims. So Parks's text leaves room for interpretations that might foster deeper emotional engagement. But such a possibility does not mean that a short play might create empathy; it shows only that a long play might have a short script. That the reader feels tempted to imagine a long performance underscores the sense that a quick parade of pilgrims would resonate less powerfully with viewers. In a quick reading or a quick performance, the play asks that the audience register the varieties of religious experience without necessarily understanding or sharing the experiences of any of the pilgrims. If such a reader or viewer experiences recognition, it is likely more intellectual than emotional. The final line may make a bid for a kind of universal empathy, but its conflation of difference reduces everyone's journey into every other, and removes the specificity that lends weight to empathic engagement.

If particular microdramas often struggle to generate empathy, figures and themes that recur across the cycle can encourage more elaborate affective attachments. As Deborah Geis has noted, the plays in *365* frequently have "permeable borders"; by complementing each other, they build structures larger than their individual dimensions might suggest.[78] Since the beginning of Parks's career, repetition and revision, or Rep & Rev as she prefers to call them, have been keywords for her dramaturgy. In her 1994 essay, "The Elements of Style," she describes her attempts to accommodate a traditional dramatic structure in which "all elements lead the audience toward some single explosive moment" with a pattern of repetition and revision to create "a drama of accumulation."[79] Confronted ten years later with the task of writing *365* plays in quick succession, Parks again employs repetition and revision—across plays rather than within them—to create a year-long drama of accumulation that, among other things, begins to compensate for the difficulty of generating intense connections within single moments. Parks's plays gain traction for the viewer or reader as they accumulate.

Such accumulation was rarely available to audiences of the *365* Festival, however. While readers of the four-hundred-page book accumulate feelings about Parks's project and some of its recurring characters and themes as they read, viewers of the local performances saw no more than seven of the brief plays in an evening. As a result, the average viewer of *365* experienced a tiny fraction of the plays in a relative vacuum. According to producer Rebecca Rugg, although performances from the *365* Festival demonstrated that audiences are "perfectly capable of accepting and enjoying a theatrical event requiring depth of thought and appreciation of metaphor and poetry," it remained "legitimately and understandably difficult for all audiences" to synthesize "a handful of short plays into a legible experience."[80] No one has attempted to stage the entire collection as a single event, but such a production would pose even greater challenges for an audience's attention, memory, and patience.

Love and Information and Time

> . . . the enigma in thinking about love is the duration of time necessary for it to flourish.
> –Alain Badiou[81]

If one examines the plays in *Love and Information* in isolation, only a handful invite extended analysis. One such play is *Piano*, an affecting piece about the riddles of memory and identity. There is very little to it on the page:

PIANO
Three people

This is Jennifer.
Hello, Jennifer.
Here's the piano. You can play the piano.
I've never played the piano.
You sit here.

He sits. He plays well and Jennifer *sings. He gets up.*

Hello.
This is Jennifer.
Hello, Jennifer.
(45)

One needs only the lone stage direction as a clue, because the other directions are implied by the conversation. The piece dramatizes with grace and economy the tragedy of memory's complexity and fickleness. It draws its appeal from the profoundly ironic fact that under certain conditions one can know something deeply yet not know they know it. A person could come to appreciate this irony by reading about the neurological distinctions among procedural memory, which helps the pianists' fingers find the keys they have found before; semantic memory, which connects a person with the name Jennifer; and episodic memory, which builds a story telling us what we have done, what we know, and whom we have met. But Churchill's play delivers these insights intuitively, beautifully, and very quickly, as a series of surprises.

First, someone who insists they have never played piano sees sheet music and begins to play, effortlessly. In Macdonald's production, the piece was a lyrical art song by Francis Poulenc, "Une Ruine de Coquille Vide," set to a Paul Eluard poem. As the song unfolds over a minute or two, its lyricism and virtuosity lend poignancy to the situation, and the moment gives the viewer time to marvel. This is one of the few examples in *Love and Information* of a self-conscious theatrical moment, a charged, heightened span of time that aims to pull the viewer outside of the stream of time and to be more than the sum of its parts. The screw turns again when the song ends, the pianist turns to his partner in the duet, sees her again for the first time, and learns her name. While the song still lingers in the audience's memory, they understand that it has already been forgotten by the man at the piano. They now presumably know *and* feel how much more than information the amnesiac loses.

The play's brevity puts the viewer in something like the amnesiac's position and winks at the structural similarity between a blank memory beginning again and again and the spectators of *Love and Information*, who can stay in one scene for only so long before it blinks to black and introduces them to another new scene. But the play also reinforces the importance of an often neglected dimension of aesthetic time: the afterlife of an aesthetic event in the memory. Unlike the man at the piano, I wager I will remember his song for a long time.

But to focus on a given scene, or to engage in any extended consideration, is largely to miss the play's point. What distinguishes *Love and Information* and *365* from more conventional plays is an experience harder to quote but easy enough to describe, the impression of moving quickly from one thing to another, and then another, the experience of hyperserial variety. Spectators by necessity scan the plays synoptically, and consider the pieces in relation to each other. The overall pace of Parks's and Churchill's microthons is their primary aesthetic intervention, and I think the aspect of these productions we are meant to identify with.

To focus on the structural rhythm in *365* and *Love and Information* begins to suggest the varieties of emotional engagement that encyclopedic theater might encourage or allow. Compared to conventional plays, microthons arguably put a greater burden on a spectator's capacities, not only because they are long but also because they are numerous. In most cases, asking the viewer to begin over and over again arguably requires more total attention and energy than letting a scene or a play run its course. The microthon format tends to disperse attention by prompting spectators to think across the series, to consider how the current play relates to those that preceded it in the series, how much of the overall event has elapsed, or how the plot of the overall event is developing, as distinct from the plot of a given play.

Reviews tend to interpret *Love and Information*'s engagement with contemporary society as straightforward mimesis. The play's "head-spinning mosaic of 50-odd mini-scenes offers a cautionary but ultimately optimistic panorama of modern, mediated life" that "ingeniously and exhaustively mirrors our age of splintered attention span."[82] It is "the story of a culture's addition to information-on-demand, told in the short attention span format to which we've grown accustomed after a generation of channel changing and Internet surfing."[83] The evening is "the theatrical equivalent of going through your Netflix queue, watching any movie for five minutes, and then starting a new one, no matter how much you enjoyed what you were previously viewing."[84] But such statements largely shy away from deciding on the play's stance toward a culture of information and do little to exfoliate its implied theses about the intimate but fraught relationship between information and love. It remains an open question whether the piece's thinness might be strategic.

One might expect an excess of information to attenuate identification; I only came to care about a few of its individual anonymous figures. But one can identify with the frustrating inability to connect deeply with stories that move by very quickly. We connect with the rhythm and texture of 24/7 time, the yearning for more time to settle in, to relax. In this way, a microthon can feel deeply familiar and charged even when, or especially when, we feel little connection to its characters. This kind of strategic frustration is a subset of a phenomenon I call rhythmic identification: our familiarity not with a human figure but with a particular pace.

If one takes rhythmic identification—familiarity not with a human figure but with a particular pace—as a central aim of *Love and Information* the play emerges in a different light. From this perspective, the play's skimming over events becomes tactical. One can discern a temporal narrative arc that uses structure to offer not a celebration but a criticism of information overload by recreating first the excitement and exhilaration of its possibilities, and then allowing accumulation to produce disorientation and exhaustion. When I saw Macdonald's New York production, which had no intermission and gave no indication how many sections there would be, by the time some eighty minutes had passed and the sixth section began, I sighed and checked my watch. When the seventh began, I wondered how much longer it would go on. Several critics agreed that over time "the premise starts to seem like a reductio ad absurdum," and more than one suggested the play should have been cut.[85] But these criticisms ignore the possibility that this might be a play built to frustrate, designed to reintroduce us to both sides of our attachment to the pace of digital culture, recreating not only the thrill of serial brevity but also the brevity of serial thrill.

An appreciation for the sometimes gradual pace of emotional involvement in theater has significant ramifications for theater and performance studies. For one, it suggests we should be careful to include in our models of aesthetic response not only flashes of insight but also less dramatic accumulations of understanding. The rhetoric of reflexive response is not limited to those enamored of mirror neurons. Buttressed by the epiphanic tropes that undergird so much Western life narrative from Augustine to *America's Got Talent*, accounts of intense aesthetic involvement tend to foreground the instant of surprise, rapture, or recognition. A lovely account by theater historian Marvin Carlson reinforces the perceived connection between immediate sensation and the spiritual:

I also have now and then experienced moments of such intensity that they might be called epiphanies. It seems to me that theatre is perhaps particularly well suited as an art to generate such moments because it constantly oscillates between the fleeting present and the stillness of infinity. . . . Such moments of apotheosis are not everyday occurrences, of course. . . . Such moments will be different for every theatergoer, but I feel certain that we all have them, and treasure them. In an art that lives by, and survives largely in, the memory, such experiences have served me as touchstones, as permanent reminders of what I have been seeking in a lifetime of theatergoing.[86]

Carlson's spiritual rhetoric makes him a serial pilgrim seeking experiences of near-mystical intensity—the revelation of epiphany, the deification of apotheosis—in the temple of the theater, and implies that the mystery of such moments can only fully be explained through something like faith. Narratives of aesthetic epiphany ring true for many. But if we seek moments of epiphany in the theater, are those moments only possible because they stand on the backs of less remarkable ones? Does Carlson's rhetoric give undue weight to memorable impressions of intense feeling and in the process downplay the less perceptible but no less essential accretion of sentiment and understanding that make such intensities possible? I would encourage scholars to ask what approaches and what vocabularies might do justice to receptive processes that accumulate, gather, or seep instead of catching us by surprise. Carlson is well attuned to the uncanny staying power of ephemeral moments. Once registered, these epiphanies serve as touchstones precisely because they have crystallized and hardened into durable memories. But by privileging the moment of shock, narratives of this kind arguably contribute to the assumption that brief performances are just as likely as others to produce intense reactions.

A clearer understanding of the temporality of feeling may also help explain generic divisions or assumptions about length that might otherwise seem arbitrary. Parks's and Churchill's shorts teach us the most about empathy when they fail to evoke it, suggesting that, for those interested in dramatic form and emotional investment, brief performances might be most useful precisely when they feel most disappointing or incomplete. The frequent failure of shorts to move us as other performances do exposes the emotional underpinnings of common dramaturgical assumptions. In particular, it suggests that the time required for audiences to identify with characters has helped to shape the normative duration of so-called full-length drama.

Taken as a whole, Parks's and Churchill's menageries of miniatures provide a survey of the lessons microdramaturgy can teach us about theater and time. Their capacious variety demonstrates the flexibility of theatrical shorts, what I have elsewhere called the heterogeneity of brief time. These cases remind us that microdramas can be infinitesimal or neverending, sluggish or frantic, sparse or crowded, fragmented or unified, comic or in rare cases tragic, transparent or opaque, unfinished or definitively resolved. Like *faits-divers* and earlier plays modeled after them, microthons continue to explore the riddle of eventfulness by first presuming that the barest scrap of experience might be noteworthy, and second by suggesting that the best record of contemporary experience might feel like a haphazard list of incidents. Like Futurist playwrights, Parks and Churchill embrace variety to fashion a hyperbolic dramaturgy that attempts both to resemble and intensify the felt pace of contemporary life, but which sometimes generates disappointment rather than astonishment. Like Beckett's shorts, but using very different means, Parks and Churchill's microthons undercut the presumption to cordon off the flux of experience into a coherent and tidy narrative. Microthons replace overarching dramatic narrative with an aleatory newsfeed, replacing linear action with a drama of assemblage. Their free-wheeling formal inventiveness might seem like the latest and in some ways the most extreme instance in a 125-year series of challenges to the temporal conventions governing scripts, but as instances of implicit metatheater, both collections ultimately underscore the tenacity of the conventions they flout: they downplay the author function but vitally rely on it; they decline to enforce the timing of performances, but their faith in dramatic form nevertheless mandates pace in more playful or subtle ways; and they make appeals for instant identification, but in the process expose the often gradual pace of a spectator's absorption.

Notes

CHAPTER 1

Epigraph: Francesco Cangiullo, *Detonation*, in *Futurist Performance*, ed. Michael Kirby, trans. Victoria Nes Kirby (New York: PAJ Performance, 1986), 268.

1. I use the American spelling, "theater," throughout but I have retained the British "theatre" when it appears in quotations, book titles, and the official names of companies.

2. Hans Jauss, *Toward an Aesthetic of Reception*, trans. Timothy Bahti (Minneapolis: University of Minnesota Press, 1982).

3. See chapter 2, note 17.

4. Future work on theatrical brevity might consider, in Europe and the United Kingdom, Anton Chekhov's comic sketches; G. B. Shaw's experimental one-acts; Irish drama by W. B. Yeats, Lady Gregory, and J. M. Synge; Brecht's learning plays; numerous expressionist plays; Artaud's surrealist fantasia *Jet of Blood*; one-acts by Pirandello, Lorca, Ionesco, Heiner Müller, Sartre, and Genet; and more recent shorts by Michael Frayn, Howard Barker, Harold Pinter, Sarah Kane, Mark Ravenhill, and others. The American tradition is at least as robust, including Eugene O'Neill's early sea plays at the Provincetown Playhouse; Arthur Kreymborg's miniature one-acts; many of Gertrude Stein's radically unconventional plays; Thornton Wilder's one-acts and three-minute plays; Djuna Barnes's shorts; and others by Tennessee Williams, Adrienne Kennedy, David Mamet, William Saroyan and Don DeLillo, plus as a growing number of contemporary shorts too numerous to list here.

5. For more on criticism about Beckett's short theater, see chapter 4 below, especially note 8.

6. An unpublished PhD dissertation by Celeste Raspanti, "Strategy of Form: The Shape of Length in Drama," University of Minnesota, 1977, shares some of the goals of this project, but it focuses on mainstream one-act and two-act plays that are relatively long by comparison; it pays little attention to the theoretical, performative, and phenomenological nuances of brevity; and it overlooks the most interesting shorts, those that deploy pace and length to reflect on the nature of time. The title of Irvin Morgenstern's *The Dimensional Structure of Time, Together with the Drama and Its Timing* (New York, Philosophical Library, 1960) promises a useful contribution to the field of time and the drama, but the book's combination of abstruse philosophy and rigid structuralism muddies the issue more than illuminating it. Kathleen George's *Rhythm in*

Drama (Pittsburgh: University of Pittsburgh Press, 1980), by contrast, is usefully grounded in the temporal texture of dramatic moments. Her subject—pacing—overlaps with mine, but does not lead her to ask questions about the relationship of pacing to length. George's book does include a microdrama as a heuristic tool. Her first chapter uses a twenty-line "playlet" to diagnose some basic properties of rhythm. Many of the authors I profile agree with George that "sometimes the best way of understanding a phenomenon is by examining it in its most pared-down form" (17). But what George considers a classroom experiment or a thought experiment becomes stage practice for authors like Beckett, Parks, and Churchill.

7. Stephen Kern, The *Culture of Time and Space, 1880–1918* (Cambridge, MA: Harvard University Press, 1983), 199–202.

8. Paul Virilio, *Speed and Politics: An Essay on Dromology* (1977), trans. Mark Polizzotti (New York: Semiotext[e], 1987).

9. Ronald Schleifer, *Modernism and Time: The Logic of Abundance in Literature, Science and Culture, 1880–1930* (Cambridge: Cambridge University Press, 2000).

10. Paul Ricoeur, *Time and Narrative*, trans. Kathleen McLaughlin and David Pellauer (Chicago: University of Chicago Press, 1988). After establishing an Augustinian view that the peculiarities and aporias of lived time tend to defy human control and understanding, Ricoeur proposes that narrative broadly construed is the major vehicle by which humans respond to time's oddity. He begins by defining narrative, following Aristotle, as mythos, including epic, tragedy, and comedy, and involving the traditional elements of plot, character, language, thought, spectacle, and melody. Ricoeur broadens that definition to include narratives either performed and witnessed or written and read, and then expands narrative yet further to include modern historiography and the social sciences.

11. Bert States, *Great Reckonings in Little Rooms: On the Phenomenology of the Theatre* (Berkeley: University of California Press, 1985), 49. For an extended description of the medium specificity of theatrical time, see Matthew Wagner's "Theater and Time," in *Shakespeare, Theatre, and Time*, and Cole Crittenden's article "Dramatics of Time," *KronoScope* 5.2, (2005) 192–212, which argues that drama's construction of time and space—what Bakhtin would call its chronotope—is categorically different than other literary forms due to drama's relentless presentness and to the inability of audience members to influence performance time.

12. In her 1993 essay, "Elements of Style," Parks distills six of her plays into visual or verbal equations. So *Pickling* is trying "to find an equation for time *saved*/saving time" and *Betting on the Dust Commander* attempts to solve for X, where X is a history trapped inside a circular vortex. In *The America Play and Other Works* (New York: TCG, 1995), 13.

13. Kalb, "Introduction," *Great Lengths: Seven Works of Marathon Theater* (Ann Arbor: University of Michigan Press, 2013), 3.

14. Greenberg, "Modernist Painting" (1960) in *The Collected Essays and Criticism*, ed. John O'Brien (Chicago: University of Chicago Press, 1995), 4: 90.

15. Worthen, *Modern Drama and the Rhetoric of Theater* (Berkeley: University of California Press, 1991), 1.

16. "Time and Theatre," in *Shakespeare, Theatre, and Time*, 12, 13.

17. Dessy, in Kirby, *Futurist Performance*, 285.

18. Drama critic Arthur Bingham Walkley on Sardou's refinement of the well-made play, a form codified by Eugène Scribe, *Playhouse Impressions* (London: T. Unwin, 1892), 80.

19. One way to begin building a more nuanced and comprehensive account of theatrical time is to combine several critics' accounts. Brian Richardson distinguishes among three distinct clocks that plays set in motion, the "story time" of the original narrative being represented, the "text time" of the particular path charted through that story, and the "stage time" needed to trace that path, and argues that the three rarely tell the same time. ("'Time Is Out of Joint': Narrative Models and the Temporality of the Drama," *Poetics Today* 8.2 (1987), 308.) In Matthew Wagner's concise account of theatrical time, the dissonance among theater's clocks (fictional action, onstage action, and real world action) and the thickness of theatrical moments freighted with past, present, and future become the *sine qua non* of theatrical activity. ("Time and Theatre," in *Shakespeare, Theatre, and Time* (New York: Routledge, 2011), 12–33.) Both Richardson and Wagner identify fundamental aspects of theatrical time, but their clarifying analyses have a tendency to make temporal experience feel more reckonable and predictable than they feel to me. My sense of theater's proliferating clocks is especially indebted to Jon Erickson's account of the multiple overlapping time scales on which theater's fundamental rhythm of tension and release unfolds, from the suspense within a single gesture to the overarching structure of rising and falling tension that shapes many performances (even as I would ask whether tension and release is the only available dramaturgical shape). ("Tension/release and the production of time in performance," in *Archaeologies of Presence: Art, Performance and the Persistence of Being*, eds. Gabriella Giannachi, Nick Kaye, and Michael Shanks [New York: Routledge, 2012], 82–99). Marvin Carlson's *The Haunted Stage* richly elaborates the ramifications of another time: the spectator's previous experience with the material represented, echoes that haunt any performance. Building on Erickson's and Carlson's work, I hope theater scholars might do for theatrical time what David Graver began to do for the figure of the actor in his article "The Actor's Bodies," which enumerates at least seven sorts of corporeal presence produced by an actor onstage. Like Graver, I want to put pressure on easy distinctions between artifice and reality, and to call attention to the assumptions that stand behind conventional ways of talking about "everyday time" and "the time on stage" as if they are clear concepts with distinct borders. (David Graver, "The Actor's Bodies," *Text and Performance Quarterly* 17.3 (1997): 221–35.)

20. William Kozlenzko, *The One-Act Play Today* (New York: Harcourt, Brace and Company, 1938), 8.

21. For more on this subject, see Rebecca Schneider on "the theatricality of time," "full of holes and gaps" in *Performing Remains: Art and War in Times of Theatrical Reenactment* (New York: Routledge, 2011), 6.

22. Filippo Tommaso Marinetti, Emilio Settimelli, and Bruno Corra, "The Futurist Synthetic Theater," *Let's Murder the Moonshine: Futurist Manifestos*, ed.

and trans. R. W. Flint and Arthur A. Coppotelli (Los Angeles: Sun & Moon Classics, 1991), 132.

23. Rockaby, in *Samuel Beckett: The Grove Centenary Edition*, ed. Paul Auster, vol. 3, *Dramatic Works*. (New York: Grove, 2006), 462.

24. *Aristotle's Poetics*, trans. S. H. Butcher, (New York: Macmillan, 1961), 66.

25. Ibid., 117.

26. One might argue that certain historical short forms, including Greek tragedies, Plautine comedies, and early modern masques, were somewhat self-sufficient. But both Greek tragedies and Plautine comedies were subsumed within larger festival programs, and masques were generally one entertainment among a number performed for a particular occasion. Many of the shorts I discuss were performed together with other short plays—in evenings of one-act plays, for example—but were generally not subordinated to longer works.

27. There are several excellent studies of the modernist cabaret, including Laurence Senelick's brief foreword to *Cabaret Performance: Sketches, Songs, Monologues, Memoirs*, vol. 1, *Europe 1890–1920* (New York: PAJ Publications, 1989); Peter Jelavich, *Cabarets in Berlin, 1901–1944* (Cambridge, MA: Minda de Gunzburg Center for European Studies, 1986); Harold Segel, *Turn-of-the-Century Cabaret: Paris, Barcelona, Berlin, Munich, Vienna, Cracow, Moscow, St. Petersburg, Zurich* (New York: Columbia University Press, 1987); and Shane Vogel's *The Scene of the Harlem Cabaret: Race, Sexuality, Performance* (Chicago: University of Chicago Press, 2009), but more work is needed on the cross-pollination between mainstream theatrical venues and cabarets.

28. For more on the modernist interest in the quotidian, see Bryony Randall, *Modernism, Daily Time and Everyday Life* (Cambridge: Cambridge University Press, 2007); Liesl Olson, *Modernism and the Ordinary* (New York: Oxford University Press, 2009); and Siobhan Phillips, *The Poetics of the Everyday: Creative Repetition in Modern American Verse* (New York: Columbia University Press, 2010).

29. Maeterlinck, "The Modern Drama," in *The Double Garden*, trans. Alfred Sutro (New York: Dodd, Mead, 1920), 122–23.

30. Maurice Maeterlinck, "The Tragedy of Everyday Life," in *The Maeterlinck Reader*, ed. and trans. David Willinger and Daniel Gerould (New York: Peter Lang, 2011), 301–2.

31. Parks, *365 Days/365 Plays* (New York: Theater Communications Group, 2006), x.

32. Marinetti, "The Futurist Synthetic Theater," in Lawrence Rainey, *Futurism: An Anthology*, ed. Rainey, Christine Poggi, and Laura Wittman, trans. Rainey (New Haven: Yale University Press, 2009), 206.

33. G. B. Shaw, "Against the Well-Made Play," in George Brandt, *Modern Theories of Drama* (New York: Oxford University Press, 1998), 101. First published as "Preface" in *Three Plays by Brieux* (New York: Brentano's, 1911), vii–liv.

34. The script to *Le Kid* is lost. Deirdre Blair reconstructs the performance from accounts by R. B. D. French, Georges Belmont, Aileen Conan, and Norris Davidson in *Samuel Beckett: A Biography*, 127–28. For more see "Le Kid, Human Wishes & *Eleuthéria*," in MacMillan and Fehsenfeld, eds., *Beckett in the Theatre*,

vol 1. See also "Peacock Theatre," *Irish Times,* 20 February 1931. Georges Pelor-son claims that Beckett contributed little more than the play's title. David Bradby, *Beckett: Waiting for Godot* (New York: Cambridge University Press, 2001), 19.

35. Bergson, *Time and Free Will: An Essay on the Immediate Data of Conscious-ness,* trans. F. L. Pogson (Mineola, NY: Dover, 2001), 12.

36. Parks, interview by Joseph Roach. 14 Nov 2006. New Haven, CT. World Performance Project. http://research.yale.edu/wpp/wpp_events.php, accessed 10 March 2010.

CHAPTER 2

Epigraph: Félix Fénéon, *Novels in Three Lines,* ed. Luc Sante (New York: New York Review of Books, 2007), 20.

1. "On Modern Drama and Theatre," in *Selected Essays by August Strindberg,* ed. and trans. Michael Robinson (Cambridge: Cambridge University Press, 1996), 84–85.

2. Strindberg, "On Modern Drama," 85. For more on Strindberg's interest in and experiments with the *quart d'heure* form, see the section later in this chapter. Strindberg contains the action of *Miss Julie* within a single interior in which the action unfolds in real time with no intermission. The play is meant to last about an hour and a half, a length which Strindberg thought, at least before he encoun-tered the *quarts d'heure,* was about as long as modern audiences would be able to sit still. Preface to *Miss Julie,* in *Strindberg: Five Plays,* ed. and trans. Harry Carlson (Berkeley and Los Angeles: University of California Press, 1983), 71.

3. Still the best history of the little theater scene in Paris of the 1880s and 1890s is John Henderson's *The First Avant-Garde 1887–1894: Sources of the Modern French Theatre* (London: George G. Harrap, 1971). See also chapter 4 of Marvin Carlson, *The French Stage in the Nineteenth Century* (Metuchen, NJ: Scarecrow Press, 1972), and Harold Hobson, *French Theatre Since 1830* (London: John Calder, 1978). Two surveys in English of the history and influence of the rise of small independent theaters written in its immediate wake are useful, if outdated: Anna Irene Miller, *The Independent Theatre in Europe: 1887 to the Present* (New York: Ray Long and Richard Smith, 1931) and Samuel Waxman, *André Antoine and the Théâtre Libre* (Cambridge: Harvard University Press, 1926). André Antoine's published diary, *Memories of the Théâtre Libre,* trans. Marvin Carlson (Coral Gables, FL: University of Miami Press, 1964), provides glimpses into the day-to-day operations of the Théâtre Libre. On the symbolist theaters, see Frantisek Deak, *Symbolist Theatre: The Formation of an Avant-Garde* (Baltimore: PAJ, 1993).

4. Senelick, Introduction to *Cabaret Performance: Sketches, Songs, Monologues, Memoirs.* Vol. 1 of *Europe 1890–1920.* (New York: PAJ Publications, 1989), 8.

5. Richard Wagner did much to inspire the idealist reaction against natural-ism, and *La Revue Wagnerienne* (founded early 1885) was the forum for a great deal of symbolist ferment. Many symbolists learned of Wagner's idea of "total art" not from Wagner's own writings but through Baudelaire's 1861 essay, "Richard Wagner and Tannhäuser in Paris," which reads Wagner through a

more poetic lens than he would likely have chosen. See Charles Baudelaire, *Selected Writings on Art and Literature,* trans. P. E. Charvet (London: Penguin Books, 1972), 341–42.

6. For more on Poe and the symbolists, see Joseph Chiari, *Symbolisme from Poe to Mallarmé; the Growth of a Myth* (New York: Macmillan, 1956); Deak, *Symbolist Theatre,* 64–69. It is no coincidence that many naturalist theatrical shorts were adapted from naturalist short stories. Both the short story and the short drama strive for compression and unity of effect, and are intended to be absorbed in one sitting. By hewing to the unities of time and place, many short stories work very much like naturalist closet dramas in which we witness life through a small window of time and space without changes of set or costume, and some—like Hemingway's "Hills Like White Elephants"—are so reliant on dialogue as to approach drama.

7. Quoted in Joe Martin, "Three One Acts: Introduction," in *Strindberg: Other Sides* (New York: Peter Lang, 1997), 303.

8. For an excellent study of the Victorian obsession with time, viewed primarily through the lens of English literature, see Jerome Buckley, *The Triumph of Time: A Study of the Victorian Concepts of Time, History, Progress and Decadence* (Cambridge, MA: Harvard University Press, 1966). For more on the cultural ramifications of this temporal revolution, see Stephen Kern, *Culture of Time and Space.*

9. Thomas Carlyle, "Shooting Niagara," in *The Works of Thomas Carlyle,* Centenary Edition, vol. 30 (London: Chapman and Hall, 1896–1899), 2–3; quoted in Jerome Buckley, *Triumph of Time,* 10.

10. Simmel, "The Metropolis and Mental Life," in *The Sociology of Georg Simmel,* trans. and ed. Kurt H. Wolff (Glencoe, IL: Free Press, 1964), 421.

11. Elinor Fuchs describes the symbolism lurking behind Ibsen's naturalist surface in "Mythic Structure in *Hedda Gabler*: The Mask Behind the Face," *Comparative Drama* 19:3 (Fall 1985): 209–21. Similarly, Erik Østerud's "Myth and Modernity: Henrik Ibsen's Double Drama," *Scandinavica* 33.2 (1994): 161–82, envisions Ibsen's work as a synthesis of metaphorical sacred drama and metonymic modern drama. Evert Sprinchorn argues that Strindberg's early work exhibits symbolically infused "greater Naturalism" and that his post-naturalistic work emerged from an extension rather than a repudiation of his naturalistic interests. Sprinchorn, "Strindberg and the Greater Naturalism," *TDR* 13, no. 2 (1968): 119–29, and "The Zola of the Occult," in *Strindberg and Modern Theatre* (Stockholm: Strindberg Society, 1975), 251–66.

12. John A. Henderson, *The First Avant-Garde,* 34–40. In the last years of the nineteenth century, Paris also saw a short-lived theatrical collective who followed Saint-Pol-Roux (1861–1940) called the *idéoréalistes,* and argued, much as Maeterlinck had, that pure symbolism is too opaque and needs a dose of the real world to make it playable. Marvin Carlson, *Theories of the Theatre* (Ithaca, NY: Cornell University Press, 1993), 290.

13. Émile Zola, "Naturalism on the Stage," in *Playwrights on Playwriting,* ed. Toby Cole, trans. Samuel Draper (New York: Hill and Wang, 1960), 9–10, (emphasis added). Further page references appear parenthetically.

14. Ibid., 11.

15. States, *Great Reckonings*, 20 (emphasis in original).

16. The visual compression of early film rested on similar logic. When German naturalist playwright Johannes Schlaf argued that dialogue can be reduced in direct proportion to the naturalism of the staging, he unwittingly made a case for the effectiveness of early silent film: "If we attentively follow the progress of a real conversation, then it is nothing short of astonishing how the spoken word is often of secondary importance. . . . how gesture, facial expression, body movement and emotional colouring are the main element if not everything. . . . Traditional drama had to resort to such crude means as the monologue or in special cases was obliged to use the aside. . . . Today we can reveal more inner life of a character in *a minute of silent action* than was earlier possible with page-long monologues or endless asides." Johannes Schlaf, "On Intimate Theater," *Neulandi* 2.1 (1898): 35–38; reprinted in Eric Ruprecht, ed., *Literarische Manifeste des Naturalismus, 1880–1892* (Stuttgart: J. B. Metzler, 1962), 104; trans. and quoted in Claude Schumacher, *Naturalism and Symbolism in European Theatre 1850–1918* (Cambridge: Cambridge University Press, 1996), 157 (emphasis added).

17. I owe the literary history of the phrase *quart d'heure* in France to Theodore Braun's article, "Un demi-quart d'heure," *Studies in the Humanities* 11.1 (June 1984), 71–74. Braun quotes many uses of the phrase in Flaubert's *Madame Bovary* that demonstrate its status as a basic and rarely divided unit of time: "de quart d'heure en quart d'heure," "un grand quart d'heure," "trois quart d'heure" (from quarter hour to quarter hour, a good quarter hour, three quarter hours) (72–73). The phrase retains its colloquial residue in contemporary French. The *Petit Larousse* entry on "heure" uses the example: "Passer un mauvais quart d'heure, traverser un moment critique, pénible, dangereux" (To spend a bad quarter hour, pass through a critical, painful, dangerous moment). Braun, 72–73.

18. Ibid., 71.

19. Jullien, *Le théâtre vivant* (Paris: Charpentier et Fasquelle, 1892). While many accounts of the origin of the phrase date it to Jean Jullien in 1892, André Antoine notes that reviewers of Guiches and Lavedan's performance of *quarts d'heures* at the Théâtre Libre in 1888 denigrated the two fifteen-minute plays as *"tranches de vie"* (slices of life) (Antoine, *Memories of the Théâtre Libre*, trans. Carlson, 66).

20. Kirk Williams, "Anti-theatricality and the Limits of Naturalism," in Alan Ackerman and Martin Puchner, *Against Theatre: Creative Destructions on the Modernist Stage* (New York: Palgrave, 2006), 101.

21. The title, *La brême*, which Gerould translates as *Meat-Ticket*, is slang for a prostitute's police card.

22. Quoted in Daniel Gerould, "Oscar Méténier and 'Comédie Rosse': From the Théâtre Libre to the Grand Guignol," *TDR* 28, no. 1 (Spring 1984), 23.

23. See Gerould, "Oscar Méténier," 15–28. At least seven of the playwrights whose plays were produced in the Grand Guignol's first season had previously staged works at the Théâtre Libre. Frantisek Deak, "Théâtre du Grand Guignol." *TDR* 18.1 (1974), 35.

24. Popular manners were scenes from the daily life of the lowest rungs of

society, like Méténier's *Meat-Ticket* or *Little Bugger*, both subtitled *A Picture from the Life of the People*.

25. Fénéon, Felix, *Novels in Three Lines*, ed. Luc Sante (New York: New York Review Books, 2007), xxiv, 27. Sante translates more than a thousand *faits-divers* penned by Fénéon for the Parisian paper *Le Matin* in 1906. The items originally appeared under the heading "Nouvelles en trois lignes," which can mean either "the news in three lines" or "novellas in three lines." Sante's slightly overstated English title succinctly makes a case developed more fully in the book's introduction, that these items are "the poems or novels [Fénéon] never otherwise wrote," and that they convert a prosaic genre into "an aggressive modernist vehicle" (viii; xxiii). Further page references appear parenthetically.

26. Some examples courtesy of Sante, xxi.

27. Méténier, *Lui!*, in *Grand Guignol: The French Theatre of Horror*, ed. and trans. Richard Hand and Michael Wilson (Exeter, UK: University of Exeter Press, 2002), 86. Further page references appear parenthetically.

28. Compare a remarkably similar newspaper *fait-divers* written by Fénéon in 1906: "Across from 29 Boulevard de Belleville, Sarah Rousmaer, who walked the streets by night, was knifed to death, last evening, by a man who fled" (72).

29. Gerould, "Comédie Rosse," 16.

30. Strindberg, Preface to *Miss Julie*, 65.

31. It's also clear that Strindberg knew Méténier's *En Famille*. In a letter written the month he started writing the first two of these plays, *The Stronger* and *Pariah*, both of which consist of a single scene, Strindberg mentions his copy of *En Famille*, which he has lent to a friend and wants to get back. Letter to the Danish actor, Carl Price, December 1888; quoted in Gerould, "Comédie Rosse," 19.

32. Strindberg, "On Modern Drama," 85.

33. Martin, "Three One Acts," 297.

34. "On Modern Drama," 84–85.

35. Strindberg quoted by Gunner Ollén, "Kommentarer," *Samlade Verk: Nio Enaktare: 1888–1892* (Stockholm: Nortstedts, 1984), 33:331; trans. and cited in Martin, *Other Sides*, 298.

36. Strindberg quoted and translated in Martin, "Three One Acts," 298.

37. See Strindberg's essay "The Battle of the Brains," from the 1887 *Vivisections*. Reprinted in *Selected Essays*, 25–46.

38. *The Stronger*, in *Strindberg: Other Sides*, trans. Joe Martin, 301.

39. Strindberg, Preface to *Miss Julie*, 75 (emphasis in original).

40. Strindberg, "Memorandums to the Members of the Intimate Theater from the Director," in *Open Letters to the Intimate Theater*, trans. Walter Johnson (Seattle: University of Washington Press, 1966), 19.

41. *Strindberg: Other Sides*, xiv.

42. Szondi, *Theory of Modern Drama: A Critical Edition*, ed. and trans. Michael Hays (Minneapolis: University of Minnesota Press, 1986), 52.

43. Chaudhuri, *Staging Place: The Geography of Modern Drama* (Ann Arbor: University of Michigan Press, 1995), 31–32.

44. Barthes, "Structure of the Faits-Divers," (1962) in *Critical Essays*, trans. Richard Howard (Evanston: Northwestern University Press, 1972), 187–95.

45. Ibid., 29.

46. Cocteau, Preface to *The Wedding on the Eiffel Tower*, trans. Michael Benedikt, in *Modern French Theatre: The Avant-Garde, Dada and Surrealism*, ed. Michael Benedikt and George E. Wellwarth (New York: Dutton, 1966), 96.

47. Poe, "The Philosophy of Composition," 164. Baudelaire translated the essay in 1859.

48. Cameron, *Lyric Time: Dickinson and the Limits of Genre* (Baltimore: Johns Hopkins University Press, 1979), 204.

49. Greenwich mean time was established as a global standard by a group of twenty-five countries at the Prime Meridian Conference in Washington in 1884, but France refused to accept it until The International Conference on Time in 1912. Kern, *Culture of Time and Space*, 12.

50. Samuel Beckett, *Ohio Impromptu*, in *Dramatic Works*, vol. 3, *Samuel Beckett: The Grove Centenary Edition*, ed. Paul Auster (New York: Grove, 2006), 476.

51. "On the absolute uselessness of the exact *mise-en-scène*," *La Revue d'Art Dramatique* (May 1, 1891), trans. and quoted in Deak, "Symbolist Staging at the Théâtre D'art." *TDR* 20, no. 3 (1976): 145.

52. For excellent discussions of the anti-theatrical tendencies in symbolist theater, see Puchner, *Stage Fright: Modernism, Anti-Theatricality, and Drama* (Baltimore: Johns Hopkins University, 2002); Patrick McGuinness, "Mallarmé, Maeterlinck, and the Symbolist Via Negativa of Theatre," in Ackerman and Puchner, eds., *Against Theater: Creative Destructions*, 149–67.

53. McGuinness, "Mallarmé, Maeterlinck . . . Via Negativa," 157–58.

54. Trans. Bernard Miall (New York: Dodd, Mead & Co., 1928), 97.

55. Maeterlinck, "The Modern Drama," trans. Alfred Sutro (New York: Dodd, Mead & Co., 1920), 116.

56. Ibid., 122–23. Sociologist Max Weber attributed late nineteenth-century Europe's increasing interest in the everyday to de-enchantment, but his descriptions of this transposition of life to a minor key evoke, as much as Maeterlinck's, modern art's re-enchantment of the quotidian: "It is not accidental that our greatest art is intimate and not monumental, nor is it accidental that today only within the smallest and intimate circles, in personal human situations, in *pianissimo*, that something is pulsating that corresponds to the prophetic *pneuma*, which in former times swept through the great communities like a firebrand, welding them together." Weber, "Science as a Vocation" (1918), in *The Vocation Lectures*, eds. David Owen and Tracy Strong, trans. Rodney Livingstone (Indianapolis: Hackett Pub, 2004), 30.

57. Maeterlinck, "The Tragedy of Everyday Life," in *The Maeterlinck Reader*, eds. and trans. David Willinger and Daniel Gerould (New York: Peter Lang, 2011), 301–2.

58. I fully agree with Katherine Worth that Maeterlinck is the spiritual grandfather of Beckett and Pinter. I would add that both also follow Maeterlinck in their compression. For more on the uncanny resemblance of Maeterlinck and Beckett, see (among others) Patrick McGuinness, *Maurice Maeterlinck and the Making of Modern Theatre* (New York: Oxford University Press, 2000); and Margaret Rose, *The Symbolist Theatre Tradition from Maeterlinck and Yeats to Beckett and Pinter* (Milan: Unicopoli, 1989).

59. McGuinness, "Mallarmé, Maeterlinck . . . Via Negativa," 161.

60. Maeterlinck, "On Modern Drama," 122.

61. Ibid., 116.

62. Gerould, "Landscapes of the Unseen: Turn-of-the-Century Symbolism from Paris to Petersburg," in *Land/Scape/Theatre*, eds. Elinor Fuchs and Una Chaudhuri (Ann Arbor: University of Michigan Press, 2002), 303–21; McGuinness, *Maeterlinck and the Making*, 66.

63. Maurice Maeterlinck, *Interior*, in *Theatre of the Avant-Garde, 1890–1950*, eds. Bert Cardullo and Robert Knopf, trans. William Archer (New Haven: Yale University Press, 2001), 45–46. Further page references appear parenthetically.

64. For an extended discussion of the naturalist artist as experimenter, see Émile Zola, "The Experimental Novel," in *The Experimental Novel & Other Essays* (New York: Cassell, 1893), 1–56.

65. The stranger makes his role explicit, "I am only a passerby, a stranger" (46). For more on old men in symbolism, see Sean Pryor, "W. B. Yeats, Maurice Maeterlinck, and Old Blind Men," *Yeats Eliot Review: A Journal of Criticism and Scholarship* 19, no. 4 (Dec 2002): 9–24.

66. Egil Törnqvist, "The Modern(ist) One-act Play," in *Facets of European Modernism: Essays in Honour of James MacFarlane*, ed. Janet Garton (Norwich: University of East Anglia, 1985), 183; McGuinness, *Maeterlinck and the Making*, 211.

67. Maeterlinck, "The Tragedy of Everyday Life," 302.

68. Harold B. Segel, *Pinocchio's Progeny: Puppets, Marionettes, Automatons and Robots in Modernist and Avant-Garde Drama* (Baltimore: Johns Hopkins University Press, 1995), 51. William Archer's appraisal is representative: "We ought not to take too literally M. Maeterlinck's description of his pieces as puppet-plays. There is, to say the least of it, a dash of symbolism in the designation. It indicates the poet's extra-mundane point of view. . . . He sees mankind as a company of puppets, dancing on an infinitesimal stage in an obscure corner of the universe, while Nature pipes the music and Destiny pulls the strings. It is primarily in this sense that his pieces may be called 'drames pour marionettes,' . . . Now M. Poe (the director of the Opera Comique production) has shown that this philosophical point of view may be illustrated just as well by flesh-and-blood actors as by marionettes. His company realised to perfection the idea of will-less creatures moving through a dream." *The Theatrical 'World' of 1895* (London: Walter Scott, 1896), 116–17.

69. Arthur Symons, *Plays, Acting and Music: A Book of Theory* (New York: E. P. Dutton, 1909), 196.

70. *Shakespeare, Theatre, and Time*, 13.

71. Maeterlinck, "The Tragedy of Everyday Life," 300.

72. Maeterlinck, *Théâtre* (Geneva: Slatkine Reprints, 1979), xii, my translation.

73. Quoted in Michael Meyer, *Ibsen: A Life* (New York: Doubleday and Company, 1971), 148.

74. Quoted in Paul Schmidt, Introduction to *The Plays of Anton Chekhov* (New York: Harper Collins, 1997), 5.

75. Maeterlinck, *The Buried Temple*, trans. Alfred Sutro (New York: Dodd, Mead, & Co., 1904), 135–36.

76. For more on Beckett's *Breath*, see Chapter 4, pp. 91–93.

77. Poe, "The Philosophy of Composition," 164.

78. Maeterlinck, "The Tragical in Daily Life," in *Treasure of the Humble*, trans. Alfred Sutro (New York: Dodd, Mead & Co., 1903), 101.

79. True, Brecht's *verfremdungseffekt* also redeployed Shklovsky in a theatrical context, but where Brecht advocated particular strategies to produce estrangement, Esslin contends that things on a stage are always already strange.

80. Consider the minimal vocabulary of Craig's design for *Macbeth*, which contained only two elements—a rock and some mist. *On the Art of the Theatre*, 22.

CHAPTER 3

Epigraph: William Shakespeare, *Macbeth*, in *Complete Works of Shakespeare*, 1.5.56–58.

1. Bruno Corra and Emilio Settimelli, *Negative Act*, in *Futurist Performance*, ed. Michael Kirby, trans. Victoria Nes Kirby, 268. Unless otherwise noted, further page references to Futurist plays will appear parenthetically and refer to this volume.

2. *Sintesi* is both the singular and the plural form. Unlike its English cognate *synthesis*, the word *sintesi* refers not only to a fusion of simple essential elements into an amalgamated unit, but also to an abbreviated summary of an idea or position, and by extension, any brief schematic account. In what follows, I use Futurist and Futurism to refer to the Italian branch of the heterogeneous international movement. While Russian Futurism and Constructivism also led to many productive reforms in theater, their theater was not primarily characterized by an impulse toward compression.

3. Gunter Berghaus, *Italian Futurist Theatre*, 6–7.

4. Mario Verdone, *Teatro del tempo futurista*, 2nd ed. (Rome: Bulzoni Editore, 1988), 165.

5. For more on Parks and the Neo-Futurists, see chapter 5. For Futurism's imaginative protagonists, see Mario Scaparro, *The Improvised Balloon* and *The Rainbow of Italy*, in Kirby, *Futurist Performance*, 305, 306.

6. Filippo Marinetti, Emilio Settimelli, and Bruno Corra, "The Futurist Synthetic Theater," *Let's Murder the Moonshine*, 132. I quote Flint's translation here because I prefer his literal handling of the pun in the original between *atti* (acts) and *attimi* (moments). Subsequent citations from the manifesto will appear parenthetically, and refer to "The Futurist Synthetic Theater," in Lawrence Rainey, *Futurism: An Anthology*, ed. Rainey, Christine Poggi, and Laura Wittman, trans. Rainey (New Haven: Yale University Press, 2009), 204–9 (hereafter abbreviated FST).

7. Three related manifestos are less relevant to the question of brevity: "The Manifesto of Futurist Playwrights: The Pleasure of Being Booed," (1910) about Futurist evenings (*serate*), which at this early date did not yet include plays; "Futurist Scenography" (1915), Prampolini's call for a genuinely abstract and expressive scenography (one that was rarely realized during the *sintesi* tours);

and "Dynamic and Synoptic Declamation," (1916) which outlines Futurist rules for recitation.

8. Puchner, "Introduction," *Poetry of the Revolution: Marx, Manifestos, and the Avant-Gardes* (Princeton: Princeton University Press, 2006), 4.

9. Marinetti would later describe theatrical activity in Egypt in the 1920s as "theatricality without theater" (*teatralità senza teatro*). "Il fascino dell'Egito" in *Teoria e invenzione futurista* (Milan: Arnoldo Mondadori, 1968), 1086.

10. Joseph Cary: "The distinguishing feature of the plays themselves was, of course, their brevity. Otherwise they were quite unremarkable." "Futurism and the French Avant-Garde," *Modern Philology* 57, no. 2 (Nov 1959), 117.

11. Taylor, *Futurism: Politics, Painting and Performance*, University Studies in the Fine Arts 8, The Avant-Garde (Ann Arbor, MI: UMI Research Press, 1979), 40.

12. Günter Berghaus's *Italian Futurist Theatre* offers a valuable history of the variety of Futurist theatrical practice but does not attempt close analyses of the *sintesi*. The chapter of Michael Kirby's *Futurist Performance* on the synthetic theater (41–65) catalogs tendencies but does not linger over individual plays. R. S. Gordon's article "The Italian Futurist Theatre: A Reappraisal," *The Modern Language Review* 85, no. 2 (April 1990), 349–61, proposes a useful rubric for categorizing the *sintesi*'s variety but remains primarily taxonomic rather than meditative. An unpublished dissertation by Georgiana O'Keefe Bazzoni, "Avant-garde Italian Drama: Futurists, 'i grotteschi,' and Pirandello" (PhD diss., City University of New York, 1983) describes a number of the *sintesi* in detail, but rarely offers more than a cursory interpretation.

Italian and French critics offer more complete accounts of Futurist theater. See in particular Giovanni Antonucci, "Introduzione," in *Cronache del teatro futurista* (Rome: Ed. Abete, 1975), 11–29 and *Lo spettacolo futurista in Italia* (Rome: Studium, 1974); Umberto Artioli, *La scena e la dynamis: Immaginario e struttura nelle sintesi futuriste* (Bologna: Pàtron, 1975); Milli Graffi, "L'angoscia della mancanza del comico nei futuristi e l'insperata soluzione del motto de spirito," *Es* 14 (Sept-Dec 1980), 75–92; Lia Lapini, *Il teatro futurista italiano* (Milan: Mursia, 1977); Jeffrey Schnapp's introduction to Marinetti, *Teatro*, vol 1. (Milan: Mondadori, 2004; Mario Verdone, *Teatro del tempo futurista*, 2nd ed. (Rome: Bulzoni Editore, 1988), 99–157; and especially Giovanni Lista, *La scène futuriste* (Paris, 1989), 185–226. Lia Lapini's article "Il teatro futurista italiano dalla teoria alla pratica," in Alessandro Tinterri, *Il teatro italiano dal naturalismo a Pirandello* (Bologna: Il Mulino, 1990): 249–64, comes to several conclusions that parallel my own: Marinetti's innovations often resemble other European theater movements, and the Futurists remain overly committed to a theatrical system they aimed to overthrow. Since my Italian is basic, I am indebted to my research assistant Chiara Montanari for familiarizing me with the Italian criticism and for translating selected articles as well as dozens of *sintesi* not yet published in English.

13. Gordon Ramsay, "Simultaneity and Compenetration in *sintesi* of the Italian Futurists," in *Futurist Dramaturgy and Performance*, ed. Paul J. Stoesser (New York: Legas, 2011) 45–56.

14. RoseLee Goldberg, for instance, begins *Performance Art: From Futurism to*

the Present (New York: Thames & Hudson, 2001) by suggesting that the "performative turn" begins around 1910 with the Futurist *serate*. Goldberg's focus on those elements of Futurist performance that anticipate later performance art programmatically downplays the importance of texts for the movement. Similarly, Steve Dixon's chapter on Futurism in his *Digital Performance: A History of New Media in Theater, Dance, Performance Art, and Installation* (Cambridge, MA: MIT Press, 2007) argues that the ancestry of digital performance forms is "precisely and inextricably linked to the philosophies, aesthetics, and practices of the Futurist movement," and goes on to outline the parallels (47).

15. Marinetti championed performance events that exceeded and trumped their scripted content. Futurist *serate* (evenings) in particular bear some resemblance to Dada and surrealist happenings, as well as those of Allan Kaprow and his peers later in the century. Like later performance art, Futurist theater often advocated improvisation, insisted on the dissolution of barriers between performers and the audience, and blurred the borders between theater and other arts.

16. R. S. Gordon, "Italian Futurist Theatre: A Reappraisal," 354.

17. Filippo Marinetti, "The Pleasure of Being Booed," trans. Rainey, in *Futurism: An Anthology*, 97.

18. "Birth of a Futurist Aesthetic," in Marinetti, *Critical Writings*, ed. Günter Berghaus, trans. Doug Thompson (New York: Farrar, Strauss, 2006), 250.

19. "Destruction of Syntax—Radio Imagination—Words-in-Freedom," trans. Rainey, *Futurism*, 143.

20. Jeffrey Schnapp, "Crash: Speed as Engine of Individuation," *Modernism/Modernity* 6, no. 1 (1999): 1–49.

21. "The New Ethical Religion of Speed," in F. T. Marinetti, *Critical Writings*, 258.

22. "Founding and Manifesto of Futurism," trans. Rainey, in *Futurism*, 50.

23. "The New Ethical Religion of Speed," in Marinetti, *Critical Writings*, 256.

24. "Destruction of Syntax," trans. Rainey, *Futurism*, 143.

25. Simmel, "The Metropolis and Mental Life," 421.

26. Strindberg, "On Modern Drama," 85.

27. Berghaus, *Italian Futurist Theatre*, 177–78. This taxonomic division obscures the fascinating way these divergent goals cross-pollinate in Futurist shorts. For one, it ignores plays that would seem to put the authors in the wrong category, such as Marinetti's *A Landscape Heard*, whose only characters are the sound of water and the sound of fire or, by contrast, Corra and Settimelli's plays *Faced with the Infinite, Passatismo* (Pastism), *Negative Act, Sempronio's Lunch*, and *Toward Victory*, all of which feature recognizable human characters in standard settings. More important, such a division distracts attention from the possibility that abstraction and verisimilitude are not necessarily at odds.

28. Franco Casavola, "Theater of Dilated Instants," in Giovanni Lista, *Théâtre futuriste italien*, trans. Giovanni Lista and Claude Minot, vol. 2 (Paris: L'Age D'Homme, 1990), 192–93, my translation from the French.

29. Roman Jakobson, *Noveishaia russkaia poeziia* (*The Most Recent Russian Poetry*, 1919). Quoted in Matteo D'Ambrosio, *Roman Jakobson e il futurismo italiano*

(Napoli: Liguori, 2009), 125. Jakobson's claim came to my attention through Harsha Ram's translation in his lecture, "Futurist Geographies: Uneven Modernities and the Struggle for Aesthetic Autonomy: Paris, Italy, Russia, 1909–1914," Yale Comparative Literature Department, February 17, 2009.

30. I use Richard Pioli's translation of the manifesto title, "Destruction of Syntax—Wireless Imagination—Words-in-Freedom," in *Stung by Salt and War: The Creative Texts of the Italian Avant-Gardist F. T. Marinetti*, ed. and trans. Richard Pioli (New York: Peter Lang, 1987), 45–54, because unlike Thompson's ("Untrammeled Imagination"), it captures the allusion to wireless telegraphy in Marinetti's phrase "Immaginazione senza fili."

31. "Destruction of Syntax," Rainey, *Futurism*, 145. Although the Futurists, in their relentless contemporaneity, cite the wireless telegraph as the inspiration for "words-in-freedom," newspaper *faits-divers* like Fénéon's had already made radical journalistic economy a familiar mode.

32. Domenico Pietropaolo, "The Dramaturgy of Simultaneity," in *Futurist Dramaturgy and Performance*, ed. Paul J. Stoesser (New York: Legas, 2011), 37–44.

33. Pietropaolo, "Dramaturgy," 40.

34. Mario Carli, *Violenza, sinfonia* (Violence: A Symphony), in *Teatro futurista italiano*, double issue of *Sipario* 260 (Dec 1967), 68. This translation by Chiara Montanari.

35. Carli, *Violenza, sinfonia*, 68.

36. Mario Dessy, *Vite* (Lives), in Verdone, *Teatro del tempo futurista*, trans. here by Chiara Montanari, 69.

37. Giacomo Balla et al, "The Exhibitors to the Public" (February, 1912), in Rainey, *Futurism*, trans. Rainey, 107.

38. William Shakespeare, *As You Like It*, 3.2.279.

39. Henri Bergson, *Laughter: An Essay on the Meaning of the Comic* (New York: Macmillan, 1911).

40. "Time and Theatre," in *Shakespeare, Theatre, and Time* (New York: Routledge, 2011), 12–33.

41. Reinhart Koselleck, *Zeitschichten: Studien zur Historik* (Frankfurt: Suhrkamp Verlag, 2000), 22. Koselleck redeploys the phrase from Ernst Bloch.

42. Bergson, "Duration and Simultaneity," in *Henri Bergson: Key Writings*, ed. Keith Ansell Pearson and John Mullarkey (New York: Continuum, 2002), 206.

43. "Variety Theater," in Marinetti, *Critical Writings*, 187; "Futurist Synthetic Theater," in *Futurism: An Anthology*, 208.

44. "Variety Theater," in Marinetti, *Critical Writings*, 187.

45. See the manifesto "La nuova religione-morale della velocità" (The New Religion-Morality of Speed), *L'Italia futurista* 1 (11 May 1916), *Europeana 1914–1918*.

46. "Variety Theater," in Marinetti, *Critical Writings*, 186.

47. Bruno Corra, *L'arte Nuova della Nuova Italia* (Milan: Studio Editoriale Lombardo, 1918), 170. Quoted in Kirby, *FP*, 25.

48. Quoted in Charles Castle, *The Folies Bergère* (London, 1984), 28.

49. Marinetti became intoxicated with the potential of variety and cabaret shows during his frequent visits to Paris beginning in his student days, as well as on a 1912 visit to Berlin (home at that time to more than eighty variety theaters and cabarets), and trips to London in 1910, 1913, and 1914.

50. "Variety Theater," *Murder the Moonshine,* 129. He did not follow through on the promise, although he once collaborated with several Russian actors to devise a three-minute version of *Hamlet* as a rehearsal exercise, and Angelo Rognoni wrote a three-line version, which I discuss later in the chapter. Marinetti's suggestion would be fulfilled near the end of the twentieth century by the The Reduced Shakespeare Company's two-hour comic condensation, *The Complete Works of Wllm Shakespeare (Abridged).* For more on the Reduced Shakespeare Company, see chapter 5.

51. Angelo Rognoni, *Hamlet.* In Lista, *Théâtre futuriste italien,* 1:226, my translation.

52. Lista, *La Scène futuriste,* 1: 72, my translation.

53. Enrico Novelli, *La Nazione,* Florence: March 10, 1916. in Antonucci, *Cronache del Teatro Futurista,* 105. Trans. here by Chiara Montanari.

54. Anonymous, *Il Secolo XIX,* Genova, February 23, 1915, in Antonucci, *Cronache del teatro futurista,* 95. Trans. here by Chiara Montanari.

55. Anonymous, *Il Secolo,* Milan, April 2, 1920, in Antonucci, *Cronache del teatro futurista,* 139. Trans. here by Chiara Montanari.

56. Ettore Albini, *Avanti!,* Milan, April 2–3 1920, in Antonucci, *Cronache del teatro futurista,* 141. Trans. here by Chiara Montanari. Mirbeau published in 1904 a collection of six comic one-act morality plays, *Farces et moralités* (Fasquelle, 1904), which use acceleration and exaggeration to satirize conventional thinking.

57. Renato Simoni, *Corriere della Sera,* Milan, April 2, 1920, reprinted in Antonucci, *Cronache del teatro futurista,* 139. Trans. here by Chiara Montanari.

58. Lista comes to a similar conclusion in *La Scène Futuriste,* 185.

59. Lista, *La Scène Futuriste,* 187.

60. "Drammi futuristi al Teatro Vittorio Emanuele di Ancona," *Corriere della Sera,* 2 Feb 1915. Quoted in Berghaus, *Italian Futurist Theatre,* 195.

61. P.B. in *L'Eco di Bergamo,* 20 February 1915, in Antonucci, *Cronache del teatro futurista.* Trans. here by Chiara Montanari.

62. Pastism is my translation. Victoria Kirby's rendering of this title as *Old Age* is somewhat curious in light of the frequent use of the word "passatismo" in Futurist writings to mean "pastism," "passéism" or "traditionalism." The story is not about old age per se, but about the premature senescence of anyone stuck in the past.

63. Virginia Woolf, "Mrs. Bennett and Mr. Brown" (London: Hogarth Press, 1928), 4.

64. Georgiana O'Keefe Bazzoni, "Avant-garde Italian Drama: Futurists, 'i grotteschi,' and Pirandello," PhD diss. (City University of New York, 1983), 87. R. S. Gordon makes a similar point ("Italian Futurist Theatre: A Reappraisal," 355).

65. Samuel Beckett, *Endgame,* in *DW,* 95.

66. Orson Welles and Peter Bogdanovich, *This is Orson Welles,* ed. Jonathan Rosenbaum (New York: HarperCollins Publishers, 1992), 51.

67. Michael Kirby points out that the extreme brevity of the *sintesi* forestalls dramatic absorption, "making the compression of the *sintesi* into a rejection of the drama itself" (*FP,* 53). Kirby views such "aesthetic nihilism" as a precursor to Dada's more explicitly anti-art performances.

68. Aronson, "Avant-garde Scenography," in Ackerman and Puchner, eds., *Against Theater*, 31.

69. Puchner, *Stage Fright*, 7.

70. "The Pleasure of Being Booed," in Rainey, *Futurism*, 121.

71. *Teatro sintetico futurista*, trans. Doug Thompson as "A Futurist Theater of Essential Brevity," in Marinetti, *Critical Writings*, 204.

72. Ibid., 183.

73. "The Variety Theater," in Rainey, *Futurism*, 163.

74. Ibid.

75. See "Killing Time: Guns and the Play of Predictability on the Modern Stage," chapter 4 of Andrew Sofer, *The Stage Life of Props* (Ann Arbor: University of Michigan Press, 2003), 167–202.

76. Sofer, *The Stage Life of Props*, 70.

77. A spectator of Émile Augier's 1855 boulevard drama *Olympe's Marriage* claimed, "Voilà un coup de pistolet qui tuera la pièce!" ("That pistol shot will kill the play!") Stephen S. Stanton, *Camille and Other Plays* (New York: Hill and Wang, 1957), xxxiii. Quoted in Sofer, *Stage Life*, 169. *Detonation*'s shot both gives birth to the play and kills it.

78. "Technical Manifesto of Futurist Literature," *Critical Writings*, 111.

79. Aristotle, *Aristotle's Poetics*, ed. Francis Ferguson, trans. Samuel H. Butcher (New York: Macmillan, 1961), 62–63.

80. I am indebted to Laura Wittman for the observation that Futurist texts convert action into myth. Wittman, "Introduction to Part Three: Stars-in-Freedom and the Dark Night of Futurism," in Rainey, *Futurism*, 418.

81. Samuel Beckett, *Waiting for Godot*, in *DW*, 1.

82. Samuel Beckett, *Endgame*, in *DW*, 100.

83. André Breton, *Manifestoes of Surrealism*, trans. Richard Seaver and Helen R. Lane (Ann Arbor: University of Michigan Press, 1972), 125.

84. Burden, Chris, *Shoot* in *Documentation of Selected Works (1971–1974)* (New York: Electronic Arts Intermix, 1971–1975), archived at UbuWeb Film & Video, accessed August 19, 2015, http://archive.is/5eHY

85. Futurist Synthetic Theater manifesto, translated by Doug Thompson as "A Futurist Theater of Essential Brevity," in Marinetti, *Critical Writings*, 205.

86. Berghaus, *Italian Futurist Theatre*, 142–43.

87. Francesco Pratella, *Autobiografia* (Milan: Pan, 1971), 120. Quoted in and translated by Berghaus, *Italian Futurist Theatre*, 143.

88. Neil Blackadder, *Performing Opposition: Modern Theater and the Scandalized Audience* (Westport, CT: Praeger, 2003), xi.

89. For more details on these tours, see Berghaus, *Italian Futurist Theatre*, 187–231. Lia Lapini makes a similar argument in "Il teatro futurista italiano dalla teoria alla practice," (Alessando Tinterri, ed., *Il teatro italiano dal naturalismo a Pirandello* [Bologna: Il Mulino, 1990]: 249–64.): Futurist theater failed to deliver a revolution in theatrical form because it relied on theater institutions already in place rather than creating new ones, and because it lacked designers and actors with the training or preparation to realize the radically new performance styles they envisioned.

90. Gordon mentions that *sintesi* are regressive compared to the *serate* and compared to their calls for total freedom. "Reappraisal," 352.

91. Matei Calinescu, *Five Faces of Modernity: Modernism, Avant-garde, Decadence, Kitsch, Postmodernism*, 2nd ed. (Durham, NC: Duke University Press, 1987), 124.

92. For Deleuze, ". . . modern painting is invaded and besieged by photographs and clichés that are already lodged on the canvas before the painter even begins to work. In fact, it would be a mistake to think that the painter works on a white and virgin surface. The entire surface is already invested virtually with all kinds of clichés, which the painter will have to break with." *Francis Bacon: The Logic of Sensation*, trans. Daniel W. Smith (New York: Continuum, 1981), 10–11.

93. Karen Jürs-Munby, introduction to Lehmann, *Postdramatic Theater*, 10.

94. Christine Poggi, *Inventing Futurism*.

CHAPTER 4

1. Beckett, *Endgame*, in *Dramatic Works*, vol. 3, *Samuel Beckett: The Grove Centenary Edition*, ed. Paul Auster (New York: Grove, 2006), 133. Hereafter, unless otherwise indicated, references to Beckett's plays will refer to this edition and appear parenthetically, abbreviated *DW*.

2. Knowlson and Pilling, *Frescoes of the Skull* (London: John Calder, 1979), 127.

3. Psalm 144:4, *New Oxford Annotated Bible*, New York: Oxford University Press, 1977.

4. Herbert Blau, "Apnea and True Illusion: Breath(less) in Beckett." *Modern Drama* 49, no. 4 (Winter 2006): 454.

5. Daniel Albright, *Beckett and Aesthetics* (Cambridge: Cambridge University Press, 2003), 1–8.

6. Martin Harries, "Theater and Media Before 'New' Media," *Theater* 42, no. 2 (Jan 2012): 7–25.

7. On the transvestitism of Beckett's media, see Albright 7–8, as well as Brater, *Beyond Minimalism: Beckett's Late Style in the Theater* (New York: Oxford University Press, 1987), 3–17; Esslin, "Toward the Zero of Language," in *Beckett's Later Fiction and Drama: Texts for Company*, eds. Acheson and Arthur (London: Macmillan Press, 1987): 35–49; Therese Fischer-Seidel, "'The Ineluctable Modality of the Visible': Perception and Genre in Samuel Beckett's Later Drama," *Contemporary Literature* 35, no. 1 (Spring 1994): 66–82; and S. E. Gontarski's "De-theatricalizing Theatre: The Post-*Play* Plays," introduction to *The Shorter Plays*, vol. 2, *The Theatrical Notebooks of Samuel Beckett* (New York: Grove Press, 1999), xv–xxix.

8. Book-length studies include Enoch Brater's excellent *Beyond Minimalism*, James Knowlson and John Pilling's *Frescoes of the Skull*, and Anna McMullan's *Theatre on Trial: Samuel Beckett's Later Drama* (New York: Routledge, 1993). Essay collections on the later work include, most notably, *Beckett's Later Fiction*

and Drama: Texts for Company, ed. James Acheson and Kateryna Arthur (London: Macmillan, 1987), and Robin Davis and Lance St. John Butler's *"Make Sense Who May": Essays on Samuel Beckett's Later Works* (Gerrards Cross, Bucks [Ireland]: C. Smythe, 1988).

See also Sidney Homan's *Beckett's Theaters: Interpretations for Performance* (Lewisburg, PA: Bucknell University Press, 1984); Ruby Cohn's *Just Play: Beckett's Theater*; and Jonathan Kalb's essential study, *Beckett in Performance*, especially "Considerations of Acting in the Late Plays," (48–68). S. E. Gontarski's "De-theatricalizing Theatre: The Post-*Play* Plays," the introduction to *The Shorter Plays*, vol. 2, *The Theatrical Notebooks of Samuel Beckett* (New York: Grove Press, 1999), xv–xxix, concisely summarizes the ways Beckett's notes and revisions in the notebooks reveal his drive toward visual concision. From among the many articles on the subject, several stand out. David Pattie's "Space, Time and the Self in Beckett's Late Theater," *Modern Drama* 43, no. 3 (2000): 393–404, argues that Beckett's late plays fragment subjectivity through the incorporation of electronic media in ways that replace the temporal and spatial conventions of his earlier work—which collapsed performance time and fictional time into a shared present—with a more ambiguous mixture of absence and presence. Keir Elam deftly traces the visual echoes of Dante in the late plays in "Dead Heads: Damnation-Narration in the *Dramaticules*," in the *Cambridge Companion to Beckett*, ed. John Pilling (Cambridge: Cambridge University Press, 1994), 145–66.

9. Cohn, *Just Play: Beckett's Theater* (Princeton: Princeton University Press, 1980), 13.

10. Yeats, "Certain Noble Plays of Japan," in *Essays and Introductions* (New York: Collier Books, 1961), 235; *Ohio Impromptu*, in *Dramatic Writings*, 476. Margaret Rose's *The Symbolist Theatre Tradition from Maeterlinck and Yeats to Beckett* (Milan: Unicopoli, 1989) argues convincingly that Beckett is a latter-day symbolist. Rosemary Pountney also connects the "spare, stylized" form of Yeats's plays for dancers, which Beckett quite admired, to Beckett's drama. *Theatre of Shadows: Samuel Beckett's Drama 1956–76* (Gerrards Cross, Buckinghamshire: Colin Smythe, 1988), 2.

11. For more on the Futurist plays, *Waiting*, *Lights!*, and *Passatismo*, see chapter 3.

12. Among the many sources that follow this line of interpretation is Herbert Blau, "Apnea and True Illusion: Breath(less) in Beckett," which describes Beckett's "microphysics of misery" (457).

13. For the fragmentation of subjectivity, see Pattie, "Space, Time, and the Self in Beckett's Late Theatre." For more on Beckett's "memory plays," see Jeanette Malkin, *Memory-Theater and Postmodern Drama* (Ann Arbor: University of Michigan Press, 1999).

14. Anna McMullan concludes that Beckett's theater "offers a rigorous interrogation of the languages and strategies of theatrical presentation and signification" because the audience "is forced to actively participate in the construction or 'deconstruction' of signification." McMullan, "Samuel Beckett as Director: The Art of Mastering Failure," *Cambridge Companion to Samuel Beckett* (New York: Cambridge University Press, 1994), 203. See also Anna McMullan, *Theater on Trial: Samuel Beckett's Later Drama* (New York: Routledge, 1993);

Charles Lyons, "Beckett's Fundamental Theater: The Plays from *Not I* to *What Where*," in *Beckett's Later Fiction and Drama: Texts for Company*, ed. James Acheson (Basingstoke, Hampshire: Macmillan, 1987): 80–97; Richard Gilman, *The Making of Modern Drama* (New York: Farrar, Straus and Giroux, 1972), 266; and Brater, *Beyond Minimalism*, 3–17.

15. Albright, *Beckett and Aesthetics*, 80.

16. Albert Camus, "The Myth of Sisyphus," in *The Myth of Sisyphus and Other Essays*, trans. Justin O'Brien (New York: Vintage Books, 1991), 1–138. Originally published in French as *Le Mythe de Sisyphe* by Librairie Gallimard, 1942.

17. Samuel Beckett to Barney Rosset, 27 August 1957, in *The Letters of Samuel Beckett*, vol. 3, 1957–1965, ed. George Craig, Martha Dow Fehsenfeld, Dan Gunn, and Lois More Overbeck (Cambridge: Cambridge University Press, 2014), 64.

18. Joseph Chaikin, *The Presence of the Actor* (New York: Theatre Communications Group, 1993), 67.

19. See Harries, "Theater and Media," 20–21.

20. *The Buried Temple* (1902), trans. Alfred Sutro (New York: Dodd, Mead & Co., 1904), 135–36.

21. Harries, "Theater and Media," 13–14.

22. Beckett, quoted in Haerdter, "Endgame: A Rehearsal Diary," in *Beckett in the Theatre*, 230–31.

23. Indeed it was written for the Sadler's Wells-trained dancer and clown Deryk Mendel. James Knowlson, *Damned to Fame: The Life of Samuel Beckett* (New York: Simon & Schuster, 1996), 377.

24. Ibid.

25. Therese Fischer-Seidel's article "'The Ineluctable Modality of the Visible': Perception and Genre in Beckett's Later Drama" characterizes the late plays as an exploration of a fundamental duality of (verbal) dramatic representation: the coexistence of spoken language and extralinguistic action. Similarly, Martin Esslin claims that Beckett's later stage pieces abstract and isolate theater's image-making potential, its ability to present to the eyes a "concretised metaphor where the story of a play suddenly coagulates in one unforgettable poetic image: Lear, naked, raging against the storm; the Pope being dressed in *The Life of Galileo*; Hedda Gabler burning the manuscript; the red carpet being unrolled for Agamemnon; Oedipus blinded." Esslin, "Towards the Zero of Language," 47.

26. As Lisa Gitelman has written, "It's not just that each new medium represents its predecessors, as McLuhan noted long ago, but rather, as Rick Altman elaborates, that media represent and delimit representing, so that new medium provides new sites for the ongoing and vernacular experiences of representation as such." Lisa Gitelman, "Introduction: Media as Historical Subjects," in *Always Already New: Media, History, and the Data of Culture* (Cambridge, MA: MIT Press, 2008), 4.

27. Martin Puchner, "Samuel Beckett: Actors in Barrels and Gestures in the Text," in *Stage Fright: Modernism, Anti-theatricality and Drama* (Baltimore: Johns Hopkins University Press, 2002), 157.

28. Beckett, *Worstward Ho*, in *Samuel Beckett: The Grove Centenary Edition*, ed. Paul Auster, vol. 3, *Poems, Short Fictions, Criticism* (New York: Grove, 2006), 482.

29. *Dream of Fair to Middling Women, Murphy, Watt, Mercier and Camier*. Beckett suppressed the manuscript for *Eleuthéria,* and it remained unpublished until after his death. For a summary of Beckett's involvement with theater before the 1950s, see the opening pages of Rosemary Pountney, *Theatre of Shadows: Samuel Beckett's Drama, 1956–1976* (Colin Smythe, 1998), 1–4.

30. Quoted in Brater, 176.

31. *Molloy,* in *Samuel Beckett: The Grove Centenary Edition,* ed. Paul Auster, vol. 2, *Novels II.* (New York: Grove, 2006), 63–64. Further page references appear parenthetically, abbreviated *M.*

32. *Malone Dies,* in *Novels II,* 252. Further page references appear parenthetically.

33. Audrey Wasser, "From Figure to Fissure: Beckett's *Molloy, Malone Dies,* and *The Unnamable," Modern Philology* 109, no. 2 (November 2011): 261.

34. Bruno Clément, *L'Oeuvre sans qualités: Rhétorique de Samuel Beckett* (Paris: Éditions du Seuil, 1994), 423, qtd. and trans. in Wasser, 262.

35. Haerdter, "Endgame: A Rehearsal Diary," in *Beckett in the Theatre,* 230–31.

36. Samuel Beckett and Alan Schneider, *No Author Better Served: The Correspondence of Samuel Beckett & Alan Schneider* (Cambridge, MA: Harvard University Press, 1998), 24.

37. Samuel Beckett to Rosette Lamont, "New Beckett Plays: A Darkly Brilliant Evening," *Other Stages* (June 16, 1983): 3.

38. Samuel Beckett, *Disjecta: Miscellaneous Writings and a Dramatic Fragment* (New York: Grove Press, 1984), 103.

39. Beckett, *Worstward Ho,* in *Nohow On: Three Novels* (New York: Grove Press, 1995), 91.

40. *Watt,* in *Samuel Beckett: The Grove Centenary Edition,* ed. Paul Auster, vol. 1, *Novels I.* (New York: Grove, 2006), 297.

41. Zola, "Naturalism on the Stage," in *Playwrights on Playwriting,* ed. Toby Cole, trans. Samuel Draper (New York: Hill and Wang, 1960), 7.

42. Beckett, *Happy Days* (New York, Grove Press, 1994), 52.

43. Anyone who takes real-world disability seriously could question the logic of Beckett's fetishization of impairment. Without defending his thematization of physical disability, I interpret his sympathetic representations of restriction as reflections of a philosophical worldview that in theory pertains to anyone.

44. Beckett in conversation with Michael Haerdter during rehearsals of *Waiting for Godot* in Berlin in 1975, recorded by Haerdter in "Endgame: A Rehearsal Diary," in *Beckett in the Theatre,* 231 (emphasis added).

45. Johan Huizinga, *Homo Ludens: A Study of the Play Element of Culture* (New York: Beacon Press, 1971), 10.

46. Beckett famously explained in an interview in 1956 (the year he was writing *Endgame, All That Fall,* and *Act without Words I* and *II*), that, "The more Joyce knew the more he could. He's tending toward omniscience and omnipotence as an artist. I'm working with impotence, ignorance. I don't think impotence has been exploited in the past. There seems to be a kind of esthetic axiom that expression is an achievement—must be an achievement. My little exploration is

that whole zone of being that has always been set aside by artists as something unusable—as something by definition incompatible with art." ("Moody Man of Letters: A Portrait of Samuel Beckett, Author of the Puzzling 'Waiting for Godot'," by Israel Shenker, *New York Times*, May 6, 1956.) Where Proust and Joyce inherited and updated an encyclopedic renaissance tradition, Beckett was anti-encyclopedic.

47. Martin Esslin, symposium on *Rockaby*. Quoted in Brater, 5.

48. Herbert Blau, *Sails of the Herring Fleet: Essays on Beckett* (Ann Arbor: University of Michigan Press, 2000), 8.

49. Vivian Mercier comes to a very similar conclusion in *Beckett/Beckett* (New York: Oxford University Press, 1977): "I am prepared to argue that the brevity of the later works is due not to any philosophical aspiration towards silence but to . . . perfectionism: the only perfectly finished piece of workmanship is the miniature" (237).

50. Schneider "Any Way You Like, Alan: Working with Beckett." *Theater Quarterly*, 5, no. 19 (Sept 1975): 35.

51. Interview with Lois Overbeck, *Women in Beckett: Critical Perspectives*, ed. Linda Ben-Zvi, 53, 52.

52. Quoted in Schneider, "Any Way You Like," 35–36.

53. Samuel Beckett to Alan Schneider, April 30, 1957, reprinted in *Disjecta*, 108.

54. Beckett, *Ill Seen Ill Said*, in *Samuel Beckett: The Grove Centenary Edition*, ed. Paul Auster, vol. 4, *Poems/Short Fiction/Criticism* (New York: Grove, 2006).

55. The sublime need not be enormous and can just as well be microscopic, as Terry Eagleton explains: "It's the farcically meager as much as the portentously boundless. . . . Samuel Beckett's degree-zero writing, which is as thin as is compatible with being just perceptible, and which shares with Swift a savage delight in diminishment, is sublime in just this sense. It seems continually surprised to find itself doing anything as importunate as actually existing . . ." (Eagleton, "Beckett and Nothing," in *Reflections on Beckett: A Centenary Celebration*, ed. Anna McMullan and S. E. Wilmer [Ann Arbor: University of Michigan Press, 2009], 33.)

56. Shenker, "Moody Man."

57. *Worstward Ho*, in *Poems/Short Fiction/Criticism*, 479.

58. *Company*, in *Poems/Short Fiction/Criticism*, 448.

59. Knowlson, *Damned to Fame*, 343.

60. Beckett, *Waiting for Godot*, in *Dramatic Works*, 40.

61. This line of argument is indebted to Steven Connor's article "Slow Going," *Yearbook of English Studies* 30 (2000), which argues that Beckett's manipulations that "trick duration into rhythm" express his "need to pucker up the agony of unrelieved elapse into something calculable and roughly predictable" (156).

62. Beckett's plays are characterized by what Terry Eagleton has called "exquisitely sculpted" vacancy. Eagleton, "Beckett and Nothing," 38.

63. Cohn, "At This Moment in Time" in *Just Play*, 34–57.

64. Cohn, "At This Moment."

65. Quoted in *Beckett in the Theatre: The Author as Practical Playwright and Di-*

rector, eds. Dougald McMillan and Martha Fehsenfeld, vol. 1 (New York: River-run Press, 1988), 231.

66. *The Unnamable*, in *Novels II, 383.*

67. Michael Worton, "*Waiting for Godot* and *Endgame*: Theatre as Text," in *Cambridge Companion to Samuel Beckett*, ed. John Pilling (New York: Cambridge University Press, 1994), 80.

68. Trinity College Dublin MS 10967/42, quoted in Matthew Feldman, *Beckett's Books: A Cultural History of the Interwar Notes* (London: Continuum, 2006), 34, emphasis added.

69. Letter to Alan Schneider, Nov 21, 1957, in Beckett and Schneider, *No Author Better Served*, 23.

70. "Minimalist music rejects segmentation and the temporal function of music. One can no longer distinguish either beginning or end; nor development, introduction, or other musical functions linked to temporality. Music has definitively become a machine to stop time" (Eero Tarasti, "Le Minimalisme du point de vue sémiotique," *Degrés: Revue de Synthèse à Orientation Sémiologique* 53 [1988]: 115. Qtd. and trans. Warren Motte, *Small Worlds: Minimalism in Contemporary French Literature* [Lincoln: University of Nebraska Press, 1999], 20.)

71. Calvin Tomkins, *The Bride and the Bachelors: Five Masters of the Avant-Garde* (New York: Penguin, 1962), 104.

72. The original script called for seven steps, but Beckett revised it to nine, apparently so as better to coordinate with the spoken lines timed to the steps.

73. James Joyce, *Ulysses* (New York: Vintage, 1986), 3.11–13.

74. Gotthold Ephraim Lessing, *Laocoön*, trans. Edward Allen McCormick (Indianapolis, Bobbs-Merrill, 1962), 77.

75. Samuel Beckett, quoted in "Addenda to *Footfalls*," Disc 2, *Beckett on Film*, DVD, prod. Michael Colgan (London: Blue Angel Films, 2001).

76. Samuel Beckett, *Texts for Nothing*, 9, in *Poems/Short Fiction/Criticism*, 325.

77. Labanotation is a comprehensive system for recording human movement as precisely as possible. The system was devised in the 1920s by Hungarian dance artist and theorist Rudolf Laban to preserve ballet choreography. Laban called the system "Kinetography"; it was renamed Labanotation by Ann Hutchison Guest in her 1977 volume, *Labanotation, or Kinetography Laban: The System of Analyzing and Recording Movement* (New York: Routledge, 1977).

78. Walter Asmus, "Rehearsal Notes for the German premiere of Beckett's *That Time* and *Footfalls* at the Schiller-Theater Werkstatt, Berlin," in *On Beckett*, ed. S. E. Gontarski (New York: Grove Press, 1986), 338.

79. Connor, "Slow Going," 163.

80. Richard Eyre, in "Addenda to Rockaby," Disc 4, *Beckett on Film*.

81. Jonathan Kalb, "Beckett after Beckett," *Salmagundi* 160/161 (Fall 2008/Winter 2009): 146, 149.

82. *Proust*, in *Poems/Short Fiction/Criticism*, 516–17.

83. Bastiaan Van Fraassen, "Time in Physical and Narrative Structure," in *Chronotypes: The Construction of Time*, ed. John Bender and David Wellbery (Stanford: Stanford University Press, 1991), 24.

84. Van Fraassen, 24, 34.

85. Letter to Alan Schneider, Oct 1, 1958, *No Author Better Served*, 29.

86. The inverse relationship between voice and lights, not clear from the script, is carefully outlined in Beckett's notes to Donald McWhinnie, the director of *That Time*'s premiere at the Royal Court. See Gontarski, ed., *The Theatrical Notebooks of Samuel Beckett*, vol. 2 (New York: Grove Press, 1999), 360, 365.

87. *Proust* in *Poems/Short Fiction/Criticism*, 515–16.

88. *DW*, 417; "solution, n.," *OED Online*, June 2015, Oxford University Press, accessed August 21, 2015. http://www.oed.com

89. Beckett in conversation with James Knowlson prior to the production of *That Time* in May 1976, quoted in Knowlson and Pilling, *Frescoes*, 219.

90. Reading University Library. MS 1639, quoted in Knowlson, *Frescoes*, 219.

91. Knowlson, *Frescoes*, 220.

92. Robert Cushman, review of "Play and Other Plays," In "Observer" (23 May 1976): 30. Rpt. in *Samuel Beckett: The Critical Heritage*, 343–44.

CHAPTER 5

Epigraph: Mark Ravenhill, introduction to *Shoot/Get Treasure/Repeat: An Epic Cycle of Short Plays* (London: Methuen, 2008), 5.

1. Caryl Churchill, *Secret*, in *Love and Information* (New York: Theatre Communications Group, 2013), 4. Further references appear parenthetically.

2. Kenneth Koch, "Very Rapid Acceleration: An Interview with Kenneth Koch," by John Tranter, *Jacket* 5 (1998), http://jacketmagazine.com/05/koch89.html/

3. Jon Jory, foreword to *More Ten-Minute Plays from the Actors Theatre of Louisville*, ed. Michael Bigelow Dixon (New York: Samuel French, 1992), vi.

4. The Actors Theatre of Louisville (ATL) invented the ten-minute play marathon in 1989 in order to solve a practical difficulty: too many scripts and too little time. Inundated by an annual flood of full-length submissions, ATL established the National Ten-Minute Play Contest and in the same year altered the submission requirements for the Humana Festival of New American Plays to allow ten-minute pieces. By fostering an artificially restricted dramatic genre, the ATL found a solution for their literary team that brought a number of secondary benefits. Ten-minute play contests allowed the theater quickly to identify promising new talent, and festivals featuring the best work provided a budget-friendly way to audition new playwrights' work in front of audiences who greet the form with refreshingly generous expectations. The short scripts also helped the ATL quickly train interns in script evaluation and provided non-strenuous but satisfying work for amateur actors. Today, the Actors Theatre, together with their co-administrators, City Theatre of Miami, reads about 1,300 entries a year to the National Ten-Minute Play Contest. In other words, the Actors Theatre's invention of a new compressed dramatic form was an institutional strategy to manage one kind of information overload. The popularity of longer one-act plays, the staple of the Humana Festival, had contributed to an increasingly democratized playwriting culture that spawned more scripts than theaters were equipped to read. Ironically, though, the ten-minute play

form has arguably exacerbated the difficulty it was invented to solve. By further lowering the perceived difficulty of writing a play, the form allowed almost anyone to fancy him or herself a playwright and allowed others to keep writing when they might otherwise have given up.

5. Jay David Bolter and Richard Grusin, *Remediation: Understanding New Media* (Cambridge, MA: MIT Press, 1999), 3–15.

6. Reduced Shakespeare Company Home Page, accessed August 21, 2015. http://www.reducedshakespeare.com/

7. Marinetti, "The Variety Theatre," in *CW*, 191.

8. Reduced Shakespeare Company, "We're Going to Washington," *Reduced Shakespeare Company Blog*, Dec 16, 2007, accessed Jan 18, 2010, http://blogs.myspace.com/reducedshakespeare (site discontinued).

9. See, for example, the annual Boston Theater Marathon produced by Boston Playwrights' Theatre ("Boston Theater Marathon," *Boston Playwrights' Theatre*, accessed August 23, 2015, http://www.bu.edu/bpt/our-programs/boston-theatre-marathon/); the Short + Sweet Festival based in Sydney, Australia, which has expanded its showcases of ten-minute plays to locations including Penang and Manila ("Our Mission," *Short + Sweet*, accessed August 23, 2015, http://www.shortandsweet.org/our-mission); and Gi60, an international festival of one-minute plays performed each year in New York and the UK ("Gi60, The International One Minute Theatre Festival, 2004–2014," *Gi60*, accessed August 23, 2015, http//:gi60.blogspot.com).

10. *One-Minute Play Festival*, accessed August 23, 2015, http://www.oneminuteplayfestival.com/about/

11. Preface to *100 Neo-Futurist Plays: From "Too Much Light Makes the Baby Go Blind"* (Chicago: Chicago Plays, 1988), 3.

12. "What is Neo-Futurism?" *New York Neo-Futurists*, accessed August 23, 2015, http://www.nyneofuturists.org/about/

13. Tim Reinhard, *George Spelvin is Alive and Well*, in *100 Neo-Futurist Plays*, 49.

14. Ralph Freud, "George Spelvin Says the Tag: Folklore of the Theater," *Western Folklore* 13.4 (Oct 1954), 250. Spelvins also sometimes appear in programs in place of double-cast actors.

15. For more on Twitter plays by the Neo-Futurists and others, see John Muse, "140 Characters in Search of a Theater," *Theater* 42.2 (2012): 43–63.

16. See the NY Neo-Futurist Twitter Plays "Favorites" page, accessed August 23, 2015, http://twitter.com/nyneofuturists/favourites. Totals from Jeffrey Cranor, "Twitter Plays," spreadsheet archive shared with the author, March 12, 2012.

17. The piece was inspired by John Cage's 1958 piece *Indeterminacy*, in which he read randomly ordered one-minute stories over a David Tudor score.

18. Kalb, *Great Lengths*, 141.

19. "12am: Awake & Looking Down," *Forced Entertainment*, accessed August 19, 2015, http://www.forcedentertainment.com/project/12am-awake-looking-down/

20. For an excellent reading of the show's Twitter feed, see Jen Buckley, "Forced Entertainment's #12AMLIVE and the Tweeting Spectator" (Conference

paper, Technology Performs Working Group, American Society for Theatre Research, Baltimore, November 2014).

21. Richard Foreman, "THE PANCAKE PEOPLE, OR, "THE GODS ARE POUNDING MY HEAD" program note to *The Gods are Pounding My Head, (AKA Lumberjack Messiah)*, Ontological-Hysteric Theater, reprinted in *The Edge*, ed. John Brokman, 2005, http://www.edge.org/3rd_culture/ foreman05/foreman05_index.html

22. Ibid. *The Gods are Pounding My Head, (AKA Lumberjack Messiah)* also rails against the pancake people.

23. Stage direction from *Abraham Lincoln at 89*, in Suzan-Lori Parks, *365 Days/365 Plays* (New York: Theatre Communications Group, 2006), 38. Unless otherwise indicated, all subsequent page references to plays from *365 Days/365 Plays* appear parenthetically and refer to this edition.

24. Parks, "It's an Oberammergau Thing," 125.

25. If the staged reading at The Public Theater in 2006 is an indication, the cycle requires four long sittings on four days to be read aloud. For details of the reading, see *365 Days/365 Plays*, 402.

26. Deborah Geis, *Suzan-Lori Parks* (Ann Arbor: University of Michigan Press, 2008), 161.

27. Mike Boehm, "Suzan-Lori Parks Offers a Play a Day," *Los Angeles Times* 30 June 2006, E-2.

28. Suzan-Lori Parks, "An Interview with Suzan-Lori Parks and Bonnie Metzgar (2006)," by Joseph Roach, in *Suzan-Lori Parks in Person: Interviews and Commentaries*, ed. Phillip C. Kolin and Harvey Young (New York: Routledge, 2014), Chapter 15.

29. See Puchner, *Stage Fright*. For more on the postmodern urge to uncloset supposedly impossible drama, see Nick Salvato, *Uncloseting Drama: American Modernism and Queer Performance* (New Haven: Yale University Press, 2010).

30. Mark Blankenship, "A Year-long Maze of Plays," *Variety*, November 11, 2006.

31. See Philip Kolin, "Redefining the Way Theater Is Created and Performed: The Radical Inclusion of Suzan-Lori Parks's *365 Days/365 Plays*," *Journal of Dramatic Theory and Criticism* 22, no. 1 (Fall 2007): 65–83; Rebecca Rugg, "Radical Inclusion 'Til It Hurts: Suzan-Lori Parks's *365 Days/365 Plays*," *Theater* 38, no. 1 (2008): 52–75; and Kathryn Walat, "These Are the Days: Suzan-Lori Parks's Year of Writing Dangerously Yields 365 Plays," *American Theatre* 23, no. 9 (2006): 26–27, 81–83.

32. Parks, *The Death of the Last Black Man in the Whole Entire World*, in *The America Play and Other Works*, 102.

33. Interview by Han Ong, 173.

34. "Elements of Style," 11.

35. Gregory Miller, "Everybody Lean Forward: Watching and Doing Times 365," conference paper, American Literature Association, May 2007.

36. Rugg, "Radical Inclusion," 54.

37. Parks, "It's a Oberammergau Thing," 137.

38. "365 Days/365 Plays," The Public Theater, accessed 24 Nov 2006, http://www.publictheater.org/365 (site discontinued).

39. Auslander, *Liveness: Performance in a Mediatized Culture*, 2nd edition (New York: Routledge, 2008), 51.

40. Despite its title, the cycle in fact contains 379 plays. Parks wrote two plays on some days, and three "Constants" that accompany the cycle.

41. For more on radical inclusion in *365*, see Rugg "Radical Inclusion," especially 56–62; and Kolin "Redefining," 65–83.

42. Sadie Dingfelder describes the production by the American Century Theater in "ACT Does Theater over the Phone," *Washington City Paper*, 15 December 2007.

43. Roberton, Campbell. "What Do You Get If You Write a Play a Day? A Lot of Premieres," *The New York Times*, November 10, 2006, 3.

44. Hilton Als, "The Show Woman: Suzan-Lori Parks's Idea for the Largest Theatre Collaboration Ever," *The New Yorker*, October 30, 2006, accessed August 23, 2015, http://www.newyorker.com/archive/2006/10/30/061030fa_fact2

45. Quoted in C. Denby Swanson, "Radical Inclusion: A Morality Tale," *The Austin Chronicle*, April 27, 2007, accessed August 23, 2015, http://www.austinchronicle.com/arts/2007–04–27/469098/

46. The festival production team hoped to build a fully and freely accessible mediated version of the festival and requested that each theater record its performances and upload videos to an online archive. The 365 Archive, if it had been completed, would have brought to fruition Kolin's suggestion that a cycle so resistant to staging "might best be realized as cyberspace, or digital theater, a theater of virtual performance(s)" allowing spectators to "see variations of the entire cycle" (Kolin, "Redefining," 81). But by 2012 only a dozen or so of the more than 6,000 performances had been archived, and the site has since been discontinued, suggesting that the 365 Festival, unlike its published counterpart, will remain more local repertoire than global archive.

47. "It's an Oberammergau Thing," 136.

48. Walt Whitman, *Leaves of Grass: The First (1855) Edition* (New York: Penguin, 1959), 8.

49. Walt Whitman, *The Collected Writings of Walt Whitman*, ed. Gay Wilson Allen and Sculley Bradley (New York: New York University Press, 1961), 10:611.

50. "Possession," in *The America Play and Other Works*, 4.

51. Parks, "Interview with Suzan-Lori Parks," by Shelby Jiggets, *Callaloo* 19, no. 2 (1996): 312.

52. I borrow this term from the title of Lance St. John Butler's *Samuel Beckett and the Meaning of Being: A Study in Ontological Parable* (New York: Palgrave Macmillan, 1984).

53. Paul Ricoeur, *Time and Narrative* (Chicago: University of Chicago Press, 1984), 3.

54. Liz Diamond, "Perceptible Mutability in the Word Kingdom." *Theater* 24, no. 3 (1993): 86.

55. Suzan-Lori Parks, interview by Han Ong, in *Speak Theater and Film!: The Best of Bomb Magazine's Interviews with Playwrights, Actors and Directors*, eds. Betsy Sussler, Suzan Sherman, and Ronalde Shavers, (Australia: G + B Arts International, 1999), 169.

56. Rugg, "Radical Inclusion," 55.

57. Suzan-Lori Parks, "Elements of Style," in *The America Play and Other Works* (New York: Theater Communications Group, 1999), 16.

58. Suzan-Lori Parks, *Venus* (New York: Theatre Communications Group, 1990), 46–47.

59. Ibid, 16.

60. Beth Rowen, "All You Need Is Love ... and Information: Caryl Churchill's *Love and Information*," *Huffington Post*, February 19, 2014, accessed August 19, 2015, http://www.huffingtonpost.com/bess-rowen/all-you-need-is-loveand-i_b_4800185.html

61. Ben Brantley makes a similar point when he says that Churchill's microthon playfully "teases, thwarts, and gluts its audience's capacity to assimilate the forms of information it considers." ("57 Bits of Emotional Knowledge: 'Love and Information,' by Caryl Churchill, at Minetta Lane," *The New York Times*, February 19, 2014, accessed August 19, 2015, http://www.nytimes.com/2014/02/20/theater/love-and-information-by-caryl-churchill-at-minetta-lane.html)

62. Caryl Churchill, *Love and Information* (New York: Theatre Communications Group, 2013), 12. Further references appear parenthetically.

63. For a trenchant discussion of the ramifications of the play's balance of constraint and freedom, see R. Darren Gobert's discussion of *Love and Information* in *The Theater of Caryl Churchill*, (New York: Bloomsbury Methuen, 2014), 187–200.

64. Suzan-Lori Parks, *365 Days/365 Plays* (New York: Theatre Communications Group, 2006), 234.

65. Horace, *The Art of Poetry*, trans. John Conington, *Theatre/Theory/Theatre*, ed. Daniel Gerould (New York: Applause, 2000), 73.

66. Qtd. and trans. Juliet Koss, "On the Limits of Empathy," *The Art Bulletin* 88.1 (2006): 139. Orig. Robert Vischer, *Uber das optische Formgefühl: Ein Beitrag zur Aesthetik [On the Optical Sense of Form: A Contribution to Aesthetics]* (Leipzig: Credner, 1873), 20.

67. John Martin, *Introduction to the Dance* (New York: Norton, 1939), 105.

68. Martin, 53.

69. Susan Leigh Foster, "Kinesthetic Empathies and the Politics of Compassion," *Critical Theory and Performance*, eds. Joseph Roach and Janelle Reinelt (Ann Arbor: University of Michigan Press, 2007), 246. See also two other works by Foster, "Movement's Contagion: The Aesthetic Impact of Performance," *Cambridge Companion to Performance Studies*, ed. Tracy C. Davis (Cambridge University Press, 2008) 46–59; and *Choreographing Empathy: Kinesthesia in Performance* (London: Routledge, 2011).

70. Foster, "Kinesthetic Empathies," 255.

71. David Krasner, "Empathy and Theater," *Staging Philosophy: Intersections of Theater, Performance, and Philosophy*, eds. David Krasner and David Z. Saltz (Ann Arbor: University of Michigan Press, 2006), 257.

72. Ibid., 258.

73. "An Interview with Suzan-Lori Parks," by Shawn Marie Garrett, in *Suzan-Lori Parks: Essays on the Plays and Other Works*, ed. Philip C. Kolin (Jefferson, NC: McFarland & Company, 2011), 189.

74. Ibid., 189–90, emphasis in original.

75. Susan L. Feagin, "Time and Timing," *Passionate Views: Film, Cognition,*

and Emotion, eds. Carl Plantinga and Greg M. Smith (Baltimore: Johns Hopkins, 1999) 172.

76. Parks, *365 Days/365 Plays*, 374–75.

77. Ibid., 33.

78. Deborah Geis, *Suzan-Lori Parks* (Ann Arbor: University of Michigan Press, 2008) 158.

79. Parks, "The Elements of Style," 9.

80. Rugg, "Radical Inclusion," 62.

81. Alain Badiou, *In Praise of Love* (New York: Profile, 2012), 31–32.

82. Ben Brantley, "57 Bits of Emotional Knowledge."

83. John Del Signore, "Theater Review: Caryl Churchill's *Love And Information*," *Gothamist*, March 8, 2014, accessed April 3, 2014, http://gothamist. com/2014/03/08/love_and_information_review.php

84. David Gordon, "Love and Information," *Theatermania*, February 19, 2014, accessed April 3, 2014, http://www.theatermania.com/new-york-city-theater/ reviews/02-2014/love-and-information_67587.html

85. David Cote, *"Love and Information," Time Out New York*, February 19, 2014. See also Beth Rowen, "All You Need is Love . . . and Information," and Andy Buck of *Theater Is Easy*, who called for more "judicious editing." ("Love and Information," *Theater Is Easy*, March 4, 2014, accessed August 19, 2016, http://www.theasy.com/Reviews/2014/L/loveandinformation.php)

86. Marvin Carlson, "The Theatre Journal Auto/Archive," *Theatre Journal* 55, no. 1 (2003): 211.

Bibliography

Acheson, James, and Kateryna Arthur, eds. *Beckett's Later Fiction and Drama: Texts for Company*. London: Macmillan, 1987.

Ackerley, Chris, and S. E. Gontarski. *The Grove Companion to Samuel Beckett: A Reader's Guide to His Works, Life, and Thought*. New York: Grove Press, 2004.

Ackerman, Alan, and Martin Puchner, eds. *Against Theatre: Creative Destructions on the Modernist Stage*. New York: Palgrave Macmillan, 2006.

Albright, Daniel. *Beckett and Aesthetics*. Cambridge: Cambridge University Press, 2003.

Allen, Greg, ed. "The Last Two Minutes of the Complete Works of Henrik Ibsen." *The Neo-Futurists*. Fringe NYC, 2005.Allen, Greg. Preface to *100 Neo-Futurist Plays from "Too Much Light Makes the Baby Go Blind."* Chicago: Chicago Plays, 1988.

Als, Hilton. "The Show Woman: Suzan-Lori Parks's Idea for the Largest Theatre Collaboration Ever." *The New Yorker*. October 30, 2006.

Antoine, André. *Memories of the Théâtre-Libre*. Translated by Marvin Carlson. Coral Gables, FL: University of Miami Press, 1964.

Antonucci, Giovanni. "Introduzione." In *Cronache del teatro futurista*, 11–29. Rome: Ed. Abete, 1975.

Antonucci, Giovanni. *Lo spettaculo futurista in Italia*. Rome: Studium, 1974.

Apollonio, Umbro. *Futurist Manifestos*. New York: Viking Press, 1973.

Archer, William. *The Theatrical 'World' of 1895*. London: Walter Scott, 1896.

Aristotle. *Aristotle's Poetics*. Edited by Francis Fergusson. Translated by Samuel H. Butcher. New York: Macmillan, 1961.

Aronson, Arnold. "Avant-garde Scenography." In *Against Theatre: Creative Destructions on the Modernist Stage*, edited by Alan Ackerman and Martin Puchner, 21–37. New York: Palgrave Macmillan, 2006.

Artioli, Umberto. *La scena et la dynamis: Immaginario e struttura nelle sintesi futuriste*. Bologna: Pàtron, 1975.

Asmus, Walter. "Rehearsal Notes for the German Premiere of Beckett's *That Time* and *Footfalls* at the Schiller-Theater Werkstatt, Berlin." In *On Beckett*, edited by S. E. Gontarski, 335–49. New York: Grove Press, 1986. First published in *Journal of Beckett Studies* 2 (1977): 82–95.

Auden, W. H. "In Memory of W. B. Yeats." In *Selected Poems*, 80–83. New York: Vintage, 1979.

Augustine, Saint. *The Confessions of St. Augustine*. Translated by John K. Ryan. New York: Doubleday, 1960.

Auslander, Philip. *Liveness: Performance in a Mediatized Culture.* 2nd edition. New York: Routledge, 2008.

Badiou, Alain. *In Praise of Love.* New York: Profile, 2012.

Barthes, Roland. *Critical Essays.* Evanston, IL: Northwestern University Press, 1972.

Baudelaire, Charles. "Richard Wagner and Tannhäuser in Paris." In *Selected Writings on Art and Literature,* translated by P. E. Charvet, 341–42. London: Penguin Books, 1972.

Beckett on Film. DVD. Produced by Michael Colgan. London: Blue Angel Films, 2001.

Beckett, Samuel. *A Piece of Monologue.* In *Dramatic Works,* 451–58.

Beckett, Samuel. *Breath.* In *Dramatic Works,* 399–402.

Beckett, Samuel. *Disjecta. Miscellaneous Writings and a Dramatic Fragment.* New York: Grove Press, 1984.

Beckett, Samuel. *Dramatic Works.* Vol. 3 of *Samuel Beckett: The Grove Centenary Edition.* Edited by Paul Auster. New York: Grove, 2006.

Beckett, Samuel. *Endgame.* In *Dramatic Works,* 89–154.

Beckett, Samuel. *Footfalls.* In *Dramatic Works,* 425–32.

Beckett, Samuel. *Ghost Trio.* In *Dramatic Works,* 433–42.

Beckett, Samuel. *Happy Days.* In *Dramatic Works,* 273–307.

Beckett, Samuel. Interview by Tom Driver. *Columbia University Forum* (Summer 1961): 21–25. Reprinted in *Samuel Beckett: The Critical Heritage,* edited by Lawrence Graver and Raymond Federman, 217–23. New York: Routledge, 1979.

Beckett, Samuel. *The Letters of Samuel Beckett: 1957–1965.* Vol. 3 of *The Letters of Samuel Beckett.* Edited by George Craig, Martha Dow Fehsenfeld, Dan Gunn, and Lois More Overbeck and translated by George Craig. Cambridge: Cambridge University Press, 2014.

Beckett, Samuel. *Malone Dies.* In *Novels II,* 171–282.

Beckett, Samuel. *Molloy.* In *Novels II,* 1–170.

Beckett, Samuel. *Murphy.* In *Novels II,* 1–168.

Beckett, Samuel. *Not I.* In *Dramatic Works,* 403–14.

Beckett, Samuel. *Novels.* Vol. 1 of *Samuel Beckett: The Grove Centenary Edition.* Edited by Paul Auster. New York: Grove, 2006.

Beckett, Samuel. *Novels II.* Vol. 2 of *Samuel Beckett: The Grove Centenary Edition.* Edited by Paul Auster. New York: Grove, 2006.

Beckett, Samuel. *Play.* In *Dramatic Works,* 353–68.

Beckett, Samuel. *Poems/Short Fiction/Criticism.* Vol. 4 of *Samuel Beckett: The Grove Centenary Edition.* Edited by Paul Auster. New York: Grove, 2006.

Beckett, Samuel. *Proust.* In *Poems/Short Fiction/Criticism,* 511–54.

Beckett, Samuel. *Rockaby.* In *Dramatic Works,* 459–70.

Beckett, Samuel. *Ohio Impromptu.* In *Dramatic Works,* 471–76.

Beckett, Samuel. *Quad.* In *Dramatic Works,* 477–82.

Beckett, Samuel. *That Time.* In *Dramatic Works,* 415–24.

Beckett, Samuel. *The Unnamable.* In *Novels II,* 283–407.

Beckett, Samuel. *Waiting for Godot.* In *Dramatic Works,* 1–88.

Beckett, Samuel. *Watt.* In *Novels I,* 69–380.

Beckett, Samuel. *What Where.* In *Dramatic Works,* 495–504.

Beckett, Samuel. *Worstward Ho.* In *Poems/Short Fiction/Criticism,* 471–86.

Beckett, Samuel and Alan Schneider. *No Author Better Served: The Correspondence of Samuel Beckett & Alan Schneider.* Cambridge, MA: Harvard University Press, 1998.

Benjamin, Walter. "The Work of Art in the Age of Mechanical Reproduction." In *Illuminations,* edited by Hannah Arendt, translated by Harry Zohn, 217–52. New York: Schocken Books, 1968.

Berghaus, Günter. *Italian Futurist Theatre, 1909–1944.* Oxford: Clarendon Press, 1998.

Berghaus, Günter. *Theatre, Performance, and the Historical Avant-Garde.* New York: Palgrave Macmillan, 2005.

Bergson, Henri. *Laughter: An Essay on the Meaning of the Comic.* New York: Macmillan, 1911.

Bergson, Henri. "Duration and Simultaneity." In *Henri Bergson: Key Writings,* edited by Keith Ansell Pearson and John Mullarkey, 205–20. New York: Continuum, 2002.

Bergson, Henri. *Time and Free Will: An Essay on the Immediate Data of Consciousness.* Translated by F. L. Pogson. Mineola, New York: Dover, 2001.

Blackadder, Neil. *Performing Opposition: Modern Theater and the Scandalized Audience.* Westport, CT: Praeger, 2003.

Blankenship, Mark. "A Year-long Maze of Plays." *Variety,* November 11, 2006.

Blau, Herbert. "Apnea and True Illusion: Breath(less) in Beckett." *Modern Drama* 49, no. 4 (Winter 2006): 452–68.

Blau, Herbert. *Sails of the Herring Fleet: Essays on Beckett.* Ann Arbor: University of Michigan Press, 2000.

Bolter, Jay David, and Richard Grusin. *Remediation: Understanding New Media.* Cambridge, MA: MIT Press, 1999.

Bradby, David. *Beckett: Waiting for Godot.* New York: Cambridge University Press, 2001.

Brater, Enoch. *Beyond Minimalism: Beckett Late Style in the Theater.* New York: Oxford University Press, 1987.

Braun, Theodore. "Un demi-quart d'heure," *Studies in the Humanities* 11, no. 1 (June 1984): 71–74.

Breton, André. *Manifestoes of Surrealism.* Translated by Richard Seaver and Helen R. Lane. Ann Arbor: University of Michigan Press, 1972.

Brook, Peter. *The Empty Space: A Book about the Theatre: Deadly, Holy, Rough, Immediate.* New York: Simon & Schuster, 1968.

Buckley, Jen. "Forced Entertainment's #12AMLIVE and the Tweeting Spectator." Paper presented to the Technology Performs Working Group, American Society for Theatre Research, Baltimore, November, 2014.

Buckley, Jerome. *The Triumph of Time: A Study of the Victorian Concepts of Time, History, Progress, and Decadence.* Cambridge, MA: Harvard University Press, 1966.

Burden, Chris. *Shoot* in *Documentation of Selected Works (1971–1974).* New York: Electronic Arts Intermix, 1971–75. Archived at UbuWeb Film & Video. Accessed August 19, 2015. http://archive.is/5eHY

Butler, Lance St. John, *Samuel Beckett and the Meaning of Being: A Study in Onto-logical Parable*. New York: Palgrave Macmillan, 1984.

Calinescu, Matei. *Five Faces of Modernity: Modernism, Avant-garde, Decadence, Kitsch, Postmodernism*. 2nd ed. Durham, NC: Duke University Press, 1987.

Cameron, Sharon. *Lyric Time: Dickinson and the Limits of Genre*. Baltimore: Johns Hopkins University Press, 1979.

Camus, Albert. "The Myth of Sisyphus." *The Myth of Sisyphus and Other Essays*. Translated by Justin O'Brien, 1–138. New York: Vintage Books, 1991.

Cangiullo, Francesco. *Decision* (1915). In Lista, 72.

Cangiullo, Francesco. *Detonation* (1915). In Kirby, *Futurist Performance*, 247.

Cangiullo, Francesco. *Lights!* (1922). In Kirby, *Futurist Performance*, 255.

Cangiullo, Francesco. *The Paunch of the Vase* (1920). In Kirby, *Futurist Performance*, 250.

Cardullo, Bert. Introduction to *Theater of the Avant-Garde, 1890–1950*, edited by Bert Cardullo and Robert Knopf, 1–38. New Haven: Yale University Press, 2001.

Carli, Mario. *Violence: A Symphony* (*Violenza, sinfonia*). In *Teatro futurista italiano*. Double issue of *Sipario* 260 (Dec 1967): 68.

Carlson, Marvin. *The French Stage in the Nineteenth Century*. Metuchen, NJ: Scarecrow Press, 1972.

Carlson, Marvin. *The Haunted Stage: The Theatre as Memory Machine*. Ann Arbor: University of Michigan Press, 2001.

Carlson, Marvin. "The Theatre Journal Auto/Archive." *Theatre Journal* 55, no. 1 (2003): 207–11.

Carlson, Marvin. *Theories of the Theatre*. Ithaca, NY: Cornell University Press, 1993.

Carlyle, Thomas. "Shooting Niagara." In *The Works of Thomas Carlyle*, Centenary Edition. Vol. 30. London: Chapman and Hall, 1896–1899.

Carr, Nicholas. "Is Google Making Us Stupid?" *The Atlantic Monthly*, July/August 2008.

Cary, Joseph. "Futurism and the French Avant-Garde." *Modern Philology* 57, no. 2 (November 1959): 113–21.

Casavola, Franco. "Theater of Dilated Moments." In Lista, *Théâtre futuriste italien*, 2:89–93.

Chaikin, Joseph. *The Presence of the Actor*. New York: Theatre Communications Group, 1993.

Chaudhuri, Una. *Staging Place: The Geography of Modern Drama*. Ann Arbor: University of Michigan Press, 1995.

Chiari, Joseph. *Symbolisme from Poe to Mallarmé; The Growth of a Myth*. New York: Macmillan, 1956.

Churchill, Caryl. *Love and Information*. New York: Theatre Communications Group, 2013.

Clément, Bruno. *L'Oeuvre sans qualités: Rhétorique de Samuel Beckett*. Paris: Éditions du Seuil, 1994.

Cocteau, Jean. Preface to *The Wedding on the Eiffel Tower*. Translated by Michael Benedikt. In *Modern French Theatre: The Avant–Garde, Dada and Surrealism*, edited by Michael Benedikt and George E. Wellwarth, 96–97. New York: Dutton, 1966.

Cohn, Ruby. *Just Play: Beckett's Theater.* Princeton: Princeton University Press, 1980.

Connor, Steven. "Slow Going." *Yearbook of English Studies* 30 (2000): 153–65.

Corra, Bruno and Emilio Settimelli. *Negative Act* (1915). In Kirby, *Futurist Performance*, 268.

Corra, Bruno and Emilio Settimelli. *Passatismo.* In Kirby, *Futurist Performance*, 269.

Corra, Bruno and Emilio Settimelli. *Sempronio's Lunch.* In Kirby, *Futurist Performance*, 271.

Cote, David. "*Love and Information,*" *Time Out New York*, February 19, 2014.

Craig, Edward Gordon. *On the Art of the Theatre.* New York: Theatre Arts Books, 1956.

Crary, Jonathan. *Suspensions of Perception: Attention, Spectacle, and Modern Culture.* Cambridge, MA: MIT Press, 1999.

Crittenden, Cole. "Dramatics of Time." *KronoScope* 5, no. 2 (2005): 192–212.

D'Ambrosio, Matteo. *Roman Jakobson e il futurismo italiano.* Napoli: Liguori, 2009.

Davis, Robin and Lance St. John Butler. *"Make Sense Who May": Essays on Samuel Beckett's Later Works.* Gerrards Cross, Bucks, Ireland: C. Smythe, 1988.

Deak, Frantisek. "Symbolist Staging at the Théâtre D'art." *TDR* 20, no. 3 (1976): 117–22.

Deak, Frantisek. *Symbolist Theatre: The Formation of an Avant-Garde.* Baltimore: Johns Hopkins University Press, 1993.

Deak, Frantisek. "Théâtre du Grand Guignol." *TDR* 18, no. 1 (1974): 34–43.

Dessy, Mario. *Lives.* In Verdone, *Teatro del tempo futurista*, 2nd ed., 69. Rome: Bulzoni Editore, 1988.

Dessy, Mario. *Madness.* In Kirby, *Futurist Performance*, 282.

Dessy, Mario. *Waiting* (1919). In Kirby, *Futurist Performance*, 284.

Diamond, Elin. "*Love and Information* by Caryl Churchill," *Theatre Journal*, vol. 66, no. 3 (Oct. 2014), 462–65.

Diamond, Liz. "Perceptible Mutability in the Word Kingdom." *Theater* 24, no. 3 (1993): 86–87.

Dingfelder, Sadie. "ACT Does Theater over the Phone," *Washington City Paper*, December 15, 2007.

Dixon, Steve. *Digital Performance: A History of New Media in Theater, Dance, Performance Art, and Installation.* Cambridge, MA: MIT Press, 2007.

Dixon, Steve. "Futurism and the Early-Twentieth-Century Avant-Garde." In *Digital Performance*, 47–72.

Duckworth, Colin. Introduction to *En attendant Godot: Pièce en deux actes*, by Samuel Beckett. London: Harrap, 1966.

Eagleton, Terry. "Beckett and Nothing." *Reflections on Beckett: A Centenary Celebration*, edited by Anna McMullan and S. E. Wilmer. Ann Arbor: University of Michigan Press, 2009. 36–37.

Erickson, Jon. "Tension/Release and the Production of Time in Performance,"

Archaeologies of Presence: Art, Performance and the Persistence of Being, edited by Gabriella Giannachi, Nick Kaye, and Michael Shanks, 82–99. New York: Routledge, 2012.

Esslin, "Toward the Zero of Language." In *Beckett's Later Fiction and Drama: Texts for Company*, edited by Acheson and Arthur, 35–49. London: Macmillan Press, 1987.

Feagin, Susan L. "Time and Timing." In *Passionate Views: Film, Cognition, and Emotion*, edited by Carl Plantinga and Greg M. Smith, 168–79. Baltimore: Johns Hopkins University Press, 1999.

Fischer-Seidel, Therese. "'Ineluctable Modality of the Visible': Perception and Genre in Samuel Beckett's Later Drama." *Contemporary Literature* 35, no. 1 (Spring 1994): 66–82.

Foster, Susan Leigh. *Choreographing Empathy: Kinesthesia in Performance*. London: Routledge, 2011.

Foster, Susan Leigh. "Kinesthetic Empathies and the Politics of Compassion." In *Critical Theory and Performance*, edited by Joseph Roach and Janelle Reinelt, 245–58. Ann Arbor: University of Michigan Press, 2007.

Foster, Susan Leigh. "Movement's Contagion: The Aesthetic Impact of Performance." In *Cambridge Companion to Performance Studies*, edited by Tracy C. Davis, 46–59. Cambridge University Press, 2008.

Freud, Ralph. "George Spelvin Says the Tag: Folklore of the Theater." *Western Folklore* 13, no. 4 (Oct 1954): 245–50.

Fuchs, Elinor. "Mythic Structure in *Hedda Gabler*: The Mask Behind the Face," *Comparative Drama* 19, no. 3 (1985): 209–21.

Geis, Deborah. *Suzan-Lori Parks*. Ann Arbor: University of Michigan Press, 2008.

George, Kathleen. *Rhythm in Drama*. Pittsburgh: University of Pittsburgh Press, 1980.

Gerould, Daniel, ed. *Doubles, Demons and Dreamers: An International Collection of Symbolist Drama*. New York: Performing Arts Journal Publications, 1985.

Gerould, Daniel. "Landscapes of the Unseen: Turn-of-the-Century Symbolism from Paris to Petersburg." In *Land/Scape/Theatre*, edited by Elinor Fuchs and Una Chaudhuri, 303–21. Ann Arbor: University of Michigan Press, 2002.

Gerould, Daniel. "Oscar Méténier and 'Comédie Rousse': From the Théâtre Libre to the Grand Guignol," *TDR* 28, no. 1 (Spring 1984): 15–28.

Gilman, Richard. *The Making of Modern Drama*. New York: Farrar, Straus and Giroux, 1972.

Gitelman, Lisa. *Always Already New: Media, History, and the Data of Culture*. Cambridge, MA: MIT Press, 2008.

Gobert, R. Darren. *The Theatre of Caryl Churchill*. New York: Bloomsbury Methuen, 2014.

Goldberg, RoseLee. *Performance Art: From Futurism to the Present*. New York: Thames & Hudson, 2001.

Gontarski, S. E. "De-theatricalizing Theatre: The Post-*Play* Plays," Introduction to *The Shorter Plays*, xv–xxix.

Gontarski, S. E., ed. *The Theatrical Notebooks of Samuel Beckett*. Vol. 2, *The Shorter Plays*. New York: Grove Press, 1999.

Gordon, Mel. *Dada Performance.* New York: PAJ Publications, 1987.

Gordon, Mel. *The Grand Guignol: Theatre of Fear and Terror.* New York: Amok Press, 1988.

Gordon, R. S. "The Italian Futurist Theatre: A Reappraisal." *The Modern Language Review* 85, no. 2 (April 1990): 349–61.

Graffi, Milli. "L'angoscia della mancanza del comico nei futuristi e l'insperata soluzione del motto de spirito." *Es* 14 (1980): 75–92.

Graver, Lawrence and Raymond Federman, eds. *Samuel Beckett: The Critical Heritage.* New York: Routledge, 1979.

Greenberg, Clement. "Modernist Painting" (1960). Vol. 1, *The Collected Essays and Criticism,* edited by John O'Brien, 85–93. Chicago: University of Chicago Press, 1995.

Haerdter, Michael. "Endgame: A Rehearsal Diary." In *Beckett in the Theatre: The Author as Practical Playwright and Director,* edited by Dougald McMillan and Martha Fehsenfeld. Vol. 1 of *Waiting for Godot to Krapp's Last Tape,* 204–40. New York: Riverrun Press, 1988.

Hanak, Miroslav John. *Maeterlinck's Symbolic Drama: A Leap into Transcendence.* Louvain: E. Peeters, 1974.

Hand, Richard J. and Michael Wilson, eds. and trans. *Grand Guignol: The French Theatre of Horror.* Exeter: University of Exeter Press, 2002.

Harries, Martin. "Theater and Media Before 'New' Media," *Theater* 42, no. 2 (Jan 2012): 7–25.

Henderson, John A. *The First Avant-Garde, 1887–1894: Sources of the Modern French Theatre.* London: G. G. Harrap, 1971.

Hobson, Harold. *French Theatre since 1830.* London: John Calder, 1978.

Hobson, Harold. "Samuel Beckett: Dramatist of the Year." *International Theatre Annual.* No. 1. London: John Calder, 1956.

Homan, Sidney. *Beckett's Theaters: Interpretations for Performance.* Lewisburg, PA: Bucknell University Press, 1984.

Horace. *The Art of Poetry.* Trans. by John Conington, *Theatre/Theory/Theatre,* edited by Daniel Gerould, 68–73. New York: Applause, 2000.

Huizinga, Johan. *Homo Ludens: A Study of the Play Element of Culture.* New York: Beacon Press, 1971.

Hutchison Guest, Ann. *Labanotation, or Kinetography Laban: The System of Analyzing and Recording Movement.* New York: Routledge, 1977.

James, William. "The Perception of Time." In *Principles of Psychology,* vol. 1, 605–42. New York: Dover, 1918.

Jasper, Gertrude. *Adventure in the Theatre; Lugné-Poe and the Théâtre de L'Oeuvre to 1899.* New Brunswick, NJ: Rutgers University Press, 1947.

Jauss, Hans Robert. *Toward an Aesthetic of Reception.* Translated by Timothy Bahti. Minneapolis: University of Minnesota Press, 1982.

Jelavich, Peter. *Cabarets in Berlin, 1901–1944.* Cambridge, MA: Minda de Gunzburg Center for European Studies, 1986.

Jenkins, Henry. *Convergence Culture: Where Old and New Media Collide.* New York: New York University Press, 2006.

Jory, Jon. Foreword to *More Ten-Minute Plays from Actors Theatre of Louisville,* edited by Michael Bigelow Dixon, vi. New York: Samuel French, 1992.

Joyce, James. *Ulysses*. New York: Vintage, 1986.

Jullien, Jean. *Le théâtre vivant*. Paris: Charpentier et Fasquelle, 1892.

Kalb, Jonathan. "Beckett after Beckett," *Salmagundi* 160/161 (Fall 2008/Winter 2009): 140–50.

Kalb, Jonathan. *Beckett in Performance*. New York: Cambridge University Press, 1989.

Kalb, Jonathan. *Great Lengths: Seven Works of Marathon Theater*. Ann Arbor: University of Michigan Press, 2013.

Kern, Stephen. *The Culture of Time and Space 1880–1918*. Cambridge, MA: Harvard University Press, 1983.

Kirby, Michael, ed. *Futurist Performance*. Italian texts translated by Victoria Nes Kirby. New York: PAJ Publications, 1986.

Knowlson, James. *Damned to Fame: The Life of Samuel Beckett*. New York: Simon & Schuster, 1996.

Knowlson, James and John Pilling. *Frescoes of the Skull*. London: John Calder, 1979.

Koch, Kenneth. "Very Rapid Acceleration: An Interview with Kenneth Koch." By John Tranter. *Jacket* 5 (1998), http://jacketmagazine.com/05/koch89.html

Kolin, Philip C. "Redefining the Way Theatre Is Created and Performed: The Radical Inclusion of Suzan-Lori Parks's *365 Days/365 Plays*." *Journal of Dramatic Theory and Criticism* 22, no. 1 (Fall 2007): 65–83.

Koss, Juliet. "On the Limits of Empathy." *The Art Bulletin* 88, no. 1 (2006): 139–57.

Krasner, David. "Empathy and Theater." In *Staging Philosophy: Intersections of Theater, Performance, and Philosophy*, edited by David Krasner and David Z. Saltz. Ann Arbor: University of Michigan Press, 2006: 255–77.

Lamont, Rosette. "New Beckett Plays." *Other Stages*, June 16, 1983, 3.

Lapini, Lia, *Il teatro futurista italiano*. Milan: Mondadori, 2004.

Lapini, Lia. "Il teatro futurista italiano dalla teoria alla pratica." In *Il teatro italiano dal naturalismo a Pirandello*, edited by Alessandro Tinterri, 249–64. Bologna: Il Mulino, 1990.

Lehmann, Hans-Thies. *Postdramatic Theatre*. Translated with an introduction by Karen Jürs-Munby. London: Routledge, 2006. Originally published as *Postdramatishes Theater*. Frankfurt: Verglag der Autoren, 1999.

Lessing, Gotthold Ephraim. *Laocoön: An Essay on the Limits of Painting and Poetry (1776)*. Translated by Edward Allen McCormick. Indianapolis: Bobbs-Merrill, 1962.

Lista, Giovanni. *La Scène futuriste*. Paris: Éditions du Centre national de la recherche scientifique, 1989.

Lista, Giovanni. *Théâtre Futuriste Italien*. Translated from Italian by Giovanni Lista and Claude Minot. 2 Vols. Paris: L'Age D'Homme, 1990.

Lyons, Charles. "Beckett's Fundamental Theatre: The Plays from *Not I* to *What Where*." In *Beckett's Later Fiction and Drama: Texts for Company*, edited by James Acheson and Kateryna Arthur, 80–97. London: Macmillan, 1987.

Maeterlinck, Maurice. *The Buried Temple*. Translated by Alfred Sutro. New York: Dodd, Mead, & Co., 1904.

Maeterlinck, Maurice. "The Foretelling of the Future." *The Double Garden*. Translated by Alexander de Mattos, 139–67. New York: Dodd, 1905.

Maeterlinck, Maurice. *Interior*. In *Theater of the Avant-Garde, 1890–1950*, edited by Bert Cardullo and Robert Knopf, 45–54. New Haven: Yale University Press, 2001. Reprinted from *The Nobel Prize Treasury*, edited by Marshall McClintock and translated by William Archer, 203–9. New York: Doubleday, 1948. Originally published as *Intérieur*, in *Théâtre* by Maurice Maeterlinck, vol. 2. Brussels: Lacombe, 1901–2.

Maeterlinck, Maurice. *The Life of Space*. Translated by Bernard Miall. New York: Dodd, Mead & Co., 1928. Originally published as *La Vie de l'Espace*. Paris: Charpentier, 1928.

Maeterlinck, Maurice. "The Modern Drama." In *The Double Garden*. Translated by Alexander de Mattos, 115–38. London: Dodd, Mead & Co., 1911. First published as *Le Double Jardin*. Paris: Fasquelle, 1904.

Maeterlinck, Maurice. "Small Talk—the Theater." In *Symbolist Art Theories: A Critical Anthology*. Edited and translated by Henri Dorra, 143–46. Berkeley: University of California Press, 1994. Originally published as "Menus propos: le Théâtre," *La Jeune Belgique* 9 (September 1890): 331–36.

Maeterlinck, Maurice. "The Tragedy of Everyday Life." In *The Maeterlinck Reader*. Edited and translated by David Willinger and Daniel Gerould, 301–2. New York: Peter Lang, 2011. Originally published as "Le tragique quotidien" (1896), in *Le trésor des humbles*. Paris: Mercure de France, 1927.

Maeterlinck, Maurice. "The Tragical in Daily Life." In *The Treasure of the Humble*. Translated by Alfred Sutro, 113–35. New York: Dodd, Mead & Co., 1903. Originally published as "Le tragique quotidien" (1896), in *Le trésor des humbles*. Paris: Mercure de France, 1927.

Malkin, Jeannette. *Memory-Theater and Postmodern Drama*. Ann Arbor: University of Michigan Press, 1999.

Marinetti, Filippo Tommaso. "The Birth of a Futurist Aesthetic." In *Critical Writings*, 249–52.

Marinetti, Filippo Tommaso. *Critical Writings*. Edited by Günter Berghaus. Translated by Douglas Thompson. New Edition. New York: Farrar, Straus, and Giroux, 2006.

Marinetti, Filippo Tommaso. "Destruction of Syntax—Untrammeled Imagination—Words-in-Freedom." In *Critical Writings*, 120–31.

Marinetti, Filippo Tommaso. "Destruction of Syntax—Wireless Imagination—Words-in-Freedom." In *Stung by Salt and War: Creative Texts of the Italian Avant-Gardist F. T. Marinetti*, 45–54. Edited and translated by Richard Pioli. New York: Peter Lang, 1987.

Marinetti, Filippo Tommaso. "A Futurist Theater of Essential Brevity." In *Critical Writings*, 200–7. Originally published as *Teatro futurista sintetico*. Leaflet. Direzione del Movimento Futurista. January 11, 1915.

Marinetti, Filippo Tommaso. "The Futurist Synthetic Theater." In *Let's Murder the Moonshine*, 131–37.

Marinetti, Filippo Tommaso. *Let's Murder the Moonshine: Futurist Manifestos.*

Edited by R. W. Flint. Translated by R. W. Flint and Arthur A. Coppotelli. Los Angeles: Sun & Moon Classics, 1991.

Marinetti, Filippo Tommaso. "Manifesto of Futurist Cuisine." In *Critical Writings*, 394–99.

Marinetti, Filippo Tommaso. "Manifesto of Futurist Playwrights: The Pleasures of Being Booed." In *Critical Writings*, 181–84.

Marinetti, Filippo Tommaso. "The New Ethical Religion of Speed." In *Critical Writings*, 253–59.

Marinetti, Filippo Tommaso. "La nuova religione-morale della velocità," *L'Italia futurista* 1 (11 May 1916). *Europeana 1914–1918*.

Marinetti, Filippo Tommaso. "The Pleasure of Being Booed." In *Murder the Moonshine*, 121–23.

Marinetti, Filippo Tommaso. "Technical Manifesto of Futurist Literature." In *Critical Writings*, 107–19.

Marinetti, Filippo Tommaso. "The Variety Theater." In *Critical Writings*, 185–92.

Marinetti, Filippo Tommaso. "The Variety Theater." In *Murder the Moonshine*, 124–30.

Martin, Joe. "Three One Acts: Introduction." In *Strindberg: Other Sides*, 297–307.

Martin, John. *Introduction to the Dance*. New York: Norton, 1939.

McGuinness, Patrick. *Maurice Maeterlinck and the Making of Modern Theatre*. New York: Oxford University Press, 2000.

McGuinness, Patrick. "Mallarmé, Maeterlinck, and the Symbolist Via Negativa of Theatre." In Ackerman and Puchner, 149–67.

McMillan, Dougald and Martha Fehnsenfeld, eds. *Beckett in the Theatre: The Author as Practical Playwright and Director*. Vol. 1. From *Waiting for Godot* to *Krapp's Last Tape*. New York: Riverrun Press, 1988.

McMullan, Anna. "Samuel Beckett as Director: The Art of Mastering Failure." In *The Cambridge Companion to Beckett*, edited by John Pilling, 196–208. Cambridge: Cambridge University Press, 1994.

McMullan, Anna. *Theatre on Trial: Samuel Beckett's Later Drama*. New York: Routledge, 1993.

Mercier, Vivian. *Beckett/Beckett*. New York: Oxford University Press, 1977.

Méténier, Oscar. *En Famille*. Paris: P. V. Stock, 1900.

Méténier, Oscar. *Meat Ticket*. In "Oscar Méténier and 'Comédie Rosse': From the Théâtre Libre to the Grand Guignol." Edited and translated by Daniel Gerould. *TDR* 28, no. 1, French Theatre (1984): 20–23.

Méténier, Oscar. *Lui!* In *Grand Guignol: The French Theatre of Horror*. Edited and translated by Richard Hand and Michael Wilson, 85–92. Exeter, UK: University of Exeter Press, 2002.

Meyer, Michael. *Ibsen: A Life*. New York: Doubleday and Company, 1971.

Miller, Anna Irene. *The Independent Theatre in Europe, 1887 to the Present*. New York: R. Long & R. R. Smith, 1931.

Miller, Gregory Leon. "Everybody Lean Forward: Watching and Doing Times 365." Paper given at American Literature Association Panel, May 2007.

Morgenstern, Irvin. *The Dimensional Structure of Time, Together with the Drama and Its Timing*. New York, Philosophical Library, 1960.

Motte, Warren. *Small Worlds: Minimalism in Contemporary French Literature*. Lincoln: University of Nebraska Press, 1999.Olson, Liesl. *Modernism and the Ordinary*. New York: Oxford University Press, 2009.

O'Keefe Bazzoni, Georgiana Frances. "Avant-garde Italian Drama: Futurists, 'i grotteschi,' and Pirandello." PhD diss., City University of New York, 1983.

Østerud, Erik. "Myth and Modernity: Henrik Ibsen's Double Drama." *Scandinavica* 33, no. 2 (1994): 161–82.

Parks, Suzan-Lori. *365 Days/365 Plays*. New York: Theatre Communications Group, 2006.

Parks, Suzan-Lori. *The America Play and Other Works*. New York: Theatre Communications Group, 1999.

Parks, Suzan-Lori. *The Death of the Last Black Man in the Whole Entire World*. In *The America Play and Other Works*, 99–131.

Parks, Suzan-Lori. "Elements of Style." In *America Play and Other Works*, 6–18.

Parks, Suzan-Lori. Interview by Han Ong. *BOMB!* 47 (Spring 1994). Reprinted in *Speak Theater and Film!: The Best of Bomb Magazine's Interviews with Playwrights, Actors and Directors*, edited by Betsy Sussler, Suzan Sherman, and Ronalde Shavers, 157–67. Australia: G + B Arts International, 1999. First printed in *BOMB!* 47 (Spring 1994).

Parks, Suzan-Lori. "An Interview with Suzan-Lori Parks." By Shawn Marie Garrett. *Suzan-Lori Parks: Essays on the Plays and Other Works*, edited by Philip C. Kolin Jefferson, 181–90. NC: McFarland & Company, 2011.

Parks, Suzan-Lori. "Interview with Suzan-Lori Parks." By Shelby Jiggets. *Callaloo* 19, no. 2 (1996): 309–17.

Parks, Suzan-Lori. "An Interview with Suzan-Lori Parks and Bonnie Metzgar (2006)." By Joseph Roach. In *Suzan-Lori Parks in Person: Interviews and Commentaries*, edited by Phillip C. Kolin and Harvey Young, chapter 15. New York: Routledge, 2014.

Parks, Suzan-Lori. "It's an Oberammergau Thing: An Interview with Suzan-Lori Parks." By Kevin Wetmore, Jr. In *Suzan Lori Parks: A Casebook*, 124–40. New York: Routledge, 2007.

Parks, Suzan-Lori. "Possession." In *America Play and Other Works*, 3–5.

Parks, Suzan-Lori. Interview by Hilton Als. "The Show Woman: Suzan-Lori Parks's Idea for the Largest Theatre Collaboration Ever," *New Yorker*. October 30, 2006.

Parks, Suzan-Lori. *Venus*. New York: Theatre Communications Group, 1990.

Pattie, David. "Space, Time and the Self in Beckett's Late Theater." *Modern Drama* 43, no. 3 (2000): 393–404.

Phelan, Peggy. *Unmarked: The Politics of Performance*. New York: Routledge, 1993.

Pietropaolo, Domenico. "The Dramaturgy of Simultaneity." In *Futurist Dramaturgy and Performance*, edited by Paul J. Stoesser, 37–44. New York: Legas, 2011.

Pioli, Richard, ed. and trans. *Stung by Salt and War: The Creative Texts of the Italian Avant-Gardist F. T. Marinetti*. New York: Peter Lang, 1987.

Phillips, Siobhan. *The Poetics of the Everyday: Creative Repetition in Modern American Verse*. New York: Columbia University Press, 2010.

Poe, Edgar Allan. "The Philosophy of Composition." *Graham's Magazine* 28 (April 1846): 163–67.

Poggi, Christine. *Inventing Futurism: The Art and Politics of Artificial Optimism* (Princeton: Princeton University Press, 2008.

Pountney, Rosemary. *Theatre of Shadows: Samuel Beckett's Drama 1956–76*. Gerrards Cross, Buckinghamshire: Colin Smythe, 1988.

Pryor, Sean: "W. B. Yeats, Maurice Maeterlinck, and Old Blind Men." *Yeats Eliot Review: A Journal of Criticism and Scholarship* 19, no. 4 (Dec. 2002): 9–24.

Puchner, Martin. "Introduction." *Poetry of the Revolution: Marx, Manifestos, and the Avant-Gardes*. Translation/Transnation, 1–7. Princeton: Princeton University Press, 2006.

Puchner, Martin. "Samuel Beckett: Actors in Barrels and Gestures in the Text." In *Stage Fright*, 157–72.

Puchner, Martin. *Stage Fright: Modernism, Anti-Theatricality, and Drama*. Baltimore: John Hopkins University Press, 2002.

Pratella, Francesco Balilla. *Nocturnal*. In Kirby, *Futurist Performance*, 299–300.

Quillard, Pierre. *La Fille aux Mains coupées*. Exeter: University of Exeter, 1976. Translated as *The Girl with Cut-Off Hands: A Passion Play*. In *TDR* 20, no. 3 (Sept. 1976): 123–28.

Rainey, Lawrence, Christine Poggi, and Laura Wittman, eds. *Futurism: An Anthology*. New Haven: Yale University Press, 2009.

Ram, Harsha. "Futurist Geographies: Uneven Modernities and the Struggle for Aesthetic Autonomy: Paris, Italy, Russia, 1909–1914." Paper presented at Yale Comparative Literature Department, February 17, 2009.

Ramsay, Gordon, "Simultaneity and Compenetration in *sintesi* of the Italian Futurists." In *Futurist Dramaturgy and Performance*, edited by Paul J. Stoesser, 45–56. New York: Legas, 2011.

Randall, Bryony. *Modernism, Daily Time and Everyday Life*. Cambridge: Cambridge University Press, 2007.

Raspanti, Celeste Rita. "Strategy of Form: The Shape of Length in Drama." PhD diss., University of Minnesota, 1977.

Ravenhill, Mark. Introduction to *Shoot/Get Treasure/Repeat*. London: Methuen, 2008.

Reinhard, Tim. *George Spelvin is Alive and Well*. In *100 Neo-Futurist Plays*, 49. Chicago: Chicago Plays, 1988.

Richardson, Brian. "Time is Out of Joint: Narrative Models and the Temporality of the Drama," *Poetics Today* 8.2 (1987): 308.

Ricoeur, Paul. *Time and Narrative*. Translated by Kathleen McLaughlin and David Pellauer. Chicago: University of Chicago Press, 1984.

Roach, Joseph. *Cities of the Dead: Circum-Atlantic Performance*. New York: Columbia University Press, 1996.

Robinson, Marc. *The Other American Drama*. Baltimore: Johns Hopkins University Press, 1997.

Rognoni, Angelo. *Hamlet*. In Lista, *La Scène futuriste*, 1.226.

Rose, Margaret. *The Symbolist Theatre Tradition from Maeterlinck and Yeats to Beckett and Pinter*. Milan: Unicopoli, 1989.

Rugg, Rebecca. "Radical Inclusion 'Til It Hurts: Suzan-Lori Parks's *365 Days/365 Plays*." *Theater* 38, no. 1 (2008): 52–75.

Salvato, Nick. *Uncloseting Drama: American Modernism and Queer Performance*. New Haven: Yale University Press, 2010.

Sante, Luc. Introduction to *Novels in Three Lines*, by Félix Fénéon, vii–xxxi. New York: New York Review Books, 2007.

Scapparo, Mario. *The Improvised Balloon*. In Kirby, *Futurist Performance*, 305.

Scapparo, Mario. *The Rainbow of Italy*. In Kirby, *Futurist Performance*, 306.

Schleifer, Ronald. *Modernism and Time: The Logic of Abundance in Literature, Science, and Culture, 1880–1930*. Cambridge: Cambridge University Press, 2000.

Schmidt, Paul. Introduction to *The Plays of Anton Chekhov*. New York: Harper Collins, 1997.

Schnapp, Jeffrey. "Crash: Speed as Engine of Individuation." *Modernism/Modernity* 6, no. 1 (1999): 1–49.

Schneider, Alan. "'Any Way You Like, Alan': Working with Beckett." *Theater Quarterly* 5, no. 19 (September 1975): 27–38.

Schneider, Rebecca. *Performing Remains: Art and War in Times of Theatrical Reenactment*. New York: Routledge, 2011.

Schumacher, Claude. *Naturalism and Symbolism in European Theatre 1850–1918*. Cambridge: Cambridge University Press, 1996.

Segel, Harold B. *Pinocchio's Progeny: Puppets, Marionettes, Automatons and Robots in Modernist and Avant-Garde Drama*. Baltimore: Johns Hopkins University Press, 1995.

Segel, Harold B. *Turn-of-the-Century Cabaret: Paris, Barcelona, Berlin, Munich, Vienna, Cracow, Moscow, St. Petersburg, Zurich*. New York: Columbia University Press, 1987.

Senelick, Laurence, ed. *Cabaret Performance: Sketches, Songs, Monologues, Memoirs*. Vol. 1, *Europe 1890–1920*. New York: PAJ Publications, 1989.

Senelick, Laurence. Foreword to *Cabaret Performance*, 7–11.

Shakespeare, William. *Macbeth*. In *Complete Works of Shakespeare*, 1255–92.

Shakespeare, William. *A Midsummer Night's Dream*. In *The Complete Works of Shakespeare*. Edited by David Bevington, 148–79. New York: Pearson, 2004.

Shakespeare, William. *The Winter's Tale*. In *Complete Works of Shakespeare*, 1527–69.

Shenker, Israel. "Moody Man of Letters: A Portrait of Samuel Beckett, Author of the Puzzling 'Waiting for Godot.'" *The New York Times*, May 6, 1956.

Simmel, Georg. "The Metropolis and Mental Life." In *The Sociology of Georg Simmel*, translated and edited by Kurt H. Wolff, 409–24. Glencoe, IL: Free Press, 1964.

Sofer, Andrew. *The Stage Life of Props*. Ann Arbor: University of Michigan Press, 2003.

Sprinchorn, Evert. "Strindberg and the Greater Naturalism." *TDR* 13, no. 2 (1968): 119–29.

Sprinchorn, Evert. "The Zola of the Occult." In *Strindberg and Modern Theatre*, 251–66. Stockholm: Strindberg Society, 1975.

States, Bert. *Great Reckonings in Little Rooms: On the Phenomenology of the Theater*. Berkeley: University of California Press, 1985.

Strindberg, August. Author's preface to *Miss Julie*. In *Strindberg: Five Plays*. Translated by Harry G. Carlson, 63–75. Berkeley: University of California Press, 1983.

Strindberg, August. "The Battle of the Brains." In *Selected Essays*, 25–46.

Strindberg, August. *Coram Populo!* In *Doubles, Demons and Dreamers: An International Collection of Symbolist Drama.* Edited by Daniel Gerould, 35–42. New York: Performing Arts Journal Publications, 1985.

Strindberg, August. "Memorandums to the Members of the Intimate Theater from the Director." In *Open Letters to the Intimate Theater.* Translated by Walter Johnson, 15–53. Seattle: University of Washington Press, 1966.

Strindberg, August. "On Modern Drama and Theatre" In *Selected Essays,* 73–86.

Strindberg, August. *Selected Essays by August Strindberg.* Edited and translated by Michael Robinson. Cambridge: Cambridge University Press, 1996.

Strindberg, August. *Strindberg: Five Plays.* Translated by Harry G. Carlson. Berkeley: University of California Press, 1983.

Strindberg, August. *Strindberg: Other Sides.* Edited and translated by Joe Martin. New York: Peter Lang, 1997.

Strindberg, August. *The Stronger.* In *Strindberg: Other Sides,* 309–17.

Symons, Arthur. *Plays, Acting and Music: A Book of Theory.* New York: E. P. Dutton, 1909.

Szondi, Peter. *Theory of Modern Drama: A Critical Edition.* Edited and translated by Michael Hays. Minneapolis: University of Minnesota Press, 1986.

Taylor, Christiana. *Futurism: Politics, Painting, and Performance.* University Studies in the Fine Arts 8: The Avant-Garde. Ann Arbor, MI: UMI Research Press, 1979.

Tomkins, Calvin. *The Bride and the Bachelors: Five Masters of the Avant-Garde.* New York: Penguin, 1962.

Törnqvist, Egil. "The Modern(ist) One-Act Play." In *Facets of European Modernism: Essays in Honour of James MacFarlane,* edited by Janet Garton, 175–98. Norwich: University of East Anglia, 1985.

Van Fraassen, Bastiaan. "Time in Physical and Narrative Structure." In *Chronotypes: The Construction of Time,* edited by John Bender and David Wellbery, 19–37. Stanford: Stanford University Press, 1991.

Vardac, Nicholas. *Stage to Screen: Theatrical Method from Garrick to Griffith.* New York: Benjamin Blom, 1968.

Verdone, Mario. *Teatro del tempo futurista,* 2nd ed. Rome: Bulzoni Editore, 1988.

Virilio, Paul. *Speed and Politics: An Essay on Dromology* (1977). Translated by Mark Polizzotti. New York: Semiotext(e), 1987.

Vogel, Shane. *The Scene of Harlem Cabaret: Race, Sexuality, Performance.* Chicago: University of Chicago Press, 2009.

Wagner, Matthew. *Shakespeare, Theatre, and Time.* New York: Routledge, 2011.

Walat, Kathryn. "These Are Days: Suzan-Lori Parks's Year of Writing Dangerously Yields 365 Plays." *American Theatre* 23, no. 9 (2006): 26–27, 81–83.

Walkley, Arthur Bingham. *Playhouse Impressions.* London: T. Unwin, 1892.

Wasser, Audrey. "From Figure to Fissure: Beckett's *Molloy, Malone Dies,* and *The Unnamable.*" *Modern Philology* 109, no. 2 (November 2011): 245–65.

Waxman, Samuel. *André Antoine and the Théâtre Libre.* Cambridge, MA: Harvard University Press, 1926.

Weber, Max. "Science as a Vocation." In *The Vocation Lectures,* edited by David Owen and Tracy Strong and translated by Rodney Livingstone. Indianapolis: Hackett Pub, 2004.

Welles, Orson and Peter Bogdanovich. *This Is Orson Welles*. Edited by Jonathan Rosenbaum. New York: Harper Collins Publishers, 1992.

Whitman, Walt. *The Collected Writings of Walt Whitman*. Edited by Gay Wilson Allen and Sculley Bradley, 10:611. New York: New York University Press, 1961.

Whitman, Walt. *Leaves of Grass: The First (1855) Edition*. New York: Penguin, 1959.

Wilder, Thornton. *The Long Christmas Dinner*. In *The Collected Short Plays of Thornton Wilder*, edited by Donald Gallup and A. Tappan Wilder, Vol. 1, 3–25. New York: Theatre Communications Group, 1997.

Williams, Kirk. "Anti-theatricality and the Limits of Naturalism." In *Against Theatre*, edited by Alan Ackerman and Martin Puchner, 95–111.

Woolf, Virginia. "Mrs. Bennett and Mr. Brown." London: Hogarth Press, 1928.

Worth, Katherine. *The Irish Drama of Europe from Yeats to Beckett*. London: Athlone Press, 1978.

Worth, Katherine. *Maeterlinck in Performance*. Cambridge: Chadwyck-Healy, 1985.

Worthen, W. B. *Modern Drama and the Rhetoric of Theater*. Berkeley: University of California Press, 1991.

Worton, Michael. "*Waiting for Godot* and *Endgame*: Theatre as Text." In *Cambridge Companion to Samuel Beckett*, edited by John Pilling, 67–87. New York: Cambridge University Press, 1994.

Zola, Émile. "Naturalism on the Stage." In *Playwrights on Playwriting*, edited by Toby Cole and translated by Samuel Draper, 5–14. New York: Hill and Wang, 1960.

Index

Note: Page numbers in italics refer to illustrations.